RESCUED BY MAO

World War II, Wake Island, and
My Remarkable Escape to Freedom
Across Mainland China

RESCUED BY MAO

WORLD WAR II, WAKE ISLAND, AND
MY REMARKABLE ESCAPE TO FREEDOM
ACROSS MAINLAND CHINA

WILLIAM TAYLOR

SILVERLEAF
PRESS

For my children and their posterity

I would like to thank Russell Gray for helping to prepare the photos and David Folkman, my brother-in-law, who assisted with the typing. And my sincerest appreciation is for my wife, Barbara. Without her constant encouragement and her hours of typing and editing, the book would never have become a reality.

Silverleaf Press Books are available exclusively through Independent Publishers Group.

For details, write or telephone
Independent Publishers Group, 814 North Franklin St.
Chicago, IL 60610, (312) 337-0747

Silverleaf Press
8160 South Highland Dr.
Sandy, UT 84093

ISBN-10: 1-933317-87-6
ISBN-13: 978-1-933317-87-8

Printed in the United States of America

Disclaimer: The content in this manuscript is written from the recollections and interpretations of William Taylor. No claims of accuracy or inaccuracy are to be construed as definite. Every effort to include only factual material has been made, but the content and stories are based on recollection as well as historical notes. All names and event references have been made with positive intention, and with the deepest respect and admiration, to best convey the stories as accurate.

If you do find a factual error, please contact us so that we can rectify the mistake in future editions. Email us at editorial@leatherwoodpress.com.

CONTENTS

List of Illustrations   6

1 The War in Europe   9

2 Off to Work in the Pacific with a
   Hawaiian Pit Stop 23

3 Destination: Wake Island 36

4 Life on Wake 45

5 Rumors of War 56

6 Japan's Initial Attack, Wake's Short-Lived
   Victory, and a Personal Turning Point 69

7 Life as a POW 109

8 Cigarette Currency and a Change of Camps . . . 142

9 Surviving the POW Life 151

10 Creative Work Detail and the Chinese Culture . 175

11 The War's Developments and
    Keeping Our Sanity 197

12 Survival and Ingenuity 205

13 News and Grim Realizations 213

14 A Move and a Chance for Escape 219

15 Freedom and Friendly Farmers 233

16 Day-to-Day Survival through China 241

17 The Kindness of the Communist Army 250

18 Rest, Journal, and a Journey 256

19 A Gobi Desert Dust Storm,
    Enemy Domain, and Travel Parties 262

20 Long Journeys, Sweet Friendship,
    and a Flight to Yenan 277

21 The American Flag, Yenan, Mao,
    and Home—at Last 289

Epilogue 298

ILLUSTRATIONS

p. 43   Photograph of Wake Island taken by Bill Taylor

p. 44   Map of Wake Island, December 1941

p. 77   Illustration by Joseph J. Astarita

p. 102   Illustration by Joseph J. Astarita

p. 111   Photograph of the *Nitta Maru*

p. 112   Photograph of original document given the POWs
             prior to boarding the *Nitta Maru*

p. 116   Illustration by Joseph J. Astarita

p. 123   Illustration by Joseph J. Astarita

p. 130   Map of barracks at Woosung drawn by Bill Taylor

p. 133   Photograph of original benjo, 1945

p. 135   Map of Woosung POW camp

p. 138   Illustration by Joseph J. Astarita

p. 146   Illustration by Joseph J. Astarita

p. 149   Map of Kiangwan POW camp drawn by Joseph J.
             Astarita

p. 159   Illustration by Joseph J. Astarita

p. 167   Illustration by Joseph J. Astarita

p. 177   Illustration by Gurdon H. Wattles

p. 180   Illustration by Joseph J. Astarita

p. 191   Illustration by Joseph J. Astarita

p. 202   Illustration by Joseph J. Astarita

p. 222   Illustration by Delane Barras

p. 225   Illustration by Delane Barras

p. 226   Illustration by Delane Barras

p. 228   Illustration by Delane Barras

p. 235   Illustration by Delane Barras

p. 244   Illustration by Delane Barras

p. 248   Illustration by Delane Barras

p. 253   Photograph of original journals kept by Bill Taylor

p. 282   Photograph and letter given to Bill Taylor from San Leung on June 20, 1945

p. 287   Photograph by James Eaton

p. 291   Photographs by James Eaton

p. 299   Photograph of first civilian memorial, 1985

p. 301   Photograph of second civilian memorial, 1987

p. 303   Photograph by Bill Taylor

Note: The illustrations by Joseph J. Astarita were printed in *Sketches of POW Life* by Joseph J. Astarita, published by Rollo Press in 1947. Astarita was taken as a prisoner of war from Wake Island with Bill Taylor. During his years as a prisoner, he drew these pictures on any kind of paper he could find and hid them in two empty Red Cross shaving cream tubes. These tubes survived many Japanese searchings as well as transitions between POW camps from China to Japan over three and a half years.

Chapter One

THE WAR IN EUROPE

As I look back on the war-torn years of the early 1940s, the conflict in Europe didn't seem so threatening to the United States. After all, Europe was far away and most Americans felt that eventually right would triumph over wrong. In the summer of 1939, the Allies—Belgium, France and England—were totally optimistic that they could contain Germany if war started. We Americans, while neutral, were also led to believe that the Allies could stop Adolf Hitler and the great German military machine. We would give support to the Allies by providing them with essential supplies: food, clothing, medicine, and many other commodities, but America would remain neutral. We would not enter the war at that time.

The United States was just pulling out of the Great Depression. People were going back to work and we were generally a nation of happy people. Oh, there were and always will be those who complain that things are just not going well, those who say the economy is terrible, immorality is rampant, Jazz and the New Swing are corrupting us, and on and on. But there were many of the upbeats who were saying, "Isn't it a beautiful day? It's great to be alive . . . well, as an American."

Unfortunately, however, there were disturbing things going on in our own country. In February 1939 the German American Bund staged "an American rally" in Madison Square Garden denouncing the nation's Jews for their hatred of German Nazis and Socialism. At the rally there were Anti-Jewish and Pro-Nazi banners hung everywhere, "The Star-Spangled Banner" was sung and the Pledge of Allegiance recited, a huge George Washington poster was on display—but President Roosevelt was booed. Fritz Kuhn, the national leader of the Bund and one of Adolf Hitler's original followers, told the crowd of twenty thousand, "We do not say they are Communists, but we do say that the Jews are the driving force of Communism."

In March of 1939 Adolf Hitler arrived in Prague, Czechoslovakia; the Spanish Civil War ended; the New York World's Fair opened, boasting the theme: "The World of Tomorrow"; Italy, governed by the Dictator Benito Mussolini, invaded the tiny kingdom of Albania; and Albania's King Zog then fled to Greece, which by that time was very nervous about Mussolini's intentions. In March Neville Chamberlain, prime minister of England, pledged military support to Poland against threats to her sovereignty. In May Italy and Germany signed a "Pact of Steel" creating an invincible block of 300 million people. Germany was to rule the land, Italy the sea. In August *The Wizard of Oz*, a Frank L. Baum children's classic, had its film premier.

At that time I was living in Los Angeles, California. I worked for Standard Oil Company of California at their training service station on the corner of Olympic and Crenshaw. Business was brisk. Gasoline was selling for ten cents per gallon and a quart of the best Pennsylvania oil, SAE 30, for only twenty cents. Hamburgers, the very best with everything on them, were about thirty cents. Nearly halfway through 1939, I left that position to manage Mobile Oil next door.

I also had a girlfriend, Helen Clifton. Helen was a lovely girl, about five feet one inch tall. Her hair, which fell just below her shoulders, was a soft dark brown with just a tinge of red. She had a lightly tanned face with a few freckles around her nose. Helen's eyes were quite large and a shade of hazel—light green with little flecks of brown. Wherever she went, people were impressed by her friendliness, humor, smile, and laughter. She also would cry during a touching movie or when she heard of a friend in distress. Helen was a delightful person to be with as she matched her moods to mine. The war seemed to be in a distant land and life was just great. What a wonderful time to live.

Then, to our surprise, in August two archenemies, Hitler and Stalin, shook bloodstained hands and signed a non-aggression pact. That stymied efforts in Paris and London to restrain Hitler and halted British efforts to encircle Germany. Stalin and the Communism he promoted were not comfortable subjects for the British. Many English diplomats believed Communism was just as great a threat to European security as Nazism.

The treaty also isolated Poland. With the pact signed on August 23, 1939, German forces, comprising 1.25 million men, swept across the Polish border from the west. On September 17, Russian troops pushed in from the east. With these two military juggernauts converging on Poland, Poland's will to resist this unlawful aggression was blown away like autumn leaves in the wind. One can only imagine the despair that settled over that beautiful land. The Polish government had no military designs on any of its neighbors. But the callous aggressions by Adolf Hitler's Nazi Germany and Joe Stalin's Communist Russia are classic examples of what happens when nations arm themselves to the teeth.

A build-up of arms in any nation, almost without an exception, eventually leads to war. And when aggression is successful, the appetite is whetted and false justification for more land, more nations, and more bloodshed overcomes principles of morality. Greed becomes the goal. That greed for riches leads to a desire for more power by the murder of innocent people. The conquerors accept the means to achieve their terrible destructive goals with absolutely no guilt for the black deeds they have committed.

The unlawful German invasion of Poland came without declaration of war. There was little opposition. Subversive elements in the country proclaimed, "Our Fuhrer, Adolf Hitler, has freed us." The Nazi swastikas flew over a divided and conquered Poland and the western two-thirds of Poland was now under German control, the eastern part controlled by communist Russia. England, France, and Poland had signed a mutual defense treaty several months before Germany and Russia had invaded Poland. On September 1st England demanded that Germany withdraw. Germany refused. So on September 3, 1939, England and France declared war on Germany. This was the true beginning of World War II. Russia was not yet included.

It was during this lightning attack on Poland that the name Blitzkrieg or "lightning war" became famous. I remember Hitler screaming to the world via radio. It was frightening. But then the war was in a distant land. Back in the United States, President Roosevelt, in response to a reporter's question, "Can we keep out of it?" replied solemnly, "I not only sincerely hope so, but I believe we can and that every effort will be made to do so."

During 1935–37 I worked for the Metropolitan Water District (MWD) on the Colorado River Aqueduct. This work consisted of bringing water from Parker Dam on the Colorado River to the parched lands of Southern California and especially to thirsty Los Angeles. Bringing the water from the Colorado River to Los Angeles was a huge engineering project consisting of eighteen-feet-wide concrete tunnels through miles of solid rock mountains, forty-feet-wide concrete-lined canals, and numerous pumping stations. Much of the tunnel work was contracted out to qualified construction companies. And almost all of the work was in progress at the same time.

In 1935 I started working for Winston Brothers Construction Company at Coxcomb Tunnel, a segment of the mammoth water project of the MWD. I continued working for them on and off for three years. I had just turned eighteen, fresh out of high school, and this was my first real job. I was hired as a construction laborer for $3.40 per day, plus room and board. During the next three years, I worked as a laborer deep underground, a cement finisher, a motorman on battery-operated trains, a chuck tender for the miners, and in various positions in other miscellaneous jobs. I matured a little during those years.

In the early summer of 1939, Helen and I became engaged. Then one day we couldn't wait any longer for marriage and decided to elope. Before actually tying the knot, I took her for a drive out to Desert Center, California, just a point on the map at that time. It is about two hundred miles east of Los Angeles on Highway 80. We left Los Angeles about noon on that beautiful summer day and headed east, riding in Helen's 1935 Ford Convertible. The top was down, and life was great and exciting. We drove through Riverside and Banning and then to Desert Center, arriving there in the late afternoon. This took us just a few miles from the Wide Canyon tunnel where I had worked several years before. I suggested, "Let me show you where I worked."

So we headed up to the Iron Mountains toward the Wide Canyon project in the Iron Mountain Range. We had completed a 3.2-mile concrete tunnel there three years before that was about ten miles from Desert Center. While traveling this narrow road, I was showing Helen the beautiful desert country, indicating points of interest along the way. I really wasn't concentrating on what was ahead, as the road was paved and in good condition. Then, suddenly, looking ahead, I saw that the road ahead had been taken out by a flash flood. There were no signs. We were about twenty feet away from where the road ended and were traveling about twenty-five miles an hour at the time. There was no time to stop. I remember yelling, "Hold on!" and then we shot over the end of the road. The wash was about four feet deep and fifteen feet wide, a deep trench. The car immediately dropped into the wash, hitting the other side with a devastating impact. I remember the windshield being smashed by our heads and watching the motor hood, strangely enough, flying through the air, flipping slowly end over end. There was a lot of dust, then a dead silence, and an eerie quiet. I looked at Helen. She had blood running down her face, and I knew she was injured. Then I noticed blood running down my face.

We were both stunned, in semi-shock. I got out of the car to look around. Helen said, "I can't move my leg, Bill." She couldn't easily move or walk. Dusk was setting in quickly and we were miles from the main highway, Highway 10. I told Helen I would go for help; there wasn't anything else I could do. So leaving her, I started toward the main highway, which I figured was about six or seven miles away. One of the spookiest things about walking at night on any blacktop road in the desert is the danger of side-winding rattle-snakes. As the air cools in the evening, these cold-blooded rattlers slither up on the roads to warm themselves on the blacktop that will keep in the heat of the sun for a few hours. I listened for their deadly rattle, but I was fortunate and I didn't encounter any snakes.

After walking about two hours, I came to the main highway where, after a short time, a man in an old four-door sedan came by. He stopped when he saw my bloodied face in his headlights. He immediately picked me up and we drove to Helen. She was in extreme pain but a very good sport, considering the circumstances. Moving her to his car, we turned around and headed toward Highway 10, then west to Indio. Indio was about fifty miles from Desert Center. In those days, Desert Center was just a wide spot in the road. Upon arriving in Indio, Helen's leg was x-rayed. There was a fracture just below the knee. Her leg was placed in a cast and the wedding plans were postponed. I couldn't thank the old man enough for helping us out of a tough situation.

Because of that most unfortunate accident, Helen and I did not get married. After that incident, we began to drift apart and she eventually moved back to her home in Ogden, Utah, where she met and married Wendell Crosby.

The year 1940 was a busy one for me. Early in 1940 I moved to Ogden, where I had graduated from Ogden High School in 1935. There, I worked for the US Forest Service by day and for Amalgamated Sugar by night. Between September 1939 and the spring of 1941, momentous events took place in the world. In October 1939 Germany and Russia destroyed Poland as a nation. More than sixty thousand Poles were killed, more than a hundred thousand were wounded, and nearly seven hundred thousand were captured. And Russia and Germany did not have a common buffer zone. How long would this demonic relationship last?

On December 15, 1939, *Gone with the Wind* opened in Atlanta, Georgia, amid a great fanfare of publicity, and was a fantastic success. Starring in this epic film were Clark Gable, Olivia DeHaviland, and a beautiful newcomer to the silver screen, Vivian Leigh. Although she was from England, she could mimic the Southern accent very well. *Gone with the Wind* was a marvelous movie in which we all vicariously lived the time and events of the great Civil War of the United States.

During the early part of 1940, the Russians, who had attacked the small country of Finland by land, sea, and air in November of 1939, were having a terrible time. They simply could not conquer that tiny country as easily as they thought, which shows how people will fight to defend their freedom and democracy. By March, however, the courageous Finns were finally forced to surrender to the Russians. What else could they do? They were outnumbered four to one in men, one hundred to one in tanks, and thirty to one in aircraft.

On April 9th, Germany stormed into Denmark by land, sea, and air. There was no resistance to the Nazi juggernaut. Then on March 18th, Mussolini and Hitler met at the Brenner Pass in Italy and discussed the idea of forming a new order in Europe comprising Germany, Russia, and Italy. Would Russia and Germany really be partners? And was Italy was just a pawn in the political drive for world domination by Adolf Hitler and the Germans?

Charles Lindbergh, a man of great integrity and the first man to fly the Atlantic from the United States to Paris, joined with many others in participating in the America First Committee. He and other well-known people in the United States were dead-set against our involvement in the war in Europe. What a tremendously tragic mistake it would have been not to help England and France. Lindbergh, great as he was, was wrong about Germany and its intentions.

On May 10, 1940, the Germans ended what was known as the Phoney War when it launched a blitzkrieg (lightning war) against the neutral Netherlands, Luxembourg, Belgium, and France. The Germans said their only reason for attacking the Low Countries was to protect them from an invasion by the Allied Forces—all Nazi propaganda. A short time later, Belgium and Holland surrendered to the Nazis.

Also, May 10, 1940, Neville Chamberlain resigned and in his place a great statesman, writer, and leader, Winston Churchill, was to form a new government under King George VI. I have nothing but the greatest admiration and respect for Churchill, for he electrified the people of England, as no one else was capable of doing.

Between May 26th and June 4th, the British Royal Navy rescued 338,226 soldiers from Dunkirk, France. For some unknown reason the Germans did not pursue the retreating British, French, and Belgian divisions, so they had time to escape the clutches of the Germans and regroup. This evacuation alone was surely one of the most important events of the war. Without the rescue of the French and British Troops, who knows what might have happened later on in the war? Saving those troops provided a great morale boost for England and lead Churchill to extol the "Dunkirk Spirit" as well as ended the possibility of seeking peace from Germany since England still had the ability to defend their country against a possible German invasion. I might add that during this stressful time, Winston Churchill stood head and shoulders above all other Allied leaders. He definitely was not like his predecessor, Neville

Chamberlain who proved insufficient during the war.

Meanwhile, moving with lightning speed, the German blitzkrieg swooped around the so-called impenetrable Maginot Line and into France. (The Maginot Line is named after French defense minister, Andre Maginot. It consisted of concrete fortifications, tank obstacles, and machine gun posts along the French areas bordering Germany and Italy. This line of defense was constructed after World War I, in the lead-up to World War II.)

The Maginot Line, built at a tremendous cost between 1930 and 1940, proved futile as the Germans simply went around the west end of the line through the Low Countries into France without even a shot being fired.

On June 14, 1940 just ten days after entering France, the German Army descended on Paris. Darkness had fallen over the capital when German troops marched into the center of the city. German tanks and armored cars swept past the trees of the Champs Elysées. What a depressing sight to behold.

French men and women wept openly; much of the city was deserted. The German High Command, intoxicated and arrogant with their success, claimed that they would occupy the rest of France within two weeks. After that, they would turn their attention to Winston Churchill and Great Britain.

To the northeast of Paris, the Germans were battering the French all along the Maginot Line. The German front now extended three hundred miles from the Rhine River all the way to LeHavre. French General Weygand had tremendous pressure placed upon him to seek an Armistice. He eventually advocated capitulation with Germany and France and signed an armistice on June 22, 1940.

As in all wars, the civilian populations attempted to flee from their invaders. In the case of France, human buzzards were demanding fortunes in gold to transport the Frenchmen in their cars. They were easy targets for the German *stukas* (dive bombers), which frequently swept down from the skies.

Meanwhile, the Russians were taking advantage of the world preoccupation of the blitzkrieg in France and the Low Countries to launch their own blitzkrieg against the three Baltic States of Lithuania, Latvia, and Estonia. The USSR had lost the three Baltic States during World War I.

On June 22nd the French surrendered to the Germans at Compiègne, France. (Hitler danced a jig at the signing.) Ironically, this armistice was signed in the same railroad car where Germany was compelled to sign total surrender after its defeat in 1918.

Terms of the treaty placed a tremendous burden on the French people. It gave Germany occupation of two-thirds of France and access to all French Channel and Atlantic ports. And France bore all the occupation costs. Germany did allow for a minimal French army, as well as a French Navy that was forced to disarm, but not surrender. Hitler feared that if he pushed the French too far they would fight back in North Africa. The unoccupied third of France was left free and was to be governed by the French people until a final peace treaty could be negotiated. The treaty was negotiated in 1942, giving Germany full occupation of France. The Germans could do no wrong. To the victor went the spoils. What a sad time for the French.

On June 18, 1940, Winston Churchill stated in a speech to the House of Commons:

> What General Weygand called the Battle of France is over. I expect that the Battle of Britain is about to begin. Upon this battle depends the survival of Christian civilization. Upon it depends our own British life, and the long continuity of our institutions and our Empire. The whole fury and might of the enemy must very soon be turned on us. Hitler knows that he will have to break us in this Island or lose the war. If we can stand up to him, all Europe may be free and the life of the world may move forward

into broad, sunlit uplands. But if we fail, then the whole world, including the United States, including all that we have known and cared for, will sink into the abyss of a new Dark Age made more sinister, and perhaps more protracted, by the lights of perverted science. Let us therefore brace ourselves to our duties, and so bear ourselves that, if the British Empire and its Commonwealth last for a thousand years, men will still say, "This was their finest hour."

Winston Churchill set about preparing for a long war with Germany. This included the destroying of the French fleet in Algeria on July 3, 1940 by the Royal Navy Force H (which was formed to replace the loss of French naval power in the Western Mediterranean) over concerns that the Germans would commandeer the French fleet.

Following Churchill's June 18 speech, Hitler ordered Operation Sea Lion, which called for the invasion of England to take place in mid-September 1940. This invasion was to encompass both a landing on the south coast combined with an airborne assault. German Admiral Raeder told Hitler that invasion of England should only be a last resort and with only full air superiority because of the superiority of the Royal Navy over the Kriegsmarine (the German navy). To prepare for the invasion, Germany started bombing convoy in England on July 10, 1940 with the intense bombings beginning on August 11, 1940. Germany believed that it would only take four days to defeat the RAF Fighter Command in southern England and only four more weeks to destroy the rest of the country and the aircraft industry. The intensity of the defense attack by the British took the Germans by surprise and completely destroyed their formation.

Greatly outnumbered, the Royal Air Force (RAF) simply would not give up. On August 28, 1940, British bombers struck Berlin for the first time, a feat that Marshall Hermann Goering had told Hitler British bombers could never accomplish. During the course of the battle, the German Luftwaffe lost several aircraft and over twelve hundred men, while the British lost 544 men. Winston Churchill portrayed the determination and courage of those pilots in a statement: "Never in the field of human conflict was so much owed by so many to so few." The Battle of Britain marked the failure of the German war machine, shifted public opinion concerning appeasement with Germany, and provided a shift in ideology that the war could be won.

On September 27th, the Reich Chancellery announced that Germany, Italy, and Japan had formed a tri-party alliance, the Tripartite Pact, thus linking Germany's military might with that of Italy and Japan. This agreement followed the invasion of the Japanese into Indo-China. That agreement seemed to indicate that Japan and the United States would be at war at some point in the future.

On October 28, 1940, Italy invaded Greece with 529,000 men. The Italian army was met by a force of 300,000 Greeks with support from the British Navy. The Hellenic army counterattacked and caused the Italian army to retreat, allowing Greek forces to take a part of Albania from Italy. In March of 1941, Italy tried an unsuccessful counterattack that humiliated Italian military pretenses and became the first Allied land victory. Following their defeat of the Italian army, the Greek army was too weak to repel the German invasion in May 1941, and for the next three years fell under Axis control. There was certainly a heavy load placed on Britain. The war did not look good for Britain at this point.

Hitler's mighty air force, the Luftwaffe, had not been able to defeat the British by bombing them from the air. It appeared that the only way to defeat them was through invasion or by destruction of the Royal Navy or the Royal Air Force. The British resistance was remarkable, and Winston Churchill proved to be a great leader.

Meanwhile, in Warsaw, Poland, the Jews were being rounded up by Germans and enclosed behind a ten-foot wall topped with glass and barbed wire, enclosing the entire city ghetto district. No Jew—man, woman, or child—was spared by the Germans.

In January of 1941, the Italians lost Tobruk, a part of Libya in North Africa to the British and the Australians. When it came down to real fighting, the Italians just didn't have the what it took. They were bullies when everything was going their way, but were cowardly and would run or surrender when confronted by an enemy determined not to quit.

In February 1941, Germany's General Erwin Rommel arrived in Tripoli under order from Hitler to reverse the setback suffered by the Axis in Libya. His troops were called the "Afrika Corps" and appeared to be quite formidable.

Bulgaria allied with Axis powers, thus giving the Germans an unobstructed path to southeastern Europe. When one looked at the whole picture, Germany was running roughshod over almost all of Europe. One wondered if they could be stopped. And if so, when?

Australia sent reinforcements to Singapore as the British were doing their best to defend the Singapore Harbor. And the United States started to send aircraft to the Pacific. This was an ominous sign of things to come.

In April of 1941 Germany invaded and captured Yugoslavia on its way to Greece. On April 27th, the Greek Army collapsed as the Germans swept into Athens.

Then in May, President Roosevelt indicated that war was imminent and declared a national emergency. He said the delivery of supplies to Britain was imperative. "This can be done; it must be done; it will be done," he said. Roosevelt told how Adolf Hitler's aim was to dominate the high seas for an attack on the western hemisphere, to eventually rule the world.

Also in May, the British put down an uprising in Iraq and occupied Damascus, Syria, thus protecting the needed oil pipeline from Mosul to Haifa.

In June Adolf Hitler made one of the greatest mistakes of the war. Germany massed troops on the Soviet border and then drove into Russia on the 22nd. That was a thoughtless move by Hitler and would eventually prove disastrous over the war's course. As I look back on this war, Churchill, Dunkirk, Battle of Britain, and Russia were all turning points that later defeated the German juggernaut.

The war in Europe was raging from England to Russia, from Norway to the hot dusty desert of North Africa, and into the turbulent Middle East. While sea battles raged in the Atlantic, where many transports carrying supplies to a troubled Great Britain were being sent to watery graves, the real impact of what was going on in the world did not seem to affect the average American. In the United States, this massive war was viewed as a distant conflict. Life went on as usual. We had yet to be awakened to the danger that confronted the world.

Chapter Two

OFF TO WORK IN THE PACIFIC
WITH A HAWAIIAN PIT STOP

E arly in the spring of 1941, I read in the classified section of the *Los Angeles Times* about large construction projects in the Pacific, on the islands of Hawaii, Midway, Guam, and Wake. I was soon excited about and considering the possibility of going to one of those exotic places. I was also excited about the prospect of a good, well-paying job. With these interests in mind, I answered the ad in the *Times* and was directed to the office of a large contracting company, Morrison & Knudsen Construction Company. M&K at that time was one of the largest construction companies in the world. Morrison & Knudsen, Bechtel, Hawaiian Dredging, Raymond Concrete & Pile, and Utah Construction, all huge construction companies in their own right, banded their resources together to form what was then known as the Contractors Pacific Naval Air Bases (CPNAB). Their work was of tremendous scope and involved heavy construction on many Pacific islands, including Hawaii, the Philippines, Midway, Wake Island, Guam, Johnston, Samoa, and Palmyra.

Each construction firm sponsored and had charge of one or more of the jobs on these islands and many construction men from the mainland United States were employed at various Pacific sites when the Japanese attacked Pearl Harbor, which took place a few months later, on December 7, 1941. Morrison & Knudsen had been awarded all construction work on Wake Island, a small atoll two thousand miles west of Oahu, Hawaii.

The Morrison & Knudsen recruiting office was in downtown Los Angeles. I told my older brother Jack (seven years my senior) about this opportunity to not only make a few bucks for ourselves, but also to serve our country. We were excited, for we saw in this opportunity a chance to make and save a considerable amount of money in as little as one year. Our brother-in-law, Harry Terrill, had already worked on Midway, and so we anticipated that this would also be a great opportunity for us.

We both passed the physical exam, which, to my relief, was no more than a stethoscope on the chest and a check of the blood pressure and pulse. At this point in time, the government was mainly concerned with getting the job done, regardless of the cost.

On July 28, 1941, we boarded the SS *Matsonia*, the luxury flagship of the Matson Line. This beautiful luxury liner was docked at a pier in Long Beach, California. Upon boarding we could hardly believe the quarters we were assigned. The SS *Matsonia* and her sister ship, the SS *Lurline*, were the crown jewels of the Matson Steamship Company. I might mention that the Matson Shipping Line controlled almost everything going to Hawaii, which included all freight (there were no shipments by air), food, building materials, petroleum products, clothing, automobiles, et cetera. Matson had a monopoly until the Pan American Clippers began flying the passengers to Hawaii in 1935.

Because of the urgency to protect Hawaii and the other outlying possessions of the United States, the government had given huge contracts to the Contractors Pacific Naval Air Bases (CPNAB). Everything was being contracted on a "cost-plus" basis. Cost-plus usually meant a five percent profit. The more money that was spent the greater the margin of profit for the contractor. There was no way a prime contractor could lose on a deal like that. While there was patriotism, there was also greed. The waste that is generated by a cost-plus contract is unbelievable. The CPNAB were the best in the world, but at the same time they reaped hundreds of millions of dollars in profit through the monopoly and the urgency to simply complete the jobs.

Therefore, when Jack and I boarded the *Matsonia*, we were given the best accommodations available. In our case, we were assigned to the top deck Royal Lanai Suites, which overlooked the beautiful Pacific Ocean. In those days the price of this suite was an outrageous seven hundred dollars for one person for five days one-way from San Francisco or Los Angeles to Hawaii.

To Hawaii on the SS Matsonia

Sailing from Long Beach, California, on July 28, 1941, was as emotional as it was exciting. Just sailing from Long Beach to San Francisco was beyond my wildest dreams. Our accommodations were out of this world! On the second or third decks of the SS *Matsonia*, there were six passengers assigned to a stateroom, or, at best, two passengers to a stateroom with an ocean view through a small porthole. There was a tiny bathroom where one could barely turn around and no access to first-class accommodations. The Royal Suite that Jack and I had, on the other hand, was a large, beautifully decorated bedroom. It had a dressing room with a separate private bath and stall shower, a telephone, and room service. It had a large sliding glass door that opened to a lanai (porch) with an eye-stopping view. This lanai ran the full width of our suite and was about eight feet deep. It also was enclosed with storm-proof sliding windows. There were chairs and a table on the lanai, so one could sit for hours and bask in the sun or just relax in the cool of the evening. For room service, all we had to do was push a button and a young steward's mate would appear at the door.

Generally speaking, the construction men going to Hawaii were tradesmen from every category. These were men who could build anything from a simple house to massive dams. They were rough, tough men qualified in their trades and willing to fight at the drop of a hat, especially if they had a few drinks under their belts. Yet, they were also the kind of men who would help a stranger in need. These men would protect and honor all women. They were rough on the outside, but gentle under the surface, although they would never admit it.

The dining room/banquet salon was spotless and very large; the tables seated six and were covered with white linen tablecloths, crystal goblets, beautiful sterling silverware, and a lovely centerpiece of exotic fragrant flowers. The dining salon could accommodate more than three hundred people at one time and was available— morning, noon, and night—to the first-class passengers only. We had for our pleasure the most exotic menus imaginable. The entrées listed described some foods we had never even heard of. Much of the language on the menu was in French, especially the wines.

There were no prices on the menus. It was all free, cost-plus for Morris & Knudsen and great for us. The contractors and Matson Line made the money, the government made out the checks, and the taxpayers paid the bill. I really can't blame the contractors or Matson Line because there just wasn't enough time to put the contracts out to bid, so the cost-plus method was the only way to expedite the work.

We were expected to dress up for dinner every night on the ship. We wore ties and suit coats and really tried to be on our best behavior. The captain sat at a table especially reserved for him and his special guests. In the background, there was also a band of five or six musicians seated on a small, raised dais (stage) that played popular numbers of the day, including lovely selections from the islands. Before the dinner began, everyone would rise as the special guests were announced, entering the room two-by-two. The musicians would play appropriate music as the guests sauntered down the aisle toward the captain's table. As they approached, the captain stood and welcomed them. These special people were usually important citizens—kings, queens, ambassadors, and presidents—of some foreign country.

I remember how one lovely evening before the meal was served the trumpet sounded, the signal that important guests were about to enter the dining salon. Everything quieted down and the music dropped to a whisper as it was announced that the maharaja and maharani of Sarawak (a small but immensely rich kingdom in northern Borneo) were about to arrive. As the musicians continued to play softly, this lovely couple entered the salon. The maharaja, probably in his late forties, was dressed in a spotless white military uniform adorned with medals and a red sash around his waist. His companion and consort, the maharani, about twenty-five, was absolutely stunning, one of the most beautiful women I had ever seen. While the maharaja was dark brown and handsome, the maharani, in stark contrast, was fair, with a gorgeous figure, about five feet, four inches. She was lightly tanned and her skin looked smooth, silky soft, and totally unblemished. Dark brown slightly wavy hair fell to her shoulders and a beautiful tiara composed of emeralds and diamonds adorned her head. She was wearing a full-length white gown with a large exotic red flower embroidered on her right shoulder. The slender stem of the flower with its dark green leaves swept down from her shoulder under her right breast, across her very trim waist and ending on her left hip. The posture of these two were as stately as anything you could imagine. They were a stunning couple and they knew it. You could see it in the way they held their heads high as her right hand rested lightly on the maharaja's left arm. Slowly they walked toward the captain's table. What a beautiful, regal couple they were. The dining room had become very quiet as everyone seemed to be entranced by the dignity and beauty of the royal couple.

Suddenly I heard some snickers, then a subdued chuckle. As they walked by our table I saw the reason for the subdued laughter. Would you believe that following about ten feet behind this royal couple was one of our construction workers bound for Wake Island? I couldn't believe my eyes for he was wearing bib overalls, his thumbs hooked under his shoulder straps, chewing something (it could have been tobacco) while grinning, nodding, and waving to everyone as he passed by. I kept hoping he wouldn't spit on the floor. I was disgusted, ashamed, and embarrassed at the time, but later I smiled and chuckled as I realized that this was an experience I probably would never forget.

Onboard the *Matsonia* were the usual assortment of well-to-do, pleasure-seeking vacationers; a large contingent of military officers, mostly Navy with some Army, and most with their families; and a rather cohesive group of college students on their way home to Hawaii for the summer. The *Matsonia* personnel were very organized and busy leading all kinds of sports, games, and social events.

During this voyage, the deep blue Pacific was relatively calm, enhanced by a light azure blue sky and puffy white clouds, a perfect blend with the dark blue water below. Early in the morning or in the evening, I usually made my way to the bow of the ship, right at the point where the starboard and port railings met. I would stand, and as the bow moved slowly up and down, I would inhale all the pure air my lungs could contain. Looking over the bow, I could see schools of flying fish racing to keep up with the ship. Many of the sporting events took place on the upper deck and there were lounge chairs scattered around the beautiful, highly polished teak deck. There was music and dancing each evening that lasted until about one o'clock in the morning. Large quantities of liquor was consumed, and as the evening wore on, many romances blossomed, some in pushed-together deck chairs. As the evening progressed couples or friends could be seen here and there, nestled up in the corners on the deck. I'm sure some of the staterooms were also busy. Cocktails, either wine or hard liquor, were available at a very small cost to all. Champagne and wines ran about twenty-five cents a serving and a cocktail was thirty-five cents. The evenings were warm and romantic. I'm sure just the excitement of being on this world-class luxury liner was enough to make any heart race a little bit faster.

My brother Jack and I, as well as almost all of the construction workers bound for the islands, had never experienced social life like this first-hand. Probably the closest any of us had come was by viewing a Bob Hope or Bing Crosby movie back on the mainland.

Another experience on the *Matsonia* that remains in my memory took place on the day my brother Jack, a carpenter named Earl Row, a plumber named Chuck Woods, and I were in our lanai suite overlooking the vast blue Pacific. We were lounging on the lanai, resting up from the previous nights' activities, and talking with our newfound friends about the uncertain future (if we had only known). Earl was toying with the venetian blinds that ran down the full length of the lanai. The storm windows were all halfway down the entire length of our lanai, there was a gentle breeze, and we were a very contented lot. Chuck was relaxing on one of the lounge chairs reading a magazine and had dropped one of his expensive leather sandals over the side of his chair. Almost absent-mindedly, Earl picked up the sandal and tied it to one of the venetian blind strings. After he had it secured, he nudged Chuck and then threw the sandal out the window, saying, "Hey, Woody, I don't suppose you want that sandal anymore, do you?" Chuck looked up just in time to see his beautiful leather sandal sailing out over the Pacific. We were all smiling and then laughing for we realized that in looking up from his magazine he had not seen the string tied to the sandal.

Chuck was hurt, you could see it in his eyes, but wanting to be a good sport he said, "I guess not," after which, before any of us realized what he was going to do, he grabbed his other sandal off his foot and threw it out the window, remarking, "I guess I can't use one very well." No sooner had he done this than Earl hauled up the one that was hanging outside the window. You can imagine the look of consternation on Chuck's face when he saw his sandal tied to the venetian blind string. We all felt sorry and rather stupid. No one ever forgot that experience, especially Woody.

First Visit to Hawaii

After six days of self-indulgence, the *Matsonia* rounded Diamond Head early in the morning, slowed down to take on pilots and visitors, and continued on to the Honolulu harbor. I will never forget my first docking at the Aloha Tower, which was more than one hundred and fifty feet tall and could be seen long before you docked. It seemed as though a good portion of the town had quit work and was there at the harbor for "Boat Day." As we slowly maneuvered into our docking space, the Royal Hawaiian Band, all decked out in freshly starched white uniforms, struck up the familiar yet hauntingly nostalgic strains of "Hawaii Aloha." Gentle trade winds drifting in around us brought in the unforgettable perfume of the island flowers. This was my very first experience with the fragrance and beauty of the islands. Even today when I visit Hawaii, its gentle trade winds bring back all those memories of my first visit to the Aloha State.

As the *Matsonia* was tied securely to the dock, passengers at the rail watched with misty eyes while those on the dock, carrying arm loads of colorful fragrant leis, waited to greet loved ones. A group of shapely, brown-skinned hula girls, in skirts made from ti leaves, festooned with flowers, performed a spectacular hip-swinging show for us. That experience was truly impressive and memorable.

As we disembarked, a distinctly unglamorous representative of the CPNAB (Contractors Pacific Naval Air Bases) greeted me. This low-salaried, white-collar emissary pointed to an olive drab Army school bus and curtly told us to get aboard. We were taken to Hickam Field, a few miles away, where we were assigned to transient quarters while awaiting further transportation. The quarters were nothing more than a big country barn—indeed a contrast to the *Matsonia*.

I had an aunt, Glenn Cannon, my mother's sister, living in Honolulu. She and my uncle, Que Cannon, who was the manager of the Honolulu Gas Company, owned several acres of ground in Aleva Heights where they had a cow, some chickens, a vegetable garden, and a gorgeous view of the Pacific Ocean. She knew we would be arriving, but somehow we missed connections at the dock. I called her home in Aleva Heights, but there was no answer. I decided to go to her home anyway on the chance that I might be able to see her. I took the bus to within a block of her home and quickly located the house. She wasn't home, but there was a note pinned on the door, with a welcome and an apology that she couldn't be home to greet me. She also had left a key to her Chevrolet Roadster Convertible and a message to have a good time.

I found the key and drove the car toward Round Top Mountain, a spectacular residential area where every lot has a view. My Uncle Lyman Gowans, and his wife, Helen Taylor Gowans, had homesteaded acres of that area years before. Uncle Lyman had been an Army pilot way back during World War I. He flew a two-seater aircraft called the "Jenney." After the War, they settled in Oahu. Aunt Helen, my father's sister, was absolutely brilliant. It was her idea to purchase property all over Oahu. They built and owned several eighteen-story high-rise apartment buildings just off Ala Moana Boulevard and became quite wealthy from their investments.

After traveling up the Pali Highway, I turned right at the Round Top sign and proceeded up a long, winding road. Reaching the top, I parked the car and got out. There was a gentle trade wind lazily drifting over this tropical island of Oahu and the air was a mild 72°F. I couldn't stop taking one deep intoxicating breath after another. From my vantage point, I had a sweeping panoramic view of more than 180 degrees and I could hardly contain myself. Looking above, I beheld intermittent cumulus clouds that came together from time to time and then separated. The rays of the hot sun were tamed by the shadows of the clouds causing the colorful beauty of the islands to change every few moments. At this point, I really fell in love with the islands—their charm, beauty, and culture.

Leaving that most enjoyable and colorful scene was difficult, and as I wended my way down from Round Top I thought it had to be one of the most beautiful places on planet earth. No wonder the islands of Hawaii are called "paradise," "the jewel of the Pacific."

A few minutes after leaving Round Top, I reached the Pali Highway, which connects Honolulu on the south side of Oahu with the city of Kaneohe on the east side. Turning left, I drove down towards the busy city of Honolulu, reaching Ala Moana Boulevard, which runs from Pearl Harbor east through downtown Honolulu, Waikiki, and out to Diamond Head. Soon I saw the Royal Hawaiian Hotel, widely known as the "Pink Palace." It was situated on Waikiki Beach and was the destination for the wealthy international traveler. The rooms and suites would be booked for months, as it was truly the playground for the rich and famous. Yes, if you wanted to see or be seen, the Royal was the place to be.

I parked Aunt Glenn's little convertible and headed for the Royal Hawaiian. The front of the hotel is known as *makai,* or "towards the ocean." The backside faces the mountains and is called *maka.* As I walked toward the open doors, the fragrance and beauty of the tropical flowers and plants coupled with the gentle trade winds made you think, "Why don't I live here?" Entering the lobby, I soon found myself on a slotted wooden boardwalk, which took me right to the famous Waikiki Beach. Large colorful umbrellas dotted the shoreline, shielding bathers from the hot tropical sunrays. It was about 250 feet from where I stood at the end of the boardwalk to the shoreline. I don't believe I've ever seen so many beautiful women and tanned men in one place. There were also older people and lots of children. The new arrivals were decked out in the latest swimwear and glistening with sun oil, awaiting a deep Hawaiian tan.

Looking beyond the shoreline about two hundred yards toward

the coral reef, there were surfers sitting on their boards waiting for the next series of waves. They were riding eight- to ten-foot surfboards, and some even longer. They would look back and when they saw a wave that would soon be breaking, they would lie down on their boards and paddle furiously with their arms to catch the wave before it rose up and broke. Once the surfboard started to move, pushed by the relentless surf, they would stand up and let the wave break and carry them to the shore.

Almost all of those *kanakas* (men) were tanned, muscular, and quite handsome. As I watched, I thought, "They are happy today. To them, tomorrow is a long way away." I was somewhat envious of them.

As I stood, mesmerized, I noticed that the sun was getting ready to lie down on the distant horizon where a golden pathway appeared as it rested on the edge of the deep blue Pacific. As the minutes went by, it gradually slipped down beyond the distant horizon and suddenly the entire sky came alive with the reflection of the setting sun on the white cumulus clouds lingering over the island. Everything seemed to stop, hold its breath, and then within minutes evening was ushered in.

The island air was so clean and unpolluted, enhanced by the fragrance of plumeria, ginger, anthurium, orchids, carnations, and countless other tropical plants and flowers. This was coupled with the swaying of the coconut palms fanned by the gentle trade winds. By that point, I was nearly overcome by the beauty of my experience. Add to the beauty the warm aloha spirit and I couldn't help but be in love with Hawaii. All that was missing was a lovely *wahine* (woman) to share it with me.

Turning at the end of the boardwalk and walking back to the lanai, I saw tables, which seated two to eight people, and banquet tables, which could seat many. They were all ready. The linens and silverware were spotless, the lights were low, and a man was playing the piano very softly at the end of the lanai. As the guests started to arrive, I noticed there were a lot of military people in their starched white dress uniforms. Was this not a sign of the times?

The Royal Hawaiian Hotel was famous for their wines, cocktails, and exotic foods. In the evening there was dancing and when the lights were turned down, there started a colorful floor show, with handsome, muscular *kanakas* and gorgeous *wahines* that simply took your breath away. Their interpretations of ancient Hawaiian and Polynesian cultures was exciting as they swayed gracefully back and forth and sang about the days gone by. It seemed that the audience was taken back to a day and time that existed long before the missionaries and white man arrived. The gentle trade winds, the distant sound of the ocean jumping over the reef, and the sky full of stars made for a pleasant experience.

As the evening wore on, I decided to walk along the beach, which was about 250 feet from the hotel at the end of the boardwalk. Noticing that the beach was nearly deserted, I took off my shoes and socks, rolled up my pants, and walked out to where the water was gently lapping the shore in a rhythmic manner. It was quiet with only the distant sound of voices and subdued music coming from the ballroom of the Royal Hawaiian. It was exhilarating and I felt very calm and content. As I walked barefoot near the water, the sand oozing up between my toes was a delightful feeling. To my left in the dim light, I could hear the laughter of several people. I wondered if they were lovers. Turning back, I decided to leave the "Pink Palace," for the pleasant memories of my visit were entrenched in my mind and I didn't want them to change.

As I walked by the registration desk on my way out, I picked up a copy of the local newspaper, the *Honolulu Star-Bulletin*. The headlines read, "Nazi Germany's lightning war against Russia is now in full swing." The news article also said there was now a two thousand-mile front in Eastern Europe and fighting all the way from Athens, Greece, to Leningrad in the north, plus a separate war in Northern Africa. It didn't register to me at that time that soon the Pacific would also be aflame and that it would be, officially, another world war.

The next day, a number of the men wanted to see downtown Honolulu, so I took three of them with me to check out what happens in the city. While driving down Beretania Street, we noticed a long line of men standing on the sidewalk. The line was about two hundred feet long, the area was nondescript, and we couldn't figure out what was going on. We stopped and asked one of the men, "Hey, what are you guys doing there? What's going on?" He just laughed and said, "You guys better park your car and get in line because this will be the last time you're going to have a woman in your arms for a long time." About then I realized that this line of men was leading to brothels. Two of the men riding with me wanted to go, so I let them out. I had no desire for anything like that. I imagine from those houses of prostitution cases of venereal diseases were transferred to many unsuspecting men. One of the sad things was that many of the men standing in that line were married and I suppose they thought, "Oh, who will know?" What a big mistake. Wouldn't it be terrible to take any disease back home to your wife and family?

I should say at this point that I knew some of my habits weren't as they should have been. I drank and smoked, and was trying to conquer these habits, but so far it had been tough.

After visiting the shops in downtown Honolulu, we headed back to Hickam Field. There I dropped off the other men that were still with me and then drove back to Aunt Glenn's home. No one was at home again, so I left a note of thanks, got on a local bus and eventually made my way back to Hickam. We were scheduled to leave for Wake Island in the morning.

Chapter Three

DESTINATION: WAKE ISLAND

T he *Matsonia*, which we rode from San Francisco to Honolulu, was paradise compared to the old, decrepit, and musty USS *Regulus*. In stark contrast to the *Matsonia* where our accommodation was a royal suite, we were now assigned to the cargo hold of this old freighter. One hold had been temporarily rigged to house large numbers of people in closely hung hammocks. Part of this space was already occupied by about one hundred screaming Cantonese Chinese laborers who had been recruited in San Francisco. The air was stifling, hot and humid, reeking of cheap tobacco smoke and stale sweat. There was little, if any, ventilation. My hammock was right next to a Chinese guy from San Francisco who was about five feet three and weighed nearly 280 pounds. Surely he was the living reincarnation of Buddha.

There were no stewards on this broken down freighter. Taking a shower meant standing in line for a warm shower and perspiring right away afterward. I worried about contracting a good dose of athlete's foot. The meals were served three times a day, but after the gourmet selection of every kind of food imaginable on the *Matsonia*, many of the men's appetites just faded away. Some ate very little, which in my book was a dumb thing to do. The food—beans, potatoes, rice, canned vegetables, canned fruit, thinly frosted cakes, among other things—was nutritious albeit very flat. Little did we know that soon we would learn how rough it could really get. What seemed unacceptable to us on the USS *Regulus* would soon seem like paradise compared to the menu at the Woosung and Kiangwan POW camps.

Things were not all bad. There was not only the humor and interesting incidents, which took place every day, but there was also the beauty of the early morning and late evening walks around the upper deck. One of the favorite places to relax was right up where the starboard and port railings met. There were times I would stand for hours watching the bow of this tired old ship rise and fall as it sliced its way through an incredibly calm, blue sea. As the bow separated the water, flying fish would appear in front of the bow and then dart ahead.

There was one evening in particular that will always remain in my memory. Just as the sun was about to set, after our evening meal, I went out on the deck to get a breath of fresh air. It had been a hot and steamy day; the clothes clung to our wet bodies, and sweat oozed out of every pore. The USS *Regulus* was heading west-south-west at the leisurely pace of ten knots per hour. As I walked up to the bow where the waist-high starboard and port railings converged, it was quiet; all that could be heard was the far away, rhythmic *thump, thump, thump* of the propellers as they pushed the *Regulus* through the dead, calm sea. It seemed as though there was hardly any movement of our ship at all, it didn't rise or fall, nor was there any sideways movement. The sun, which had been unbearable during the day, was now a giant red ball of fire, resting on the distant rim of the ocean behind a few cumulus clouds. You could almost feel that the sun also wanted to cool off after it had spent so much energy making us uncomfortable day after day.

As the sun sank beneath the far horizon, it lit up the clouds above us and the entire sky became alive. The reflection of the sun's rays upon the clouds was spectacularly beautiful. As the rays of the dying sun lit up the underside of the clouds, it made the impression of an outline of a small town, perhaps in mid-western America. As the sun sank lower and lower, beyond the horizon, more lights became visible in this make-believe town. The glow from this beautiful little village gradually dimmed one light at a time until there was just a faint glow, then nothing. Our little village had retired for the evening, and darkness descended softly on the sea until finally there was just the *thump, thump* of the pistons turning in the engine room below.

Standing at the railing and looking over the bow, I was mesmerized as the *Regulus* sliced through a gradually darkening, clear, calm sea. Occasionally, a flying fish would dart out of the water just in front of the bow. Gradually the damp, hot air of the day became cooler and I welcomed the refreshing breeze. It was a good time to be alone.

On the morning of August 19, 1941, after twelve days of boredom, stifling heat, and food that could have been better, we had our first glimpse of Wake Island, a dot in the Pacific, two and a half square miles of blisteringly white coral. Time stood still. It was quiet, and suddenly we all seemed to realize that we were alone in the midst of an immense deep blue ocean called the Pacific, thousands of miles from home.

Arrival at Wake Island

We were so happy to see Wake, knowing that this was the end of our long journey from Hawaii. We were so anxious to get off that miserable, foul-smelling, rusty freighter called the USS *Regulus* that we could hardly contain ourselves. After dropping the *Regulus* anchor, we boarded several small landing crafts (there was no dock), which whisked us through the reef and a small channel, which was cut between Wilkes and Wake. Wake Island is actually an atoll comprising three islands (Wake, Wilkes, and Peale).

It was so good to get on land again. I then understood the difference between "sea legs" and "land legs." After being on the *Regulus* for eleven days I had finally gotten a feel for the rolling pitch of our ship. I had acquired sea legs, so my first steps on Wake Island were a little difficult. Walking on land felt awkward, as my legs had become accustomed to the pitch and roll of the boat. While getting off the landing craft onto firm ground, I had the desire to roll as I walked, but the land does not roll, so I kind of spread my legs a little as I waddled along, just to keep my balance. After a short time, the rolling feeling went away and I was back to reality.

The glaring hot sun beating down on the white coral was almost blinding to the eyes. I hurriedly put on my Polaroid sunglasses. What a difference they made! The gentle breeze that blew across the lagoon also helped. And there were white billowy cumulus clouds that drifted over the island, giving us some temporary relief from the blinding rays of the hot tropical sun overhead. In the distance you could hear the booming surf as the waves hit the outer reef, and you suddenly realized and hoped that the ocean didn't get angry at the island and just wash over it. The highest point on the island was only about twelve feet above sea level and the coral reef was the only protection we had from a sea that could turn absolutely devastating and terribly destructive.

I noticed as I was boarding the flatbed truck that there were a lot of birds—thousands! I thought that might be a problem for any planes landing or taking off, but apparently not.

There were benches fastened to the bed of our flatbed truck and soon Jack, Chalas Loveland, "Mac" McCurry and I were on our way down the coral road to Camp 2, which was about five miles away. As we drove down the road, I was impressed by the work that had already been accomplished in such a short time. The island was alive, with construction going on everywhere. Many men thought: "This is a construction job; we will be here nine months and then back to the States." How little we knew about what was to come.

After checking in at the office, Jack and I were assigned quarters in one of the one-story, long H-shaped barracks that had recently been constructed. Each wing housed about forty men, with eighty men total in one barracks. Where the two wings joined, there was a passageway that contained many showers, toilets, urinals, and washbasins. All in all, the living conditions were not bad. Each man occupied a wooden partitioned area eight feet wide and eight feet long. The exterior wall facing out was screened from four feet up and the screen covered almost the entire outside width of the stall. The two sidewalls were solid wood. The entrance to this little stall also had a solid partition five feet wide, leaving a three-foot entrance that could be sealed off by a curtain. The stall was furnished with a twin bed, a shelf, one electric outlet, and one fixture with a green shade that hung in the center of the ceiling. There were no glass windows, just shutters over openings, as the emphasis was on natural circulation by the gentle trade winds. All my belongings were in a steamer trunk, which was delivered to my stall in the afternoon. This was my new home and the end of my first day on Wake Island.

I was excited about working on Wake and always looked forward to each day's new adventure. After a long day of work, I would walk the northern shoreline with my friends Chal and Lauchlin "Mac" McCurry, looking for Japanese glass fishing balls and beautiful shells, which could be found out near the reef, about 250 yards north of where Peale and Wake met. The reef fascinated me and in the weeks and months that followed, I would spend much of my leisure time out where the waves were breaking. The days were scorching hot, but everything cooled down in the evening. There were lots of gentle rain showers that would come and go. We had movies almost every night. The "movie theater" was more like a drive-in movie set-up, with a large, outdoor screen—but without cars or women. We would sit on the long wooden benches in our shorts, eat popcorn, candy, and enjoy the latest films produced in the United States. Often a gentle warm rain would fall and Chal,

Mac, and I would just sit, watch the movie, and get wet in the warm water coming from the heavens, so pure and refreshing.

All of the water used on the island was salt water, except for the distilled water for drinking and cooking. An interesting sight was someone taking a freshwater shower in the rain under the eaves of a building. The pure fresh water from the sky was most welcome. As there was no fresh water source on the island, water for culinary purposes was distilled. Salt water from the ocean was used for showers, toilets, washbasins, laundry, et cetera. It wasn't as nice as the wonderful fresh water at home, but I didn't mind that little hardship at all.

There was no alcohol permitted on Wake, but of course at the Pan American Hotel on Peale there was liquor for the world travelers to enjoy as they were stopping in overnight. There were no women on the island, either, except Dan Teeter's wife, Florence. A lot of the men had a hard time handling this, especially those with families at home.

Dan Teters, an employee of Morrison & Knudsen Construction Company, was general superintendent of all the civilian workers on Wake. Dan had made an agreement with Henry Morrison, president of the company, that he would accept the assignment to run all of the work on Wake if Henry would let Dan bring his wife, Florence, with him. Henry agreed and so the lovely, energetic Florence Teters became the only woman on Wake. Actually, this was a smart thing to do because she not only was very attractive, but she was also friendly. Everyone who saw her on the beach, in the canteen, at the movies, or just walking around camp, felt her presence. I saw Florence walking along the beach one afternoon in shorts. She was alone and seemed very happy. There was no question about it—she was a great morale booster. She was well liked, but I'm sure she also made men long for their wives, families, and sweethearts on the mainland.

One of the most memorable sights I enjoyed while on Wake was watching the sun come up in the morning. The sky would gradually light up as the rays from the sun bounced off under the white cumulus clouds. Then the rising sun, first a glow, then a sliver of light, and finally this gigantic ball of fire, would sit on the distant horizon, forming a pathway right to where I was standing on the shore. Then the heat would set in and you knew it was just going to get hotter throughout the day. In the evening, the sun would depart, its glory dimming as it descended gradually into the sea. When this happened, the entire sky would glow with the most beautiful colors imaginable.

Once a month we would also enjoy a full moon. When this happened the moon, looking huge, would appear on the distant horizon after a hot afternoon had passed and evening was being ushered in. The moonrise was not white like we were used to on the mainland, but a beautiful light orange. It would gradually rise up from the far away edge of the ocean and within thirty minutes change to a glistening white, unrolling a lovely path of light to the shore. The moon was enormous and you felt like you could almost walk out and touch it. Early the next morning, from the opposite side of Wake, you could watch the same full moon change from a glistening white to a glorious light orange and gradually descend into the ocean. It was breathtaking to catch the rising and setting of both the sun and the moon in one day. It is an experience one can only enjoy on a boat or on a small island like Wake.

Conditions on Wake Island: August 1941

I was completely amazed by the contractors' progress on Wake, considering that just nine months before it was absolutely void of human habitation except for the Pan American base on Peale. When we arrived on August 19, 1941, we found comfortable dormitories, a post office, a hospital with all of the modern equipment, a recreation hall, a commissary, a laundry that would wash and iron all clothing, a library, and two mess halls, each seating 550 men with the kitchen in the center. We also had a baseball field and tennis

Photograph of Wake Island taken by Bill Taylor

courts. We even had airmail service from mainland USA to Wake via Pan American Airways.

There were well-built banquet tables about ten feet long that were used for all of the meals. The food on Wake was the best that could be purchased from the mainland. Everything that was perishable was brought over in refrigerated containers and tasted as fresh as the day it had been packaged. There was also a large refrigeration plant on the island.

When you walked into the dining room at the end of a hard day at work, all of the food for that night was on each table, which seated about ten men. A typical meal consisted of boiled, mashed or scalloped potatoes, sweet mashed potatoes, prime rib (so tender you could eat with a fork), fried chicken, boiled chicken, ham, lamb chops, fish, peas, carrots, beans, spinach, red beets, soup (a different variety each day), milk, coffee, tea, root beer, pies, cakes, and on and on. In the morning it was cereal—hot or cold, scrambled eggs, sausage, hot cakes, toast, muffins, orange juice, tea, milk, hot chocolate, and more. During the years that followed in prison camp, everyone remembered, in detail, all of those wonderful meals we had on Wake.

Almost every night we had an outdoor Hollywood movie. For instance, on Thursday, August 28, 1941, the movie was *The Villain Still Pursued Her*, starring Anita Louise and Alan Mowbray. On Monday, September 15th, the movie was *Algiers* with Charles Boyer and Hedy Lamarr.

So what did we have to worry about? For a guy wanting to get paid three times what he could make on the mainland, it was just great. However, I must note that a majority of the men were married with families on the mainland, so even though they were paid great wages and bonuses to entice them to stay after their contracts expired, most of them could hardly wait to get on the boat or the clipper and return to "the good old USA." I was not one of these. From the day the Regulus docked on Wake, I just wanted to let the dollars stack up in the bank on the mainland.

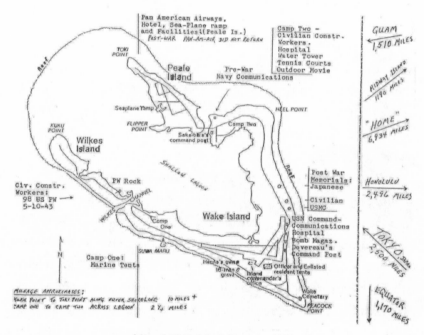

Map of Wake Island, December 1941

Chapter Four

LIFE ON WAKE

I n 1934, CEO of Pan American Airways, Juan Trippe, a trans-oceanic aviation pioneer, became fascinated with the idea of developing an airline that would connect mainland United States with the Philippines and Asia. He plotted a transoceanic route from San Francisco to Honolulu, Midway, Wake, Guam, Manila, Hong Kong, and Shanghai.

He then asked for and received permission from the Navy to use Wake for five years. The Navy was ecstatic. Why? Because in 1922 the United States had signed the Five Power Naval Limitation Treaty, also called the "Shantung Treaty," a mutual agreement limiting fortification of the little Pacific islands. The Treaty was with Japan, France, and Great Britain. Then in 1935 we permitted Pan American Airlines to use Wake as a stepping-stone for refueling aircraft on their way to the Philippines, Australia, Japan, China, and elsewhere. Pan Am gave the United States an out, because Wake was not being "fortified," but was just going to be used as a commercial refueling station, so there was no violation of the Treaty. Because of this, Congress finally began to recognize the importance of and strategic location of Wake. It should be noted, however, that many of the islands controlled by

Japan already had been or were being fortified, such as Kwajalein in the Marshalls, Saipan, and others. Japan, however, completely disregarded this treaty and armed the Marshall, Caroline, and Mariana Islands, among others in the Western Pacific years before WWII. The United States, on the other hand, held to their part of the bargain.

The aircraft Pan American used were thirty-two passenger Martin seaplanes, called "clippers" after the sailing ship that plied the open seas the century before. The Pan Am Clippers, amphibious aircraft driven by four propeller motors, were the largest commercial airplanes in the world at that time. When flying from San Francisco to Honolulu, however, the planes could carry only twelve passengers because the extra fuel needed for the long trip took up more weight. Now, one could travel from San Francisco to Hong Kong in six days instead of the three to five weeks by ship. This method of travel was new, expensive, and exciting. It was used by royalty, the rich and famous and their companions, and politicians. Yes, Pan Am airlines offered world-class, five star hospitality to all who flew with them.

The Pan American facilities were on Peale Island, the second largest islet in the chain of three (Wake is 2.14 square miles or 1,367 acres, Peale is .4 square miles or 256 acres, and Wilkes is .31 square miles or 197 acres). The seaplanes docked there and the passengers would disembark onto a landing pier and go to the twenty-six-room hotel facing the lagoon. On "Clipper Night" the hotel was a beehive of activity. One could hear the laughter of the guests mingling with each other as they enjoyed their exotic cocktails, the clink of brightly polished silver placed atop snowy white linen, and the romantic music playing in the background. Soft, tropical trade breezes drifted through the bar and dining rooms, while the romantic excitement of the moment floated in the air. Overnighters savored their moment on that small coral atoll out in the middle of the Pacific.

The westbound clippers usually arrived in the early afternoon after a twelve-hundred-mile hop from Midway, and the eastbound clippers arrived just before dark after bucking headwinds for nearly fifteen hundred miles in its flight from Guam. Clippers headed in either direction left early each morning. Between six o'clock and six thirty each morning, one could hear all four motors rev up as the clipper moved out into the lagoon and taxied toward the barrier reef that separates Peale from Wilkes. Turning gracefully around, the plane gradually increased the tempo of its engines as it headed down the lagoon toward the center of Wake. In less than a minute, it would skip across the lagoon, leaving a salty spray behind, then rise gracefully, clearing Wake by a mere one hundred feet. What a thrill for the passengers, for they were part of the future. And what a thrill for me as I saw the East and the West drawing closer to each other, whether either party liked it or not.

Watching the clipper ships arrive and depart was an experience in itself. Many an afternoon, I would watch for that small dot on the horizon, which grew larger and larger. Then in less than a minute, you could hear the hum of the motor as that "beautiful bird" drew nearer. It would fly overhead, then bank, circling the island and landing gently upwind on the emerald green lagoon. It was a sight to behold and one never to be forgotten.

In November 1941, when the clipper landed and took off from Wake, all of the window blinds in the plane were pulled down. Many of the travelers going to the United States or Asia were diplomats and all seemed to be in a hurry. A few of the better-known passengers were James Roosevelt, Ernest Hemingway, Japanese Ambassador Kichisaburo Nomura, and Saburo Kurusu. There was a sense of urgency in the air from September through November of 1941.

After-Work Activities on Wake

During these marvelous months, I could hardly believe that we were actually working on a tropical island in the Western Pacific and earning a large income. I thought about how my friends on the mainland would have given anything for this opportunity and was not too concerned about the ominous signs that things were not going well in other parts of the world.

There was a little newspaper on Wake that was published almost daily. Actually, it was a news bulletin comprised of about four eight-by-fourteen-inch pages called the *Wake Wig Wag*. Everybody looked forward to reading its colorful contents. The compiler and editor was Louis Cormier. The first item in the bulletin was the schedule of the Pan American clippers comings and goings from Wake. The next item was information about the movie set to play that night. For example, on Wednesday, September 17, 1941, the movie was *Three Loves Has Nancy*, starring Robert Montgomery, Janet Gaynor, and Franchot Tone, with the notation "Tonight at 8:00." There were also other interesting items in the *Wig Wag*, such as a fire bulletin notice that said, "Brother, if you're hankerin' to squirt a little water, don't use the Fire Department hose. 'Cause you hadn't oughter!'" Then there was a notice for all to remember to tie their laundry bags securely, thereby preventing loss of clothing or laundry slips, which could occur during handling. There was also a note to pick up dry cleaning (it was so nice to always have our clothes cleaned for free). Another sheet was the news, and on one particular day it brought President Roosevelt's "Shoot First" order ringing in our ears.

Meanwhile, tension was mounting throughout the nation and the president's fiery order was still stirring up supporters and opponents against his policy. There is always opposition and there was no exception when Senator Bennett Clark of Missouri and Representative Hamilton Fish of New York both blasted the president, accusing Roosevelt of jeopardizing our national security. My thoughts were, "Go ahead, Mr. President. You are doing the right thing." We had to help England, for they were taking the brunt of the Nazi onslaught, or we would stand a good chance of later fighting the Nazis on American soil.

War was like an ominous dark cloud on the horizon that was moving inevitably closer to America. The war in Europe was like an uncontrollable devastating typhoon. It was a long way away from us, but we could in a sense see the lightning flashing across the horizon, and we knew that soon would come the inevitable deafening thunder, with the vicious hurricane winds of war, and then the uncontrollable destruction. Would the United States be able to withstand the onslaught? But then on Wake, did we really have anything to be worried about?

To us on Wake, the war was a long way away. Or was it? The United States was beginning to cut off a large percentage of the oil that was shipped to Japan. Of course that made the Japanese angry. Those of us on Wake didn't want to think about the events that were happening elsewhere. We were living in a dream world and we resented any thought of change. During those months, I would wonder what the high-flying aircraft over Wake at night were doing. No one seemed to care.

Going out to the reef on the north end of Wake was an exciting experience. When we had a day off work, Chal, Mac, and I would head for the reef, looking for glass balls that had broken away from the Japanese fishing nets. They ranged in size from three inches to two feet in diameter and were of little value. What we really wanted and searched for were the cowrie and aleva shells found out in the reef. There were many of these shells that had broken off from the reef and washed ashore. The truly valuable and beautiful shells were found out in the water at a depth of four to six feet between the shore and the reef. You had to watch out for the rising and falling of the tide, the moray eels, and the giant clams. Eels look like snakes but are actually fish, except they have no pelvic fins. They grow to an average length of about five feet and have a long and slippery body. As they hide in their holes and crevices with only their head protruding, they can strike at passing prey in the blink of an eye. The multicolored giant clams, which ranged from two inches to two feet wide could be seen through your diving mask and would look like just a fringe of gentle billowy color attached to the lips of the grooved shells, gently waving back and forth in the crystal clear water, trying to entice small fish, octopuses, eels, or anything else that happened to be passing by. When they get their prey close enough, the trap is sprung, and the two shells close with lightning speed over the prey that can last for several meals. As you look through your mask at these beautiful mollusks, they appear so innocent and attractive, yet are so dangerous and deadly to the unsuspecting who might come within their range of grasp.

I had a spear made of quarter-inch reinforcing steel about five feet long, flattened on one end into the shape of an arrowhead. Being curious, one day I stuck the spear into a clam, which was about twelve inches wide, and in an instant the spear was clamped tight by the lips of the clam. I could not pull the quarter-inch smooth steel rod from the grip of the clam, so I grabbed my knife and ducked down to where the clam was anchored to the coral, cutting the clam away. I brought it to the surface and after about ten minutes of slicing and cutting the lips, I was able to get my spear loose. I thought that if I had been alone in just a little deeper water and happened to step on one of the larger clams, it could clamp down on my ankle and cause terrible pain. Eventually the tide would come in and I would drown.

The octopuses we would see out on the reef were quite small, about three feet or less from the end of one tentacle to the end of the opposite one. When an octopus emerges to find food, it often lures its victim by wiggling the tip of an arm like a worm. Or it glides near and pounces on a crab, sinking its beak into the shell and injecting a toxic poison. Only a few species of octopus can poison humans. If you came upon an octopus unexpectedly, there may be an explosion of what looks like ink forming a cloud that blocks your view of the octopus. The octopus does this by drawing water in with its mouth cavity then expelling it with great force along with melanin—the same pigment found in human hair and skin—thus escaping under a cloud of black water. It was marvelous to see this animal in action and to observe nature's method of providing protection for these oceanic creatures.

I remember one day I went shell hunting out by the reef. I went out nearly to the edge of the reef where the waves were pounding thunderously on the coral ring, which surrounded the islands like a string of precious white pearls. The tides on that day were quite low and when I reached the reef, the water level was just above my waist. I was trying to find live olive or cowrie shells attached to the coral. I became so engrossed in my hunt that I let the time slip by. Suddenly I realized that the water was up to my armpits. About four hundred yards from shore, I started swimming toward it. It now looked farther away than it had been an hour before. I didn't panic, but I didn't want to encounter a shark, barracuda, giant clam, or Portuguese man-of-war. A lot of things flew through my mind. I stopped for a minute to rest when I saw the water to my left rippling and moving toward me rapidly. All I could do was stand with the water now up to my shoulders and watch this "thing" boil straight towards me, verge to the right at the last moment, and then vanish. I didn't waste any time, and my speed at that time probably would have qualified me for the Olympic team. To this day I have no idea what caused the turmoil on the water. It wasn't a shark as there was no dorsal fin, so probably it was a school of fish—but who knows?

Searching for olive and cowrie shells was a favorite pastime of many of the men on the island. The shells that were found alive and attached to the coral were the only ones of real value. Alive, these beautiful shells were absolutely stunning. They had to have the meat removed from the inside. This was accomplished by burying the shells in a shady spot in about an inch of sand and leaving them for about a week, giving the island ants time to eat the meat, leaving the shells clean as a whistle. Ants clean the shells better than any other method. If the shells are found alive, they retain their vibrant color better. There were different colored shells, some brown with white spots, some black with white spots, and some white with a yellow border and blue on top. Some men wrote home for eighteen-carat gold wire, which they used to make gorgeous bracelets, necklaces, pins, and hairpieces. They sent the shell-adorned jewelry back home to their wives and girlfriends. I didn't think much of this practice at first, but I later learned that years ago these beautiful shells were used as a medium of exchange in the South Pacific, South Asia, Africa, and South America.

There were animals and plants in our part of the lagoon, which distinguished Wake from Peale and Wilkes. We had a swimming pool just off the lagoon, which actually was just a man-made pool that was constructed by bulldozing a hole in the white coral sand seventy feet long and forty feet wide. One day one of the construction workers decided to go swimming before dinner. After swimming a while and stirring up the sand a little, he sat on the edge of the pool with the water up to his waist just resting when he felt something wrapping itself around his leg. He pulled himself to the top of the coral bank separating the pool from the lagoon and as he did, he saw he was in the grip of an octopus with six-feet-long tentacles. He yelled for help, the men came running, and in a few minutes the octopus was captured, killed, and hung up outside the canteen. Because the octopus had no anchor in the sandy-bottomed pool, it couldn't pull the man down into the water, in its typical mode of operation. We all laughed about the incident later, but then we always wondered just what was swimming around in the lagoon and the reef.

Wake also had a lot of hermit crabs, soft-bellied crabs that live in the empty shells of other crabs. As the hermit crab grows, he has to look for another larger home, which another of his kind has abandoned for an even larger one. They live in the lagoon in the water near the reef and come ashore at night to scavenge anything that is dead.

When we first landed in August, I noticed that there were no palm trees and wondered why. There were many small bushes, about three-to-four-feet tall, and some small ironwood trees that grew to a height of about fifteen feet with trunks three-to-four-inches in diameter and with few growth rings. Interestingly, when these young trees were cut and placed in water, they were not buoyant at all. They were so heavy that they would just sink, which probably explains their name of "ironwood." Wake and Peale had ironwood, but Wilkes was almost barren of vegetation. Wilkes Island, instead, had migratory birds—tern, boatswain, boobie, frigate, and plover that built their nests on the coral. When they were nesting, it was almost impossible to walk there for fear of stepping on them or their nests. It was as if they expected you to be careful of them. I had heard there were places like this in the world, but never expected to witness the sight of these beautiful birds at close range. Because Wake was so isolated, there were no predators to harass them.

Experiencing a Typhoon

It wasn't long before I knew the answer to my question of why there were no palm trees and why the ironwood trees were so young. Every few years a typhoon storm hits Wake. The term, "typhoon," comes from the Chinese words *tai fung* and means "big wind." Essentially the same as a hurricane, typhoons consist of high velocity winds accompanied by a tremendous amount of rain blowing around a low-pressure center, which is called the "eye of the storm." These storms are rated from a category 1, which has winds of seventy-four miles per hour, to category 5, with winds exceeding 155 miles per hour. The diameter of a typhoon can reach and exceed three hundred miles. The worst place to be when one approaches is directly in the center or the eye, as the winds surrounding this area are the strongest. When a typhoon strikes head-on and you're halfway through the storm, everything suddenly becomes very calm with no wind, no rain, and a clear sunny sky. The ocean, however, remains violent and serves as a reminder that the worst is yet to come. This dead spot, or the eye, can be about fifteen miles in diameter, so if the storm were moving at seven miles per hour, you would have about two hours before the other side of the typhoon reaches you, the moment when the tremendous damage takes place. Suddenly, within thirty minutes, the wind comes and stirs up the stillness with winds up to 125 miles per hour. At that point, the wind is coming from the reverse direction, battering from the left instead of the right. The resulting damage can be an enormous loss of property and even lives. If a large typhoon directly hit Wake, a tremendous surge of water ten to fifteen feet above normal would completely cover the island, destroying everything that wasn't anchored down.

Well, none of us expected a typhoon to hit Wake and in fact we hadn't even given the possibility much thought. In mid-November 1941, however, we were notified that a typhoon was headed directly toward us. We didn't know the exact velocity of the winds, but we were told it was above one hundred miles per hour and moving towards us at ten miles per hour. We were told that it would reach us in approximately forty-eight hours. We immediately started to tie down anything that was loose or vulnerable to such violent winds. On that particular day, I had been working with a friend named Roger Buxell, who had desired to be a pilot but was turned down by the Army (no Air Force at the time) due to a hearing defect a couple of months before. As I recall, you had to be a perfect physical specimen or you couldn't qualify as a cadet in the Army Air Corps. Roger and I were working in a large warehouse when the wind started to steadily increase. Stepping out of the building onto the road, I looked toward the southeast end of the island, the direction from which the wind was blowing. The cumulus clouds were no longer a soft billowing white, but were then one large mass of menacing dark clouds moving towards us with alarming speed. Roger shouted, "Look at the reef over by Peacock Point!" When I turned to look where he was pointing, a sudden fear went through my body. Gigantic waves were pounding the reef continuously, throwing spray thirty to forty feet into the air. It was an awesome sight, but at the same time you realized that if the wind velocity increased further, soon the whole ocean would rise up and sweep over the island, taking everything with it.

Roger and I hurried back into the warehouse and crouched behind a concrete retaining wall where we could still see outside, as the large double doors were wide open. The wind howled, and debris banged through the doors and against the sheet metal walls of the warehouse. I saw one piece of corrugated sheeting fly by the doors, twisting and turning, and the thought came to me, "If that piece of metal hit anyone it would cut them in half." Roger and I were scared, for we knew if the wind increased, the next thing we would see, and maybe the last thing we would see, would be a wall of water smashing everything and everybody.

We waited and waited, then gradually, after several hours, the wind quieted down. We stepped out of the warehouse to assess the damage. It appeared that while there was damage to many of the buildings, most of it was minor. Wondering why we weren't dead, we learned that Wake had been spared the center of the typhoon's fury, and that for some unknown reason the typhoon had veered north, leaving our island behind. It was estimated that the winds that hit us had a velocity of about eighty miles per hour. Imagine what a one-hundred-sixty-mile-per-hour storm would have done. (If it had been such, you can be sure I wouldn't have lived to write this account.) There is nothing that will bring more fear into your heart than when the elements take over and you realize that you are helpless. And now I knew for myself why there were no palm trees on Wake, just small, fast-growing shrubs and ironwood trees.

Chapter Five

RUMORS OF WAR

After the terrifying typhoon threat, many of the men became a little more apprehensive, realizing for the first time that we were on an island in the western Pacific that could become very hostile and realizing that we were closer to Tokyo than to Honolulu. There was a definite uneasiness, complicated by the drone of airplanes overhead at night. Suddenly the money didn't look as good and some men made the decision to return home.

In August of 1941, 173 Marines and five officers of the 1st Defense Battalion arrived on Wake under the command of Major Lewis A. Hohn. They brought with them four three-inch anti-aircraft guns, three five-inch guns, thirty thirty-caliber and eighteen fifty-caliber machine guns. No one was surprised; Wake was to be fortified as quickly as possible and having Marines on the island was just part of the fortification.

While I was just a civilian iron worker on Wake, I wondered why so much attention had to be focused on building permanent facilities of reinforced concrete and structural steel, such as the bachelor officers' quarters, barracks, and recreation facilities—sparing no expense and making for a perfect target for ships at sea. It has been very difficult for me to understand the order of priority for work on Wake prior to WWII. Work on Wake began January 9, 1941, and during that eleven-month period, it could have become almost impenetrable if the focus would have been on the construction of pillboxes, gun emplacements, revetments at the airfield for the aircraft, two runways instead of just one, and many facilities built partially underground to be nearly invisible from the air. We would pay for the oversight.

We had complete trust in the US Navy. They had never indicated to us that Wake was in danger of attack from the Japanese, but we felt that if there was any danger, we would be protected. Looking back on the situation as it existed and with the information we now have, I believe the government knew and had plenty of evidence that we were on the very brink of war with Japan and in harm's way if it came. Wake would be high on the Japanese list to attack, and undoubtedly without warning. Therefore, it was a race against time. Would there be enough fortification? Probably not, as it would require uninterrupted progress for at least another year and Wake had already been made comfortable and self-supporting for the workers arriving, as I described before.

Did Admiral Husband E. Kimmel, the commander in chief of the Pacific Fleet, know about the threat to Wake in case there was war? Of course, it was no secret; Wake was vulnerable in case of war. However, if it came to armed conflict, it was thought by almost everyone that Japan could be handled quite easily. Their navy was not modern, we thought; their army could not stand up to ours; their aircraft were almost all biplanes. Their morale was good—but would they fight? Were we in for a big surprise! We must remember that Japan had never lost a major foreign war in more than two centuries. In almost every category our government was misinformed, and especially on the Japanese's will to fight. They were great warriors—from a man willing to follow the spirit of Bushido and fight to the last drop of their blood as well as their enemy's blood. They believed it was an honor to die for their country. "Surrender" was not in their vocabulary, and they felt anyone who surrendered was a coward and should die. Cruelty to the vanquished was normal to the conquering Japanese. They considered themselves a superior race and were willing to give up their lives for the emperor.

On November 27, 1941, on Oahu, Admiral Kimmel held a meeting with top Navy and Army brass to discuss what measures should be taken in preparation for the war that was certain to become a reality. The US Military leaders knew that Guam would be almost impossible to defend, as it was in the middle of many islands controlled by Japan in the Western Pacific. Wake and Midway were questionable as work on these two islands was progressing rapidly, but would it be completed soon enough? The safety of the civilians on Wake was never brought up in the Navy's roundtable discussions. In a sense, it seems that the civilians weren't important.

Any attack on Hawaii was out of the question, they thought. Yet even as the meeting progressed, six aircraft carriers, nine destroyers, and two battleships, among other war ships, were already plowing their way through the cold North Pacific to a rendezvous north of Oahu. Surprise was the objective of Admiral Isoroku Yamamoto, commander in chief of the combined Japanese fleet.

On November 27th, Admiral Kimmel received a message from Washington, which stated: "This dispatch is to be considered a war warning. Negotiations with Japan looking for stabilization of conditions in the Pacific have ceased and an aggressive move by Japan is expected within the next few days."

Additional warnings indicating Japan's intentions to attack the United States were known by American intelligence. "Magic" was the code word for secret Japanese messages intercepted, decoded, and translated before Pearl Harbor was attacked. In the fall of 1940, our code breakers were able to read some of the highest-grade diplomatic codes used by Tokyo, its embassies, and consulates, worldwide. This was a year before the Japanese attack on Pearl Harbor.

Why would Japan risk war with the United States? We have to look outside of the attack on Pearl Harbor to get the answers. There was no question the Japanese could see that if they didn't act quickly within a few months, their supply of oil would be gone and the fortifying of Wake, Guam, and Midway would greatly reduce their chances for success. The war on the European front also undoubtedly had its affect on Japan's thinking.

Admiral Kimmel was aware of the potential of a fortified Wake. The Japanese were too. After all, Wake was only about two thousand miles from Tokyo, closer to Yokohama than to Pearl Harbor. A heavily fortified Wake would be an insult to the Japanese. We had already put an embargo on petroleum in July of 1941 and in a sense we were squeezing Japan and letting them know: "Do not expand into Southeast Asia." It was "hands off" Hong Kong, the Philippines, Indo China, Burma, et cetera. We were telling Japan what they could and could not do in our warnings to go no further with their expansion of the Japanese Empire. Our military, however, greatly underestimated Japan. No one thought Japan would attack us. That is, unfortunately, just exactly what they did.

Admiral Kimmel also knew that there were 1,146 civilian contractors plus seventy workers from Pan Am on Wake. He and his staff, however, indicated little concern for our safety as he felt that we would be kept out of harm's way. We all felt that if there were trouble, the Navy would get us off the island. On the other hand, we were probably better off not knowing what was in front of us, because if we had known, many would have left on the next boat out, even if it were the *Regulus*. Like most government officials, Admiral Kimmel never conceived that the Japanese would move so quickly and so efficiently in so many directions at the same time. It was a stunning concept—overwhelming—and it worked.

On October 15, 1941, Major James P. S. Devereux arrived on Wake to relieve Major Hohn as commander. On November 2, 1941, another two hundred Marines arrived on Wake. We now had 388

Marines on hand to defend the ten-mile perimeter of the three islets of Peale, Wake, and Wilkes. All of the Marines were established in Camp 1 on Wake, which the contractors had occupied previous to Camp 2 being built.

And so life went on. On November 28, 1941, Commander Winfield Scott Cunningham arrived on Wake to serve as island commander in charge of all government activities, which included all military personnel, Pan American workers, and civilian contractors. Major Walter L.J. Bayler, a Marine in charge of Marine Communication Personnel arrived from Oahu, Hawaii, on November 29, 1941. Their job was to establish an air-ground radio facility to guide Army bombers being shuffled toward bases in the Philippines, Australia, and elsewhere. Major Bayler was assisted by the arrival of Captain Wilson and six Army personnel of the USASC (US Army Signal Corps), who were to provide a radio guard for the Army bombers being shuttled to forward areas in the Pacific.

In late November, the Marine Fighter Squadron VMF-211 was ordered to report to Admiral Halsey's task force, which consisted of the carrier USS *Enterprise* accompanied by heavy cruisers—*Northampton, Chester,* and *Salt Lake City*—plus eight destroyers. This was a top-secret mission; no one knew about this except the very top brass. The pilots of VMF-211 had no idea where they were going. In fact, they were just told to report for training for one day. They reported without any gear or clothing—not even a toothbrush.

After they boarded the *Enterprise* and had put out to sea, they were informed that this was a top-secret mission and that the destination was Wake Island. Because of the secrecy surrounding their departure, it became apparent that the rumors about war with Japan were being taken seriously by the Military. Even as serious as the situation looked with Japan, however, Washington was concentrating almost all of its resources on the war in Europe.

On December 4, 1941, the huge Japanese Naval Armada led by Admiral Yamamoto was only three days away from attacking Pearl

Harbor. On that same date Halsey's task force was within two hundred miles of Wake. When the VMF-211 Squadron, which included twelve F4F Grumman fighters, left the *Enterprise*, a Navy PBY Catalina (an amphibious patrol bomber) met them. This meeting was necessary as the F4Fs were not equipped with navigational or direction finders, so the PBY had to lead them to Wake. Because of their lack of equipment, visual contact with land was imperative, and so with this handicap, the squadron didn't have much to offer to the defense of the island. Because there were so many shadows cast on the water by a sky full of cumulus clouds, if the enemy attacked, you could not chase him too far out of sight of land, or you just might not return.

Many disappointments greeted the VMF-211 upon their arrival on Wake Island. The landing strip, while long enough, was not wide enough to handle more than one plane. This meant only one plane at a time could take off or land. Also, there were no revetments (shelters) to protect the aircraft in case of an attack. And as a final frustration, there were no maintenance manuals or spare parts for the aircraft.

These circumstances were all indicative of the mind-set of our Military in the Pacific. The feeling in Washington was that if Japan decided to attack the United States, it would be a fairly short war. The Military knew Japan had a fair-sized navy and that they might be able to invade some of the small nations in Southern Asia, although they didn't anticipate that Japan could also take the heavily fortified Corregidor in the Philippines, Hong Kong, or the seemingly impenetrable Singapore. While the United States recognized that Japan was a power in the Pacific and probably would have some success at the beginning of any conflict, they believed Japan would run out of oil and other essential resources quickly. The United States was concentrating on the war in Europe at that point, so Japan's immediate threat was temporarily ignored. In the meantime, we would build up our defenses, fortify our territory in the Pacific, and then we would be in a position to hem in Japan to the point where they could not maneuver.

The concept and strategy might have worked if we had another year to finish the fortifications, including those on Wake, Guam, and the Philippines. The Japanese knew we weren't fully prepared for them, and they wouldn't wait much longer. The result was that America's extended plan didn't work and that Japan became infinitely better prepared than anyone in our government ever imagined. In short, we had not planned far enough ahead. We were not fully prepared and we greatly underestimated the ability of Japan's military as well as their national courage and determination for a victory at all costs. The Japanese strategy was to hit the United States first, then to attack Asia. We would put up resistance, but we were up to our necks in Europe, so maybe, just maybe, an attack on the United States, a devastating attack, would keep us at bay until it would be too late to retaliate.

What did we learn from this shortsightedness? We were to learn very soon to never underestimate the power of the enemy!

Wake's Involvement in the War

It seemed to me that because Washington was indecisive about Wake's role militarily, Congress had let two vital years slip by before they actually realized that Wake was important to the United States. In those days, Wake Island was a dot out in the Pacific the United States could just as well forget. Wake was a waterless, very small atoll, 2.5 square miles (6.5 square kilometers). The highest point was only eleven feet above the blue Pacific, which could at times get quite angry. About every ten years, a typhoon would hit Wake. When this happened, the ocean would rise up and literally wash over the island. Given time, however, structures could be built that could endure the fury of a full-blown typhoon with winds up to 175 miles per hour. We could build and overcome this type of a natural disaster. But Congress fiddled and dawdled and let time pass by. They failed to realize that we needed Wake to be the eyes and ears in the Pacific and an outpost for the States.

In the spring of 1939, Congress had before them a Naval appropriation bill for fiscal year 1940 in which they were asking two million dollars for improvements on Wake (bear in mind that Pan American was already on Wake and had been since October 21, 1936, working under a contract with the US mail service to the Far East.). Congress finally proceeded to authorize the construction work on April 25, 1939, but dropped Wake from the appropriation bill, which passed on May 25, 1939. So the work was authorized, but the money was not approved and Wake received nothing. Because the appropriation bill concerning Wake Island was dropped, a very important year of fortification was lost.

And then there was the Five Power Naval Limitation Treaty (or the Shantung Treaty), a mutual agreement signed in 1922 stating that Great Britian, the United States, Japan, France, and Italy would respect each other's rights by not arming the little Pacific islands under their own possession.

In 1940 Congress finally came to its senses and hurriedly appropriated more than five million dollars for aviation facilities on Wake and then in 1941, a whole year later, appropriated an additional ten million dollars. Now that the United States began to realize that Japan was committed to a policy of aggression and conquest in the Pacific, it was decided to maximize development on Midway and Wake. But the money came a little too late. That single year of fortification work foregone in 1939 probably lost us the island in December 1941.

Just before the attack on Pearl Harbor and Wake, the Wake airbase was still under construction by 1,146 civilians contractors, headed by superintendent Dan Teters. A large number of buildings were either being started or were nearly complete. Camp 2 was just across the bridge from Peale to Wake. Across the lagoon on the opposite tip of Wake, near the channel separating Wake and Wilkes, was the smaller Camp 1 for the Marines. The new ship channel through Wilkes was halfway completed.

Large stores of all kinds of construction supplies, machinery, and equipment for operating the base had been received on the island. Had the island not been attacked, all might have been in place by the summer of 1942. The military defense consisted of the First Marine Defense Battalion equipped with six five-inch coast defense guns, twelve three-inch anti-aircraft guns, four searchlights, eighteen fifty-caliber and fifty thirty-caliber machines guns, and miscellaneous small arms.

Late in November of 1941 a small carrier task force commanded by Vice Admiral W. F. Halsey, USN, supported by Rear Admiral R.A. Spruance with two heavy cruisers and a few destroyers in addition to the carrier *Enterprise*, made a high speed run west from Pearl Harbor to a point northwest of Wake. On December 4, 1941, twelve F4F (Grumman Wildcat fighters) of VMF 211 commanded by Major Paul A. Putnam, were launched from the *Enterprise* to fly to Wake Island and their rendezvous with destiny and fame. As one can see, America was trying desperately to beat the clock.

At this time the population of the island consisted of seventy-two Navy men, six Army Signal Corpsmen, 379 men from the First Marine Defense Battalion, and 59 men with VMF-211, for a total of 516 military personnel. There were 70 Pan American Airways employees and 1,146 Contractor Pacific Naval Air Bases employees for a total of 1,216 civilian personnel. We had a grand total of 1,732 inhabitants on this small coral atoll before the Pacific Theater's onset.

At this point, on Wake, we were about to be in trouble. The island was about 25 percent prepared to wage battle. War was looming and the government knew it, but did not make the fortifications needed in time, nor seemed to have the intention of doing so.

According to the coded messages that Japan was sending in the six months before Pearl Harbor, it was clear that the Japanese Military was planning offensive moves against the United States, Great Britain, and the Dutch East Indies. At the same time, full-scale espionage against the United States was in progress, as can be seen from the exchange of messages between Tokyo and its diplomats in the capitals of the West. These communications contained factory production, defense emplacements, military movements, et cetera. In short, Japan was taking the steps that any country takes in preparing for the eventualities of war. Also, Japan, as a member of the Axis Powers (with Germany and Italy), was being pressed to make the ongoing global conflict. The war in Europe was going well for Germany, and if Japan was really going to attack Southeast Asia, only the United States stood in the way. Since these messages were available to the government a year before Japan attacked Pearl Harbor, one wonders why we were caught off guard.

Our country knew the Japanese were prepared to launch some kind of an offensive in the Pacific, and the government thought the target would probably be the Philippines, which was under United States administration at the time. The Japanese had invaded China in 1937, causing the United States to declare an oil embargo and in 1940 the Japanese were granted military access in French Indochina by the Vichy Government in France. This Vichy Government was a new government in France that was controlled by the Nazis after Germany had invaded and overthrown the French. These moves only furthered the strength of the Japanese in the Pacific.

Japan's thinking was that Great Britain and the Netherlands were too involved in the war in Europe to mount any significant response if Hong Kong, Singapore, Indochina, Burma, and Indonesia were attacked. They were correct in this observation. This left the United States, the protector of the Philippines, Wake, Guam, Midway, among others, the only nation standing in their way.

As the United States saw the picture, the only way the United States could really be hurt by the Japanese was if they attacked the Philippines or Pearl Harbor. The Philippines would be a target, but they would never overrun Corregidor; it was considered impregnable. Hitting Pearl Harbor when the fleet was in port and striking Hickam Field when almost all of the Army's Air Force was stationed there was unthinkable. Admiral Husband E. Kimmel, General Short, and other top brass could not even conceive of an attack on the islands, mainly because they believed that the Japanese Navy would never be able to get within striking distance without being detected.

But the Japanese fooled everyone. Or did they? Did the United States know of a pending attack? Let's take a look at the information we had prior to December 7, 1941.

The following is a series of communiqués our government had received, many of which were decoded at least a day before Pearl Harbor and Hickam Field were attacked:

Communiqué No. 222 from Honolulu to Tokyo, November 18, 1941: "The warships at anchor in the Harbor on the 15th were as I told you in my No. 219 on that day. Area A—A battleship of the *Oklahoma* class entered and one tanker left port. Area C—3 warships of the heavy cruiser class were at anchor. 2. On the 17th the *Saratoga* was not in harbor. The carrier *Enterprise*, or some other vessel was in Area C. Two heavy cruisers of the *Chicago* class, one of the *Pensacola* class were tied up at docks 'KS.' 4 merchant vessels were at anchor in Area D. . . . 3. At 10:00 a.m. on the morning of the 17th, 8 destroyers were observed entering the Harbor. Their course was as follows: In a single-file at a distance of 1000 meters apart at a speed of 3 knots per hour, they moved into Pearl Harbor. From the entrance of the Harbor through Area B to the buoys in Area C, to which they were moored, they changed course 5 times each time roughly 30 degrees. The elapsed time was one hour, however, one of these destroyers entered Area A after passing the water reservoir on the Eastern side."

Now for communiqué No. 123 from Tokyo to Honolulu, which was received on December 2, 1941: "In view of the present situation, the presence in port of warships, airplane carriers, and cruisers is of utmost importance. Hereafter, to the utmost of your ability, let me know day by day. Wire me in each case whether or not there are any observation balloons above Pearl Harbor or if there are any indications that they will be sent up. Also advice [*sic*] me whether or not the warships are provided with anti-mine nets." This was not translated until twenty-eight days later, December 30, 1941, weeks after the attack on Pearl Harbor.

Communiqué No. 254 from Honolulu to Tokyo, December 6, 1941: "1. On the evening of the 5th, among the battleships which entered port were and one submarine tender. The following ships were observed at anchor on the 6th: 9 battleships, 3 light cruisers, 3 submarine tenders 17 destroyers, and in addition there were 4 light cruisers, 2 destroyers lying at docks (the heavy cruisers and airplane carriers have all left). 2. It appears that no air reconnaissance is being conducted by the fleet air arm." In addition to the communiqués, there were continual visual signals from the east coast of Oahu and Maui. These signals were made almost daily until December 7th.

With all of the above information, why were we caught off guard? Knowing there was growing tension between the United States and Japan and with all the coded Japanese information we were receiving, you would think we would be on constant alert. Why this lackadaisical attitude?

As I have mentioned before, Hawaii was a great place to live, especially for the Military. There were parties every night, the liquor flowed like a river, it was a fun place to be stationed, and nobody ever, ever thought we would be attacked right at home. Yes, we grossly underrated the Japanese's ability to wage a war against the United States. We underestimated their intelligence system, drive, loyalty to the emperor, bravery, and determination to succeed. And we considered them racially inferior (which alone was enough to make them angry). And so, to a great extent, we had a racial war on our hands.

The Japanese were and are a proud people. They had been so successful in their past conflicts that they had absolutely no intention of being defeated by anyone, especially the arrogant Americans. This great Asian war consisted of so many opposites—skin color, culture, language, morals, ancestry, heritage, et cetera. Sometimes there are leaders of countries who lead their people along the wrong paths. But according to my experience, if you are able to become friends with a Japanese person, without any conflicts in the way, you are lucky, as the Japanese are wonderful people from a great nation.

Chapter Six

JAPAN'S INITIAL ATTACK, WAKE'S SHORT-LIVED VICTORY, AND A PERSONAL TURNING POINT

And now back to Wake and my story. December 8, 1941 will always remain special in my memory. It's amazing how you remember certain dates and times—where you were, what you were doing, the weather, the hour. This is how it was for me when I found out about Pearl Harbor's bombing, which had taken place just the day before. Because Wake is across the international date line, when it was seven o'clock in the morning, Sunday, December 7th in Honolulu, it was five o'clock in the morning, Monday, December 8th on Wake Island.

There were beautiful cumulus clouds that morning. The weather was perfect with a slight breeze. On this eventful day I arose early, washed with salt water, dressed in shorts (we didn't wear long pants, as they were too hot), and hurried to the mess hall for breakfast. Everything and anything was set out for breakfast: bacon, scrambled eggs, hot cakes, sweet rolls, mashed potatoes, prunes, peaches, pineapple, watermelon, cantaloupe, coffee, hot chocolate, orange juice, pineapple juice, toast, butter, a choice of many syrups, and milk—all in great abundance.

After breakfast, it was quickly off to work. Outside the mess hall, we boarded the flatbed trucks in order to be taken out to our areas. On this particular day, I had been assigned to work with Roy Stephens, Joe Goicoechea, and several other ironworkers on the new power plant to be built on Peale Island. The foundation had been excavated. In place of the exterior walls were the wooden forms two feet high and seven feet wide that would hold the reinforced concrete in place until it set up. There were also four interior walls that ran across the entire length of the footing. Our job was to place one-inch steel reinforcing bars twelve inches apart, each way, forming a mat of twelve inches square, 1.2 inches from the bottom of the frames. Then we made another mat twenty-two inches from the bottom. I might mention that all of the reinforcing steel had to be sandblasted before being put in place. Sandblasting is a very physically demanding job. Roy Stephens, who was six feet three inches, and I, being five feet eight, did all of the sandblasting. Roy outweighed me by one hundred pounds.

After the forms are built and the steel is in place, the concrete is poured. The entire island is made up of coral from which all of the aggregate was prepared. This was our sand and rock, and for every yard of this aggregate, six ninety-pound sacks of cement were used. The cement was shipped over from Honolulu, two thousand miles away, so you can imagine the cost of just one yard of concrete on Wake Island.

After working for about an hour, a pickup truck drove up and our rebar superintendent, Dutch Raspe, jumped out and yelled down to us, "Hey you guys, we're in a war! Japan just bombed Pearl Harbor a couple of hours ago." We stopped working. Nobody seemed too excited. One of the guys yelled back, "So what do we do now?" Dutch shrugged his shoulders and replied, "I don't know. We can stay here, I guess, or take the next boat out." What none of us realized was that there wouldn't be another boat home for almost four years.

After Dutch left, we kept on working. The magnitude of what had happened just didn't sink into our heads. We were comforted

by the thought that the Navy would protect us and in the meantime
we could finish our quite lucrative contracts. Almost ten minutes
to noon, I climbed out of the foundation of the power plant and
boarded the back of the flatbed truck that was waiting to take us
back to camp to lunch, a distance of about a mile and a half.

A carpenter climbed up on the truck and took his seat next to me
on a bench. We sat there for a minute or two waiting for Roy and Joe
and the rest of the men to fill the seats. As I looked southwest, toward the airport, I noticed a large number of bombers flying low over
Peacock Point. I thought, "Boy, Uncle Sam sure got here quickly."
They were very low, about fifteen hundred feet above ground level. In
a sense, they just seemed to be gliding in for a landing. It was an unreal scene. Everything was quiet and seemed so peaceful. Then I saw
the bombs dropping from the aircraft and exploding on the runway
where we had eight of our precious twelve F4F Grumman Wildcat
fighters exposed. There wasn't a sound. Time seemed to stand still.
We just sat there and watched. Then, suddenly the sound reached us
and we could see and hear the devastation that was taking place.

I just sat there for a few frozen seconds, then I heard the explosions and the chatter of machine guns as the bombers strafed
the island. I jumped off the truck on one side and the carpenter
jumped off the other side. He was hit by machine gun fire as the
bombers passed over us. I ran out onto the Pan American runway,
just as nine more enemy bombers flew over the runway. I flattened
out on the ground, only this time I was looking up at the bombers
as they flew over the base. They were low and strafing everything.
As I lay on my back looking up, it seemed like I could almost touch
them. The bomb bays were wide open and I could see the bombs
dropping out. Everything was in chaos, the ground seemed to be
jumping out of control as the bombs hit. I later learned that there
were three groups of bombers, nine planes in each group, flying in
"V" formations, two groups hitting the airfield and the other group
hitting Pan American.

As I lay on my back, I wondered if the Pan American Philippine Clipper ship, which had been on its way to Guam early in the morning and had then returned to Wake, was still intact and if the passengers were okay. Well, the attack on Pan Am destroyed much of the facility, but the Philippine Clipper ship was not too damaged. It had been strafed with a lot of holes in the fuselage, but nothing mechanical had been damaged.

The pilot, John Hamilton, a lieutenant in the Naval Reserves, later decided that he would try to fly to Midway Island, one of the many stops the Pan Am planes made on their way across the Pacific. He then ordered everything off the clipper that wasn't necessary for the flight to Midway, loaded up all of the personnel from the hotel and the passengers, taxied down the lagoon toward the reef on the northwest end, and turning at the reef, he revved up his four motors. I watched as they started the long way down the inside of the lagoon—slow at first, then picking up more speed. The clipper raced down toward the end of the lagoon. You could tell the clipper was doing all it could to pick up the necessary speed to get above the island at the end of the lagoon. Just when you thought the clipper wasn't going to make it, it gained enough altitude to barely clear the island by about ten feet. Then it gradually gained altitude and soon was just a little dot on the horizon, winging its way to Midway.

I was stunned by the attack. I got up and ran through the bushes toward the ocean on the north side of Peale. I fell down as I ran through the tangled mass of growth and then suddenly I saw a gigantic Albatross bird, about two feet away. It leaped back and screamed at me and I could see down its throat. I was startled and yelled, then got up and ran right out into the ocean about two hundred feet away and let the breakers wash over my head. After about ten minutes, I calmed down and made my way toward camp. I walked across the bridge connecting Peale Island to Wake. As I approached the camp, I decided to stop at the mess hall to see what was going on there. When I opened one of the screen doors and stepped inside, I was

shocked by the sight of tables loaded with delicious food. There
was everything you wanted, and the steam was still rising from the
hot food. In later years, while a prisoner of the Japanese, I had the
vision of that feast in my mind. But the most striking sight was not
the tables laden with food, it was that not one person was eating and
there was nobody in the hall. After waiting a few minutes, I walked
back outside into the blazing Monday sunshine.

Some of the barracks and other buildings were on fire. I decided to go over to the hospital to see if any help was needed. Upon
entering the hospital, I beheld a sight that would make anyone's
heart turn over. There were wounded men who were waiting for
treatment, men who were mortally wounded, and others who were
already dead. Our facilities were meager. We had two doctors to
care for the men who were wounded and dying, and our medicine
and drugs were grossly inadequate. As I stood in the hallway looking at the carnage the bombers had caused, I was stunned, numb.
It had happened so quickly. No one was ready for this war that had
suddenly appeared on our doorstep. Everything had just come to a
stop. I thought, "These guys who are wounded, dead, or dying had
breakfast with me just a few hours ago."

As I look at those moments in time, I can fully understand why
it is so important to have the basic training that all branches of the
service receive. Navy, Army, Air Force, Marines, and Coast Guard
personnel receive basic training that prepares them to act in unison
in times of chaos. They may be in shock, but the inner instinct takes
hold and they fall back on that training they received when they entered the Military. He is much better prepared when a situation such
as this arrives unexpectedly. This preparation was the reason the
Marines reacted so quickly when we were attacked on Wake. But I
never spoke with anyone who was there—Marine or civilian—who
wasn't frightened after the initial attack.

I suppose one of the things that has bothered me over the years
is that some of the Marines expected everyone to react as they did,

which could not happen when so many civilians were involved. Over the next weeks, however, the civilians learned to respond. Some two hundred of the 1,076 civilians were actually serving with the Marines on three-inch and five-inch guns—fifty- and thirty-caliber machine guns. The other eight hundred also served in various capacities, running the heavy equipment, assisting at the airport with the repair of the F4F Grumman fighters, moving the very heavy three-inch guns almost every night, taking care of the logistics of food, et cetera. In short, the Marines would never have been able to sustain themselves without the great deal of support they were given by the civilians in their efforts to withstand the Japanese assaults. In recent years, the Marines I have been acquainted with have reaffirmed this. Commander Cunningham has said of the civilians, "When it came to helping out, there was a limit to the number of untrained civilians who could be absorbed into Military units and it was clear that their greatest value would be in providing food and work crews."

The modernization of the Military's fighting equipment on Wake was so far behind that it was criminal to expect the Marines or anyone else to compete with the enemy. Almost everything that was sent to Wake for defense was out of date, from the bolt action 1913 Springfield rifles, to the World War I helmets, to the immobile three-inch anti-aircraft guns with heavy outriggers that were very difficult to move. Had the civilians not manually moved these guns almost every night, the Japanese bombers would have destroyed the batteries within two or three days after their initial strike. I might also note that it took thousands of sacks of sand to protect these guns. Commander Cunningham said that he was familiar with the five-inch guns sent to Wake, that they were taken off an old battleship from WWI. They were good for coastal defense, but were almost immobile and very difficult to move. The three batteries of four three-inch guns each augmented the five-inch guns. There were also eighteen fifty-caliber machine guns, which were to be used against low flying aircraft, landing boats, or infantry, thirty thirty-caliber machine guns, and a small number of rifles and pistols. This pretty well completed the firepower that we had to use against the Japanese. We also had six large searchlights with their own generators.

We could say that our defense was quite productive, but really it was not very good. Our three-inch guns were ineffective against high altitude raids, and of the anti-aircraft guns, only one was capable of putting shots where they might do some damage. Furthermore, Devereux's battalion was less than half of what they needed; one of the anti-aircraft batteries was entirely without a crew. The situation was about as hopeless as it could get. The outlook was dim, but we were not willing to give up without a fight—even to the end. A makeshift defense by the Marines and civilians was hastily organized, hoping for the miracle that never happened. The Japanese took advantage of our weakness.

On that afternoon of the 8th of December, Dan Teters, our superintendent, told all who were not manning the guns to head for the bushes, dig a hole, and wait for further orders. We were told not to return to the barracks that were still standing. For the rest of the day, we just tried to adjust to the circumstances. I headed for the brush on Wake along with my brother Jack and Chalas Loveland. We stopped about two hundred yards south of our camp, dug a small foxhole in the coral gravel and waited for someone to tell us what was needed and where we could help. We didn't have to wait long, for one of the things that can decimate an army, especially if they have to stay in one area, is sanitation. So covered latrines were built everywhere. I dug my own hole and covered each bowel movement with coral sand and gravel, and then waited for the next bombing, speculating about what would happen next. There seemed to be plenty of distilled water and there was a good supply of food. There was speculation from the beginning that the Navy would come to Wake, bringing food and medical supplies, as well as arms, more Marines, more aircraft, et cetera. Then they would evacuate the civilians.

Then December 8th passed without further interruption and an uneasy night settled in. Sleep in a foxhole did not come readily or comfortably under the stars, listening to the endless crashing of waves on the coral reef while anxiously wondering what the next day would bring.

The morning of the 9th of December was beautiful with a few white cumulus clouds and gentle trade winds moving across the island and soon the most gorgeous sunrise. The first rays lit up the whole sky, then the sun emerged from the bottomless sea—a breathtaking sight. Everyone was wondering what would happen next. What a change forty-eight hours had made in all of our lives! Two days ago it was Sunday, a day of relaxation, swimming, searching for shells, looking through a great library, eating wonderful food, enjoying the unbelievable climate and gentle breeze. Then, twenty-four hours later, we received a devastating surprise blow by the enemy, and within fifteen minutes, everything changed. So there we were on December 9, 1941. We were in the midst of World War II.

We were all confused and depressed by the devastating attack the day before, the loss of life, and the loss of flight crewmembers and airplanes. The VMF 211 Squadron had nine planes in the first raid either lost or damaged. Captain Platt asked Second Lieutenant John Kinney, a Marine pilot, to take charge of repairing the damaged aircraft with whatever parts he could find. John was a university graduate with a degree in electrical engineering, with an uncanny ability to make irreparable things work. So, within twenty-four hours of the first raid, Lieutenant Kinney, with the help of Technical Sergeant Hamilton, had one fighter repaired and another nearly ready, making a total of five usable planes. Lieutenant Kinney was indispensable in the battle for Wake.

Because there were no revetments to shelter the planes, one of the civilian cat-skinners (bulldozer operators), Max Boesiger, started to make revetments, air raid shelters, and a big command post from which Major Devereux could operate more efficiently.

The atmosphere on the island became rush-rush as everyone became involved in the tasks at hand, which included protecting the three-inch and five-inch guns. McCurry was on a thirty-two-caliber machine gun. Chalas, my brother Jack, and I volunteered to do all we could to protect the big artillery pieces. In the back of our minds was always the question, "What would happen next?"

The Japanese had hit us around 11:55 a.m. the day before, and we determined that they would likely attack us close to that hour again. In a meeting the day before, Commander Cunningham, Major Platt, and Colonel Devereux decided the Japanese had taken off from Roi in the Marshall Islands in the early morning of the 8th. Roi was about six hundred miles south of Wake, and because most pilots do not like to fly over the water in the dark, it was decided that the next bombing raid would be around noon. So we waited, and about 11:45 a.m. the lookout on the water tower reported that twenty-seven twin-motor bombers were bearing down on Wake at an altitude of around twelve thousand feet. We had two fighters

The contractors' camp was well demolished. Shown above is the contractors' warehouse. Behind and to the left can be seen the conveyor belts and gravel piles where many of the men were able to take shelter. At the extreme left lie the remnants of the garage and machine shop.

facing the attack of the twenty-seven enemy bombers. Soon one enemy aircraft just blew up and another was hit. In a few seconds the bombers were gone.

Over by Camp 2, the men were moving around when the bombers struck again. Chal, Jack, and I had taken Cunningham's advice to stay away from the camp. We were near our foxholes when the bombs hit. The strike this time hit not only the barracks, but also the hospital and other buildings. It was again coupled with the seemingly unending strafing by the enemy machine guns. The casualties were devastating: fifty-five men wounded, thirty-five mortally. The cries of the wounded and dying filled the air and there was fire everywhere. We had two doctors—Dr. Mason Kahn, a Navy doctor, and Dr. Lawton E. Shank, the civilian doctor—who worked feverishly operating and patching up the wounds of those who were wounded in the first raid. They had been up all night and were dead tired when the second raid swept across the island. There was no place to run, and even if a shelter was nearby, there wasn't time to get there. The only thing one could do was dive under a bed or pull something over his head. When something like this takes place, one moment everything seems to be going smoothly and then the next moment is total confusion, fear, explosions, fire, and then quiet again, only then with a lot more wounded men to care for. Luckily, neither doctor was injured.

On this second raid, the Japanese didn't get away scot-free. They lost three bombers and perhaps four others that were shot up, trailing smoke as they disappeared from sight.

By the time the raid was over, many of the contractors were working with the Marines. Major Devereux realized that the next time the enemy came to drop their bombs, they probably would target the five-inch Navy guns and the three-inch anti-aircraft guns. The three-inch anti-aircraft guns were spread in three groups of four guns to a battery, one on Peacock Point, one on Wilkes, and one at the end of Peale. After the raids of the 8th and 9th, Major Devereux made an order that the three-inch anti-aircraft guns be moved to a new location about seven hundred yards away. He felt the Japanese were taking pictures every time they attacked the island. Moving the guns may sound like a small task, but it was a hefty job, especially in the dark, to relocate a battery of three-inch anti-aircraft guns, as each battery was surrounded by thousands of sandbags. These guns also had heavy outriggers. The gun alone weighed more than eight tons, and that's not counting the monstrous outriggers. Before the war, it had taken a minimum of two weeks to get these batteries in place. We, the Marines and civilians, moved the battery on Peacock in twelve hours. This was an excellent maneuver by Devereux, one that probably saved many lives as the days went by. I was in the group of men that moved the guns on Peacock Point and we didn't finish the moving a moment too soon.

The civilian contractors have been blamed for much of the chaos that occurred right after the first attack. But over a period of many years, not only have the Marines vindicated the contractors, but the Navy and others have also vindicated them once they realize how necessary the construction workers had been in a time of war. Before a month had passed, the government organized the Seabees (Construction Battalion of the United States Navy). They realized how indispensable construction workers were to any Military operation.

One of my friends, Ike (Isaac J.) Wardle had some comments after the men returned home at the end of WWII. Here is the story of the attack from his vantage point:

> After the first bombing at noon on December 8th, the whole island, including the Marines, were in a state of shock and frustration. Dan Teters, Commander Cunningham, and other officers assembled us and told us to gather in small groups, to get food, water, supplies, and to hide in the brush and to keep out of sight and shift for ourselves. (What else was there to say?)

On the night of December 8th, we were asked to help at the airport. About two hundred contractors showed up with all of the equipment necessary to make the runway unfit for enemy landing. We placed dynamite charges over the entire runway. All of the wiring was interconnected to a central control. We then were asked to go to Wilkes Island where we covered large culvert pipes with four feet of dirt. The next day, the 9th, we helped the Marines dig in. The Japanese missed us on their next bombing run. Dan Teters sent word for all of us to come over to Wake to the Bachelor Officers' Quarters (BOQ) that night at dusk for further instruction.

The Marines needed men to help man the five-inch guns at Peacock Point, so I went. When I arrived, I helped for a short time and then was called away to help gather and clean gasoline barrels. This meant taking them to the power plant where we steamed them out, then filled them with distilled water, as all of our drinking water on the island had to be distilled. This had to be done, or in a few short days there wouldn't be any fresh water for anyone. Two of the contractors, Jack Wolf and Joe Williamson, and others kept the water plant running twenty-four hours a day. Yes, I'm responsible for the gassy water we were given to drink after we surrendered.

Each night, Chalas Loveland, my brother Jack, and I went to the various anti-aircraft guns to help move them and get them ready for the next day's anticipated attack. The moving and filling of sand bags was really hard work. Though food became quite critical, we were able to manage relatively well. At least twice a day, meals were served from trucks that traveled around the island. We were quite fortunate to have a good supply of food, enough to sustain life. We knew that if we were not given relief within a month, our food supply would dwindle and eventually run out. Although we were distilling our drinking water, in time that supply would also run out. We didn't dwell on this, as we were so sure that the Navy would soon evacuate all of the civilians. We had rumor that a small task force had been assembled in Hawaii and that within a very short time, maybe a week or two, we would be on our way home. Our spirits were high.

At about a quarter to four on the morning of December 11th, we saw lights flashing back and forth about five miles out at sea and we knew something was up. These lights were coming from a Japanese Task Force whose objective was to capture Wake and kill all defenders. They were first just going to soften us up with heavy artillery fire from cruisers and destroyers who were gradually circling the atoll, drawing in a little closer all of the time. The Japanese probably thought the invasion of Wake would be a very simple task, but they were in for a surprise!

The Japanese Task Force was comprised of fifteen enemy ships and 450 landing troops under the direction of Rear Admiral Sadamichi Kajioka. Admiral Kajioka was part of the Japanese Fourth Fleet, commanded by Vice Admiral Shigeysoshi Inoue. (Actually Admiral Inoue had implied that the Japanese Navy was old fashioned and that in the future the naval wars would be won by aircraft carriers. For this radical assumption, he was sent to Kwajalein.) Their homeport was Roi, in the Marshalls, about six hundred miles south of Wake.

Guam's Capitulation

After Pearl Harbor was bombed, the war in the Pacific was rapidly centered on the islands controlled by the United States. Wake and Guam were to be taken by the Japanese, the first objective being Guam, where there were only 424 sailors and Marines, plus 326 native home guardsmen and militia. The Japanese wanted to be sure that Guam would be taken without too much trouble, so the task force consisted of 5,500 Army men, four cruisers, a mine layer, four destroyers, along with four Army transports. Vice Admiral Inoue assigned Rear Admiral Sadamichi Kajioka to be the commanding officer.

When Guam was attacked on the 8th of December 1941, the defenders capitulated so quickly that the shelling of the island never took place. Guam just turned itself over to the Japanese. The cruisers and destroyers didn't have to fire a shot. The Japanese invasion forces were so pumped up that Vice Admiral Inoue decided that Wake would go the same way, quickly, and that is where he made a big mistake—one that armies have made since the beginning of time. He underestimated the enemy, therefore he decided that Wake would fall with little or no resistance. So he cut way back on the number of troops he felt were needed to conquer Wake. The invasion force that was assigned to Wake consisted of the flagship, *Yubari*, a light cruiser; two submarines; four transports; six destroyers (the *Hayate*, *Oite*, *Matsuki*, *Kisaragi*, *Yayoi*, and *Mochizuki*); and two light cruisers, *Tenryu* and *Tatsuta*.

Wake's Resistance

The Japanese realized that there would be very little resistance as the Americans had lost most of their fighter squadron, their facilities had been destroyed, and aerial photos showed major destruction resulting from the second raid. Everything pointed to a quick victory.

The weather on the night of the 10th of December did not help the enemy's invasion plan, as the seas were rough. The small landing craft, with their flat bottoms, capsized in the waves. Admiral Kajioka decided to get in a little closer to the island. As he gradually moved in, he wondered why there was no action and thought the Americans were possibly sleeping.

The Americans surely were not sleeping. They were fully aware of the Japanese task force. At about 3:15 a.m. of the 11th, Commander Scott Cunningham received word from Marine Gunner

Hames at the battalion command post, telling him, "Major Devereux reports ships sighted on the horizon and requests permission to illuminate the searchlights." Cunningham knew that the range of our six five-inch guns would be inadequate against the larger naval guns the cruiser would be using, so he instructed us: "Don't turn on the searchlights and hold your fire until they come within range of our five-inch guns, and then I will give the word to Devereux to fire." Cunningham climbed into his clothes as quickly as he could and ran out to his pickup. Within five minutes he was at the magazine command post. Inside, everything was quiet and now they waited as the word went out that there was to be no unnecessary noises, no lights, and no firing of guns. They were to keep conversations low and nothing was to move at the airport.

Time went by oh so slowly as the specks on the horizon moved in gradually from three o'clock to five o'clock that morning. There was a boom, and not from the surf—the enemy had opened fire. The Japanese had surrounded the atoll and were coming in closer and closer. At six o'clock, Cunningham gave the order to Gunner Hames to commence firing. He relayed this information to Peacock, Wilkes, and Toki Point. Lieutenant Barninger opened up on Peacock Point and hit a light cruiser on the second salvo. The cruiser turned and ran, but not before two more salvos hit as it tried to get out of range.

McAlister opened up on Wilkes where there were three ships in sight. Focusing on one of the three, he hit it head-on and it immediately exploded. Then a second ship was hit. Finally, the third ship, which was probably carrying the 450 landing troops, was hit.

Now the guns on Peale got in on the action. The guns had been waiting for something to come within range. Soon, three ships slipped by Wilkes and turned toward Toki Point on Peale Island. The ships were within range and soon Lieutenant Kessler's man on Battery B opened up, hitting the lead ship. The enemy returned fire and destroyed our communication lines. But Battery B kept on firing and the enemy finally turned tail and ran.

Within less than an hour, the battle was over and won. The Japanese had received their first loss of the war and we still had four F4F Grumman Wildcat fighter planes left, ready to put in their punches.

During the land and sea battle, our F4Fs were quiet and stayed out of range. After the battle was over, the Japanese retreated home towards the Marshalls as fast as they could. The lack of air power from the Japanese was very surprising to everyone, which gave us control of the sky. We had control of the sky because of the four aircraft, aircraft that Lieutenant John Kinney had put together after the devastating attack on December 8th.

Major Putnam, along with Captains Elrod, Tharin, and Freuler, took off and within ten minutes had found the enemy. Two groups of two F4Fs swooped down on the retreating ships, strafing and bombing with the two one-hundred-pound bombs each of the planes carried. The Japanese threw up all the anti-aircraft fire they could muster, but this did not deter the four fighters. After dropping their bombs, they returned quickly to Wake, refueled, loaded two more one-hundred-pound bombs and more ammunition for the machine guns, and they were on their way to battle again. Lieutenant John Kinney and Sergeant Hamilton traded off with two of the pilots on the second time out. Captain Hank Elrod put a bomb directly down the smoke stack of a destroyer, and a few minutes later, it blew up and sank. Soon the remnants of the Japanese task force—bewildered, scattered, and demoralized—were on their way back to Roi.

The Japanese reported later that the Americans' courage and efficiency was remarkable in that the little F4F fighters accounted for one sunken destroyer and heavy damage to two light cruisers and one transport. Because Admiral Kajioka maneuvered his task force much too close to Wake in the early morning of December 11, 1941, when he could have shelled us from sixteen or seventeen hundred yards away, he allowed the Japanese to be decimated by the vastly inferior Americans. Our five-inch guns had a range or 15,850 yards (about nine miles). The Japanese cruisers could hit Wake from 26,118 yards (about fourteen miles) out. All they had to do was sit out in the ocean out of the reach of our artillery, but they didn't. They just kept coming in closer and closer until they were only seven thousand yards, or about four miles from our shores. Once again, never underestimate the enemy.

That battle on Wake Island on December 11, 1941 was of great importance to the morale of our nation. After the attack on Pearl Harbor and then the surrender of Guam, there was a great mental depression throughout the nation. There was nothing positive, nothing to cheer about. Then along came the attack and defense of Wake and our first victory over the enemy. A movie depicting the December 11th story was made shortly after the victory and was very popular with the folks back home, however highly inaccurate it may have been.

The defeat of the Japanese fleet in their attempt to take Wake Island on December 11th was a bitter pill for the Japanese to swallow. Rear Admiral Sadamichi Kajioka was terribly embarrassed. He had lost face, but not nearly as much as Vice Admiral Shigeyoshi Inoue and Isoroku Yamamoto, admiral of the combined Japanese fleet. There was anger, embarrassment, loss of face, and frustration that a small group of Marines and civilians could defeat the Imperial Forces of Japan. The Japanese were furious, as they had already published a news release from Tokyo that they had taken Wake. They wondered, "How could this have happened?!"

One of the main reasons we were so successful on December 11th was because the bombers didn't really hurt our gun positions. At great effort we moved those three-inch and five-inch guns and sand bags, day after day, and so the Japanese bombed where they had been the day before, destroying nothing. These pilots returned back to Kwajalein Island and reported that Wake was nearly defenseless. That was true. We really didn't have too much to work with; the Marines were expected to fight with rifles that were used in WWI;

our artillery was antiquated; and we had no radar for our four F4F Grumman fighters. In short, we should have been defeated, but it didn't happen and the Japanese were furious; they were determined to take this pesky little island.

After the Japanese had been defeated on this initial attempt to take the island, they retreated, angry and determined to come back again. This time they would take Wake at all costs. Word had gone out in the newspapers and on the radios around the world that the island had been taken—a great victory for the emperor. Now that this was known to not be true, the Japanese were more determined to show the world that Wake would be taken. A great naval force, including the task force that had attacked Pearl Harbor on December 7th, was quickly assembled in Roi for this mission.

Because of the attack on December 7th, and the unexpected success of the Japanese Navy in the assault on the American Navy, Pearl was stunned. No one thought for a minute that the Japanese would ever attack Hawaii. The general opinion was that the Japanese would be an easy enemy to fight, that the battle would be short, and that they would retreat to their homeland. It was once again a case of underestimation.

But America was stunned too. How could this happen? Who goofed up? Who was to blame? But very soon the blame was laid on the shoulders of Admiral Husband E. Kimmel. Admiral Kimmel was really a fine qualified Naval officer. He was brilliant and forceful and quickly organized a task force to save Wake. In Washington, President Roosevelt was pressured into firing Admiral Kimmel, as he was blamed for not recognizing the danger to Hawaii. But firing Kimmel was a mistake. After Kimmel organized the relief task force that was to reinforce Wake in mid-December, Kimmel was notified of his release and Vice Admiral William S. Pye was named to succeed him. Pye was a complete failure. He was a deskman, a statistician; he was not a fighting man like Admiral Kimmel or Admiral Chester A. Nimitz (who eventually replaced him). Who suffered for this decision during those trying times? It was the Marines and civilians on Wake.

After the Japanese attempt to take Wake on the 11th, we were relieved somewhat. We were still alive, we had not been conquered, we had caused the Japanese to retreat for the very first time in the war, and the enemy knew that we were willing to go all out to save Wake and its defenders against all odds. Most of us contractors were helping out by providing logistics vital to the defense of Wake, such as sand-bagging the guns, moving them at night, preparing the food, doing anything to help the cause, and awaiting the next day's bombing attack. We also felt that very soon there would be another major attack. Could we hold out? We had done it once, but we felt that when they returned the next time they would be ten times stronger.

As I mentioned, the task force that Admiral Kimmel organized was then under the direction of Admiral Pye, and he proved to be a very careful and hesitant leader. On tactics he was very good, but on getting the job done, he was indecisive and fearful that he might fail. Admiral Pye was not the leader we needed! Julius Caesar said many centuries ago, "He who hesitates is lost." How true that is, even today.

Well, Pye hesitated. He knew the Japanese Naval Force was going to come back to Wake and that their base of operations was only six hundred miles away at Roi. This was a race against time. Could the task force from Hawaii get to Wake in time? It would be several days (250 miles) before the task force would have reached Wake with the badly needed reinforcements and supplies. Pye ordered Admiral Jack Fletcher to refuel several of our destroyers. Unforutnately, after a delay of two days, they were ordered to turn around and come back to Hawaii. If they had continued on to Wake, they would have beaten the Japanese by at least one day. What a great Christmas present it would have been for the defenders of Wake, as well as something for those at home in the United States to celebrate. But Pye hesitated, and all was lost.

Pye also knew that he was only going to be in charge for less than a month before he was replaced by Admiral Nimitz, so he wondered why he should take a chance at failing during his short term. When Pye "gave up," his attitude permeated throughout the fleet, and Wake then became expendable. When this order to return was given to the Marines who were in the relieving task force, they actually cried.

So there we were, Marines and civilians, fighting a lost cause. The full impact didn't hit us at the time. It was just endure, fight on and on, and maybe something might happen to save the day for us. Well, it wasn't going to happen.

We did gain hope, however, when we learned that Admiral Kimmel was sending us reinforcements which included thirty- and fifty-caliber machine guns, anti-aircraft five-inch and eight-inch artillery, a radar, medical supplies, food, clothing, another four hundred Marines, and additional aircraft, consisting of fourteen Brewster buffaloes and eighteen Dautless dive bombers—all of which were desperately needed. And there were orders to remove most of the civilian contractors. I supposed that that meant that any remaining contractors would be used to build up the base. Needless to say, this news buoyed our spirits, as we hoped our US counterparts would arrive before the Japanese fleet.

In what manner did we live as we awaited either friendly forces or the enemy? We were in the bushes and trees going out on work parties at night. We lived in shallow little trenches that had been dug out of the coral rock and sand. We ate twice a day. I remember that one day I got a Hershey's candy bar. When I took off the foil paper, I noticed that maggots had beaten me to the chocolate. I brushed them away and ate the candy anyway, wondering how in the world they got through the wrapper. Boy, that was a treat! When you are hungry, almost anything in the form of food looks and tastes good. Water is so important for survival. Without our distilled water supply, we wouldn't last very long on the island. We were actually living in a very precarious situation and the Japanese were aware of this, so the water distillation plant was protected on both sides.

We had a lot of civilian contractors on the island who were forty to sixty-five years in age. It would be anybody's guess how long most of them would live under conditions like this. I was sure that diarrhea, malnutrition, and other health conditions would take their toll.

It was one day after another, being bombed almost every day. I remember one day I was sitting in the Navy communications dugout when the sirens went off and we knew we were going to be bombed again. This time it seemed that there was a lot of enemy aircraft. I could hear the bombs drop on the south side by Peacock Point. Then the bombing became louder and more intense. It was like a giant walking across the island—*thump*, *thump*, closer and closer. Then a very close explosion! There were six of us in the communications dugout. It was crowded and a guy by the name of Dick Fuller was sitting on my lap. Everybody was very intense. I told Dick, "Boy, that one was very close." He said, "Yeah, the next one will get us."

No sooner did he say that than there was a tremendous explosion right outside the entrance to the dugout. Sand, dust, and bits of coral filled the air inside the room. Then there was an eerie quiet. The dust settled down and we all just sat there, looking around in a dazed silence. Pretty soon one of the guys ventured outside, then the rest followed until I was the only one left in the dugout. After about a minute, I heard someone calling me, "Hey, Bill, come on out and see this crater that was left by that last bomb." I got up, moved through the dust and stuck my head out the dugout, then I took a few steps up and I could see a huge crater, about twenty-five feet across and ten feet deep at its center. Now that might not seem like a really large hole until you realize it was in coral sand. To make a crater that large in coral sand would require at least a five-hundred-pound bomb. I sat down on the edge of the crater and realized that if it had been about twenty feet closer to our shelter, I wouldn't have survived.

From the 8th to the 23rd of December, the contractors were of tremendous help to the Marines as more than five hundred men answered Dan Teters' call for help.

Using bulldozers and other CPNAB (Contractors Pacific Naval Air Bases) equipment, the contractors built sturdy bomb shelters with reinforced roofs at all major battle stations and many minor ones. They erected airplane revetments and personnel shelters at the airfield for VMF-211. Whenever Japanese bombers spotted Marine aircraft guns, civilians would help move those big cannons and then enclose their new positions with high, protective walls composed of thousands of sand bags. The Military also found other important jobs for the contractors: getting machine gun ammunition; filling sandbags; fashioning camouflage and portable barbed wire barriers; building covered latrines and burying human excrement; distributing food, water, and reserve ammunition to caches scattered across the atoll; and moving ammunition to every Marine battery and machine gun position. Electricians repaired field telephones operating out of Major Devereux's command post. And Dan Teters organized an all-civilian catering service, which cooked and delivered two hot meals a day to the entire garrison. This alone was a task the Marines could not have done by themselves.

As the days rolled by and rumors of evacuation from the island grew, we all felt that we could hold out, never doubting that Uncle Sam was going to be there when the chips were down. As we were bombed almost every day, anxiety became more intense. Everyone knew that the longer it took for help to arrive from the United States the more precarious our situation would become. The Japanese were not bombing us for practice, but to soften us up for their next invasion attempt. We thought, "Come on, Uncle Sam, give us help before it is too late." And so on the night of the 22nd and early in the morning of the 23rd of December we finally knew that the Japanese were not going to give up on taking Wake. They had been embarrassed, defeated in their first major battle with the

Americans, caught in a published lie about the outcome, and were determined to defeat us, no matter what it took. This time they arrived in force.

At the time of arrival it was very quiet. It was eerie, but we just knew something or somebody was out there. It was very dark, but we had starlight and a moon, which gave some light. We were just waiting for something to happen. Was our Uncle Sam finally coming to our aid or was the enemy really going to invade before we received help?

As we peered out over the reef, we couldn't see the enemy, but we felt that something was going to happen very soon. At around one o'clock on the morning of December 23rd, the northern horizon took on a life of its own. There were lights flashing all over the ocean on the north side of the island. The low clouds emphasized that this was a large enemy force that was not concerned about being discovered.

All kinds of thoughts went through our minds as we waited. What had become of our relief force that was supposed to arrive with more fighter aircraft, more Marines, more ammunition, and more artillery? They should have arrived by that time. Had they been engaged by the Japanese and defeated or was it all just rumors and scuttlebutt that there was help on its way? Then came the thought in the back of our minds, "Were we expendable?" This was a thought that had never entered our minds before. Maybe help was a little tardy, but then Uncle Sam would show up, right? It was getting awfully late for that, however.

It soon became apparent that the Japanese were intent on taking Wake. Out there on the water, Vice Admiral Sadamichi Kajioka, the very same admiral who was defeated on December 11th, had been given an unusual second chance. Now he was in charge of this new attempt to conquer Wake. This time he was determined to be ready, and he was prepared. Nothing would be accepted except absolute victory over this small group of stubborn defenders who were fighting with great courage and antiquated weapons.

This time the Japanese used battle-hardened marines who were determined to force their way onto the island, regardless of the number of men that would be killed or the number of ships that might be destroyed. It was a battle they were going to win at all costs.

From midnight until two thirty in the morning, there were reports that the Japanese had landed on Peale, in the lagoon near Toki Point, and other places on the island. We only had faint starlight and as time passed, we had more reports that half a company of Japanese Special Naval Landing Forces (SNLF) had landed on Wilkes' south shore and that the battle was on. Fourteen civilian contractors suffered fatal wounds in action on Wake Island on December 23rd, the same number that the Marines had lost that bloody morning. Japanese casualties were very heavy, but the invaders kept pouring more soldiers onto Wake.

On Wilkes Island, the Japanese had been eliminated, but Devereux thought that the Japanese had taken Wilkes when he saw the enemy flag flying at several different locations. The telephone lines had also been destroyed, so there was no communication or any other reports from Wilkes. It is easy to see why he thought Wilkes was gone. Even though our forces had suppressed the enemy on Wilkes, as well as on the south side of Wake, he still had good reason to be concerned, as the Japanese had come ashore in waves of one- to two-hundred marines. These Japanese Marines were brave men and were not going to be denied victory. Even after hundreds of his men had been killed, Admiral Kajioka ordered several thousand more into the battle.

The US Marines had held their own in some parts, but there were only eighty-seven on the south end of Wake and Wilkes, besides about twenty-seven civilians for assistance. These Marines had received excellent training before the war. In their training they learned that Marines never surrender, even though it may mean losing their lives.

While all of this was going on, and while Devereux believed that Wilkes and south Wake had fallen, the situation became desperate and he quickly told Commander Cunningham about this grave state of affairs. There seemed to be no hope that we would receive any help from the US forces; it was too late for that. The Japanese were pouring onto the island; victory for the valiant defenders of Wake just wasn't going to happen. It was clear that Admiral Kajioka would soon be looked upon as a hero by all of Japan. It seemed to Devereux that all was going to be lost. Gregory Urwin, in a talk given to the Wake POW Organization, stated:

> Had Devereux been an aggressive infantry tactician, he might have employed Major George Potter's troops or something more than a static headquarters guard. Unlike his subordinates on Wilkes and on the main islet west of the airfield, it never occurred to Devereux to land an offensive sweep or even to probe Japanese positions to develop a reliable idea of their strength. Nor did he think to extend Potter's front far enough to the right to link up with Battery E, which would have added a minimum of fifty more leathernecks to his force. Devereux also neglected to advance Potter's defensive perimeter to shield Dr. Kahn's hospital seven hundred yards to the south. Potter's left flank began at a point one hundred yards below the C.P. and then angled away to the northeast crossing the "north-south" road and petering out in the brush beyond. Devereux merely covered his own command post and yielded his wounded and the initiative to the Japanese.
>
> The sluggish behavior of Potter's line represented a failure in American leadership. Elsewhere on the atoll, other Marine officers accomplished far more with considerably fewer Marines. Devereux and

Potter opted to play it safe and failed to take control of the situation. Any laurels earned during Wake's final hours of resistance belong to their subordinates.

Major Devereux's conduct stands in contrast to the feats Captain Platt and Lieutenant Poindexter performed the last morning of the siege. Once Devereux lost contact with a unit or battle station, he assumed it had been annihilated. After Lieutenant Kessler reported Japanese flags on Wilkes, Devereux wrote off the islet and its sixty-eight Marine defenders. Captain Platt would have checked such stories with a personal reconnaissance; Devereux did not stir from his C.P. If he had stuck his head out the door, he would have seen Japanese planes circling overhead as they pulled out of their strafing passes against American resistance to the west. Nor did the major send out any stray patrols to reestablish contact with any cut off elements of his command. Without considering that the enemy might have bypassed American strong points, he interpreted attack on Battery E and Corporal McAnally's machine guns as signifying that all American troops on the main islet's southern leg had been killed or captured.

To account for his actions of the 23rd of December, Devereux attempted to blame his lapse on his detachments slashed phone line and defective walkie-talkies. Had he known the truth about the tactical situation, the major implied, the story of Wake might have been different. But Devereux prematurely arrived at certain fatal conclusions; the appearance of Japanese troops near his command post did not prove that all the Americans at Peacock

Point, the southern beach, and Camp 1 had been slain or dispersed.

Devereux can be faulted for forgetting Colonel Harry Picketts' 1939 shore defense plan which is how to react to a hostile landing by retiring to the nearest strong point, then to go on the offensive the moment the enemy's initial drive has spent itself. Now it's interesting to note that this is what Platt, McAlister, McKinstry, and Poindexter had done on their own. Devereux failed to do likewise.

Devereux can be faulted both for forgetting the Pickett plan and for a low opinion of his own leathernecks. He failed to imagine that his subordinates were capable of surviving or battling on without his dictating every move; his tendency to see the worst in others robbed him of confidence at the very time he needed it most.

(The method of defense of Wake can be argued back and forth. It seems that everyone on the sideline has their own opinion of what should have been done and how it could have been done. This is always the case, especially by those who are not directly involved. If you do this and it works out you're a good guy and everyone thinks you're a genius. However, if it doesn't work out, then you're a bum and should not ever have been in command.)

Now in defense of Devereux, if all these other things that should have been done by the Marines were put into action, well, we might have been able to resist for a short time, but inevitably we would have been overrun because the Japanese already had made a successful landing. They were in the brush, ditches, and bomb craters on Wake, the main isle.

Admiral Kajioka was determined not to fail a second time. He had ordered one thousand more landing troops to hit the beach, and if that wasn't enough to make the invasion successful, he was prepared to ground six destroyers and commit their crews of 150 in each to the conflict. So you can see with an additional 1,900 men as a back up to those who were already on the island, the battle was decided. Therefore, the additional troops were not needed to insure victory for the Japanese.

(This was interesting; most of those sitting by a blackboard in some classroom explaining all the different ways the battle could or should be fought, had never been under fire.)

Now . . . on this crucial morning of December 23, 1941, both Devereux and Commander Cunningham had a tough decision to make. Cunningham had received information from Pearl that the relief force of the Marines, fighter planes, ammunition, food, et cetera would not be arriving at Wake. Cunningham was stunned, so much so he decided to not tell Devereux. Cunningham knew at that time that Admiral Pye, who succeeded Admiral Kimmel, was not going to risk committing ships, men, aircraft, submarines, et cetera to the defense of Wake. In short what was meant by this decision was Wake is going to fall in the hands of the Japanese and you are expendable.

This was complete mental devastation to the Marines on board the relief task force when they heard the order. They actually cried, "How could we not help our Marine friends? This is not what we have been taught. We have been trained that Marines never surrender." But this relief force that was supposed to rescue Wake was canceled two hundred miles away from Wake. Admiral Kimmel, who was fired because of the Pearl Harbor fiasco, was released of his command just at the time he was needed the most. Admiral Pye was put in charge of the fleet and what a mistake that was. Admiral Pye knew that his term of command was going to be very short, two or three months, then he would be relieved, so he didn't want to go out in defeat. Therefore, he personally canceled help to Wake.

There was a tremendous loss of morale in the Navy and Marines when Pye canceled the relief force to Wake. After this fiasco, Pye was released and given an obscure command way down the line. For the rest of the war he was out of sight.

Cunningham had also sent a message to the USS *Triton*, which Cunningham thought was still in Wake's waters. He ordered the USS *Triton* to attack the Kajioka Fleet and was puzzled when he received no reply. After his attempt to get an answer from Oahu or the USS *Triton*, Cunningham received a laconic message from Hawaii that read, "Units 7-2-4 and 7-2-3 are returning to Pearl and no friendly vessels would be in your immediate vicinity today. Keep me informed." How easy for Pearl to send this message to Cunningham. How devastating for Cunningham to receive it.

More time was of the essence. It was obvious that the enemy was going to take Wake. Within a few hours the war on Wake would be over. Then the thought came to Cunningham, what do we do now with certain defeat staring us in the face?

At this point, at seven thirty on the (morning of the) 23rd, Cunningham asked Devereux if he thought surrender was justified. Devereux was stunned. Marines never quit. We will fight to the end. Devereux tried to change Cunningham's mind. Then for several minutes they debated the question. Finally Cunningham said, "There are no friendly ships within twenty-four hours." Devereux said, "Not even submarines." "Not even submarines," replied Cunningham. Devereux then said that Wilkes had fallen (which it hadn't), and he did not have the right to make the decision, that it was the prerogative of the senior official present. After several minutes of who would do what, Cunningham took a deep breath and authorized Devereux to surrender the atoll, provided he felt the garrison could no longer hold out.

Surrendering was not in Devereux's battle book. Even while believing that "Marines never surrender," he carried out Cunningham's decision, which was probably the most important Military decision he had ever made. At approximately eight o'clock in the morning, Gunner Hames entered the Major CP just as Major Devereux hung up and was told that Cunningham had surrendered the island to the Japanese. Gunner Hames, a POW from World War I, just stared at the major for a few seconds. Devereux then told Hames to fix a white flag on a stick and said, "It's too late, John, Commander Cunningham has ordered us to surrender." Gunner Hames stood for a moment, saluted and said, "Yes Sir," and left. As Hames walked away, he shouted, "Major's orders, we're surrendering." Devereux, on hearing Gunner Hames, ran to the doorway and said, "It's not my order, God damn it!"

Meanwhile during those final hours of the battle, about seventy or eighty civilians, including myself, had taken shelter in a tunnel under an aggregate pile near Camp 2. After we had been there for several hours, the word came to us at about eight thirty in the morning that the island had surrendered to the Japanese. We all just stood there and wondered what was coming next. We had read stories about the cruelty of the Japanese—murder, rape, torture, beatings, and starvation. Many of us knew about the rape of Nanking and the massacre of some 220,000 Chinese civilians, which included women and children, in less than one month. Who were these people? Were we also going to be tortured and killed?

Surrender to the Japanese

We didn't have to wait very long, for soon someone appeared at the end of the aggregate tunnel and shouted, "We've surrendered to the Japanese! Come out immediately!" We sat there for a minute in a deadening silence. Then someone said, "I think we ought to have prayer." No one volunteered. Then someone said, "Ask Bill Taylor." Believe you me, I'm sure that anybody could have done better. But I agreed to the request and offered a short prayer, just requesting Heavenly Father's support for all of us before we walked out of the tunnel into the tropical morning sun.

As I walked out of the tunnel and as my eyes adjusted to the bright light, I saw civilians standing around. Then I saw my brother, Jack, standing naked in a truck with about twelve other naked prisoners. I walked over to the truck where Jack was standing, holding on to the top of the side railing. He looked at me then said, "They made us take off our clothes and climb into this truck." I could see fear in his eyes and as I looked around, almost everyone else also had fear in their eyes. Jack said, "What do you think they're going to do, Bill?" "I think they are going to kill all of us," I replied, "These guys are just taking small groups at a time so that there won't be a general uprising."

Many of the prisoners were forced to strip and kneel. Their wrists were wired together with telephone wire behind their backs. Their ankles were tied behind their backs. Then the ankles and wrists were all tied to a single wire that ran from the ankles, around the wrists, then around the neck. When this was done the prisoner was in a kneeling position with the feet and hands behind with a wire around the neck. This was a terrible position for anyone tied up like this for even a short time because if you leaned forward at all, the wire would choke you. After a few hours of this torture, one would often die of suffocation. This torture was very cruel.

After I spoke to Jack, a jeep drove up and stopped. There was a moment of hesitation, then a Japanese officer dressed in a spotless white uniform stepped out. Everything seemed to stop. He surveyed the situation, then walked over to a Japanese officer who seemed to be in charge of the landing force. I learned later that this officer was Admiral Sadamichi Kajioka, supreme commander of the Japanese Task Force. He was the same admiral that was in charge of the task force that tried to invade and take Wake back on the 11th of December. That was a disaster, a failure in their book. Admiral Kajioka was most fortunate to be given control of a second attempt to take the island and he was willing to sacrifice and even run aground six destroyers, which would give the Japanese more than three thousand men to take Wake. This extra supply of men was not necessary as the first landing force was successful.

The officer in charge of the landing force saluted Admiral Sadamichi Kajioka. Kajioka acknowledged the officer's salute and then they talked for the next fifteen minutes. You could tell that this was more than just the supreme naval officer in charge congratulating another officer for capturing the island. Soon they were speaking to each other in loud voices. They even yelled at each other several times. Then it seemed the officer in charge of the landing force was overruled and forced to accept Admiral Kajioka's decision. Admiral Kajioka then got back in the jeep and drove away.

After this heated discourse between Admiral Kajioka and the Japanese colonel who was in charge of the actual fighting force, all prisoners were told to stop taking their clothes off, then to kneel down on the hot, rough road that led away from the aggregate pit where there was a large group of men. We were forced to kneel down at five men abreast, row after row. This we did and soon there were about nine hundred men in 180 of these rows, kneeling in the hot sun in rows five feet apart for about one thousand feet.

To keep everything in order for the Japanese and to keep us in control, the Japanese set up machine guns about forty feet apart and parallel to the road. Two Japanese soldiers were on each gun, their fingers on the triggers. Everyone was told to be quiet and we were. The sun beat down on us relentlessly. We only heard the surf crashing against the coral reef. Then suddenly there were Japanese fighter planes, "Zeros," buzzing us one after another. They flew about ten to fifteen feet above the ground, and as they passed over us, they fired their machine guns. It was spooky because we didn't know which of the pilots would go berserk and take us out.

We were so grateful, though, for the trade winds that still gently blew over us. Even with the trade winds, it soon became apparent that we could only be able to stay in the position for a short period of time. Dehydration was going to be a huge problem. It doesn't take long for the sweat to run down your face into your eyes, trickle down your chest, and then for the thirst to kick in. There were many of the men that were not tanned from the sun. These men were going to get burned badly if something wasn't done quickly. The Japanese on the machine guns were very young and they were under strict orders to keep us under control. All it would have taken was for someone to break, then jump up and run toward a machine gun manned by a young inexperienced soldier, then chaos would ensue.

After about three hours of torture, kneeling on the coral road, we were told to get dressed and to do so in a hurry. Men stumbled here and there trying to find their clothes. I was one that didn't have to strip, but I thought, "Why not take some extra clothes?" So I did. The shirt I decided to take had a pair of glasses in it. I removed the glasses and placed them on a piece of coral thinking someone would recognize the glasses and pick them up.

After we dressed, we stood in line then boarded trucks that took us down to the airport. When we arrived at the airport, we were told to disembark on the landing strip. I got off the truck and almost immediately saw my brother Jack. When he approached me, he said, "Boy am I glad to meet you. Hey, those are my clothes you have, where are my glasses?" I told him, "I don't have them but I know where they are."

Water was brought out to all of us on the airstrip. We could hardly wait to get a drink. The Japanese gave us water that had been

As cattle herded for slaughter, we were brought to the airport. Tired and weary, we were kept there for two days enduring the blazing sun and cold nights. Gasoline-tainted water and a bit of stale bread was our fare. On Christmas Day, we were taken to the barracks, which by this time were encircled with barbed wire.

in fifty-gallon drums that previously had been filled with aviation gas. The barrels simply had been emptied of gas, then filled with drinking water. We drank this water, but some of the men got very ill. I'm not sure why I didn't get ill from the water too.

The night of the 23rd of December was awful. At about nine o'clock, it began to rain. It was a drizzle at first, then as the rain got heavier and heavier, the Japanese ordered us to go into a vacant hangar. Then they shoved us, pushed us, and packed us like sardines in a can. I was deep in this horde of men. The huge sliding doors were closed and there we were in the dark. There was no room to lie down. The air soon became stifling. Men were getting ill. I finally couldn't stand any longer and so I worked my way down between several men and wormed myself into a non-standing position. There, I was able to rest. I would say we were there for about four hours. Many of the men were vomiting. Eventually we were permitted to come out of the hangar. The rain had stopped and the air outside felt so good. Water, food, and shelter, the necessities, really become the most important things in our lives when everything else is taken away.

On the 24th of December 1941, Christmas Eve, we spent the day on the broiling airport runway. At about seven o'clock that evening someone started singing "Silent Night." Soon almost everyone was singing. About halfway through the song, the Japanese told us to stop singing, and so we did. We were so alone. It was a difficult night for us.

As the morning sun rose on the 25th, the Japanese let us move back into the barracks that were still standing. When we arrived at the compound, I noticed that a barbed wire fence had been erected around the barracks that had not been destroyed. There was also about a one-half acre of ground that was bare. There we spent Christmas Day, 1941.

We were hustled in the barracks and where one man slept before, there were now five to ten men. Many of them were wounded. It was awful, but still better than the airstrip or the road where we all could have been killed. We slept on the floor of the barracks, shoul-der-to-shoulder. There was a wounded guy named Clarence next to me who was in terrible pain. The smell was unbelievable. The day after we moved into the barracks, the medics came and took him away. I learned later that he died the next day.

Because the island had been stocked with food when the war started, we started to get meals that were healthy. But we knew this would soon end and that the food supply would vanish. When that happened, it was anybody's guess how we would survive.

During the next two weeks, the Japanese let us out of the com-pound in small groups. A few of us had a gallon can or two of food hidden in the brush. There were beets, potatoes, tomatoes, spinach, canned fruit, et cetera. We were able to get a hold of all this dur-ing the weeks between the first attack and the day we surrendered. I found my buried supply and brought it back to camp. But there just wasn't any storage room in the barracks. And a one-gallon can was a lot of food. It had to be eaten quickly before it spoiled. The Japanese didn't seem to mind our extra supplies of food. They let us do what we wanted to, knowing that we were just going to be there for a short time.

After I had brought my first can of food into the barracks, I knew that I had to do something different, and quickly. We were so crowd-ed that there was absolutely no room for any canned food. Then I got an idea. Why not dig a little cave under the concrete floor of one of the showers that wasn't in use? But how could I keep it secret from the Japanese? They would become highly suspicious and then probably get mean. I wasn't sure what I would do with the coral sand that I scraped out from underneath the concrete slab. I didn't pay too much attention to what anybody else thought. I just took the lid off an old gallon can and used it as a sand scoop, then went out behind the shower and started digging. Nobody paid much attention to me. I scraped the coral sand out from underneath the slab and filled the can over and over. I spread the sand I dug up away from where I was digging. Within two days and nights I had dug an opening under the concrete slab about three feet wide by twenty-four to thirty inches high. Inside I widened the little cave to about four feet wide and nearly seven feet long. Then at the end of the little hole inside, I went down another foot and there I placed my canned goods. It also served as a place to sleep. And it was one of the safest places to be in case of a naval bombardment from the sea. After finishing this little cave, I got a hold of a mattress and worked it inside.

I did all of this within two or three days. It felt so good to have my own quarters. No one else had anything like it and I felt proud about what had been done. There were those who were curious, but nobody followed suit. My brother Jack really liked it and asked if I would share my little cave with him. So he moved in. There was little room when we were both in there, but I felt it was still worthwhile.

I was amazed at how small the Japanese soldiers were. They were about five and one-half feet tall and about 120 pounds. They wore the craziest footwear I had ever seen. These shoes, slippers, sandals or whatever, were made out of cloth, except for the sole, which was grooved rubber. The most interesting part of this shoe was the toe area. The sole was flat and in one piece, except where the big toe was. So when you slipped in your foot, the big toe went into its own little pocket. Leaving the big toe separate would give the toes considerably more traction.

These Japanese soldiers didn't have any idea about how to use the toilets. One day as I was walking by the shower area where we had toilets, I happened to glance in to where I could see one of the toilets. A Japanese soldier was standing on the rim of the toilet and facing the wall. There was a pipe running up the wall behind the toilet. This Japanese soldier was standing on the rim of the toilet, squatting over the bowl facing the wall and hanging onto the pipe behind the toilet. I just laughed to myself.

The Japanese we saw, all of them except a few officers, had terrible-looking teeth. Most had teeth that were bent and decayed. A lot of them were missing teeth in front. As I looked at them, I wondered, "How in the world could these little people with a different culture and background ever think of defeating the United States?"

A Pivotal Choice: Quitting Smoking

I had picked up a bad smoking habit over the years. When I started to smoke in high school I just considered something that a lot of people did. It was a social thing. Men smoked cigarettes, cigars, and pipes, and many men chewed tobacco. Some even made their own cigarettes. They used a small piece of paper, put a little tobacco in it, rolled up the cigarette, twisted the end, and they had made their own cigarette. We called this, "rolling your own." I became very good at the practice of rolling.

When I was sixteen, my friend John Volker took me to Liberty Park next to Ogden High School and taught me how to inhale the smoke. It was tough at first, but then I persisted and within a month I was addicted. Cigarettes in those days cost ten cents for a pack of twenty. There were ten packs of cigarettes in a carton, which cost one dollar. I didn't try to quit. All my friends smoked, even the girls we went with were smoking. It was the social thing to do.

When I went to work on the Metropolitan Water District of Southern California after I graduated from high school, I worked in the huge tunnels, which were to bring water to the Los Angeles area from the Colorado River. It was exciting work. The base of the tunnels was eighteen feet in diameter. We were drilling through solid rock. Then later we formed and poured concrete to make an eighteen-foot pipe that ran for miles through the mountains. Throughout all of this time I smoked and drank.

My brother Dick (Richard) had been living in Hawaii, but he came to work with me and we rented a home by Palm Springs. It had no water, no sanitation, no heating, and no cooling. It was just a roof over our heads. At that time Richard tried to get me to read the Book of Mormon, a book of scripture in the church we had both been raised in. I told him to forget it. I had never gone to church and I wasn't going to change. This discussion went on for weeks and almost drove us apart. Finally, I told Dick I would read the book, only if he would never mention it again.

This book fascinated me and as I was reading, a strange feeling came over me. I thought, "If this is what it's all about, why not go out and talk to the Lord?" I walked out about a hundred feet from the house, scooped away the hot sand, knelt down and started talking to Heavenly Father. I fervently prayed and there I received a strong feeling of peace and my own conviction that the book was true. I got up, went back to the house, and sat down. I knew that if I really believed in this book of scripture that I would have to adhere to the principles of the church. That meant that I would have to give up smoking, drinking, and other bad habits. The most difficult habit for me to overcome was smoking. I had tried everything to quit smoking, but when I went to Wake Island, that bad habit was still right by my side.

And so there we were in prison camp on Wake. The future was not bright. At any time we could be slaughtered. The enemy that had taken us prisoners had a reputation of torturing and beating. One of their hallmarks of brutality was exterminating conquered people. So why were we any different than other people they had fought and conquered, especially as we were only a little dot thousands of miles from Hawaii, and only seventeen hundred miles from Tokyo? The Japanese could easily do away with us. And if we hadn't surrendered, we would have been terminated.

Through wheeling and dealing, I was able to obtain a carton of Camel cigarettes: ten packages total. This was like gold. In fact it was better than gold. On this particular evening, I was walking inside and around our compound on Wake with this valuable carton of Camel cigarettes under my arm. As I walked around the inside of our POW compound, I started to talk to my Heavenly Father. I have found out over the years that Heavenly Father hears every prayer—

every sentence we pray in sincerity. He listens to everyone who calls on His name. How all of this is accomplished, I don't know. Now on this particular night, near the end of the year 1941, I poured out my heart to him. I know I was heard. During my conversation, I talked about a lot of things, but then I talked to the Lord about cigarettes. I finally said vocally, "Heavenly Father, I have tried to stop smoking for years. I haven't been able to do it. Now tonight I would like to make a covenant with you. If you will get me through the bad times ahead, I will never smoke another cigarette again, and also I will serve you to the end of my life—forever."

After my prayer, I walked into the barracks and gave the carton of Camel cigarettes away. I had made my commitment to the Lord and that was that. Now because I had made a binding commitment with Heavenly Father, I will show later how this commitment saved my life as a prisoner in China. I also learned that we should never underestimate the power of prayer. It is truly the way to talk to Heavenly Father. He listens.

Chapter Seven

LIFE AS A POW

The days went by and soon 1941 was history and 1942 was ushered in. There was no celebration for the new year. It was just welcomed in with little fanfare. We all held our breaths and wondered what was going to happen next. The days went by quickly. The Japanese had worked out details for us. I remember working in the carpenter shop destroying a number of saws there. I was assigned to sharpen the saws, but instead I made it impossible for anyone to use them. It was a small thing to do, but somehow it made me feel better. The Japanese were also going through our records every day. There were rumors that the civilians were going to be taken to a neutral nation and that the Marines and other Military were to go to Japan as POWs. Then we heard that most of us were going to go to Japan and others were going to stay on the island. This last rumor was the one that was going to be the most accurate. We were nervous. We counted the hours and minutes and watched with each new day, wondering, "What will this day bring?"

We watched the sun bring in the new day. First a glow overhead in the east turned the cumulus clouds from a faint glow to a brilliant red, orange, and purple. Then, in a few minutes, the tip of the sun would show and, as it rose, it created a beautiful pathway of light right to our shore. Then in the evening the reverse happened as the sun set after a blistering hot day. As the sun went down, there was again the path of light in the gorgeous colors of the rainbow, sinking beyond the horizon as the sun lit up the cumulus clouds once again. It was wonderful to see all of this, for it seems to clear your mind as you feel as though this gorgeous sun was going to see you through your challenges.

Through the misery we were enduring, the moon also had a soothing effect as it made us feel that everything would eventually be better. When the moon rose in the early evening, it would rest on the edge of the ocean in all of its resplendent orange beauty, casting a pathway to where we were standing, only then the trail was a stunningly beautiful pathway of silver. You felt as though it was all especially for you. It was so fascinating, for on the same day you could see the rising and setting of the sun as well as the rising and setting of the moon over our island that was so small compared to the rest of the world.

The beauty of the sun and moon paired with the startling clarity of the stars in the heavens only caused us to stare in wonder about what was coming next. Many thought an agreement would be reached for the evacuation of the civilians. We were going to be shipped out to a neutral country that wasn't in the war, and everyone thought the Marines were headed to a POW camp somewhere in Japan. Then others thought we would be split up. I personally thought we would all go together. I was wrong. On the morning of the 10th of January 1942, when I got up and looked across the lagoon and South Wake, I saw an ominous sight, a huge ocean liner. It was a luxury liner called the *Nitta Maru*. It was anchored about a quarter of a mile off shore so that the ship would not go aground on the jagged reef.

The Nitta Maru: *The old luxury liner in which Bill Taylor and other POWs were transported to the POW camp in China*

The Trip on the Nitta Maru

When the war started, the *Nitta Maru* was commissioned into the Japanese Navy. It was large and was built as a luxury liner that could easily be converted into a transport, and that's what happened. No longer would it be taking travelers to the distant ports of the world. It was wartime, and one of its first assignments was to go to the Wake atoll and pick up prisoners of war to take to Japan.

There was a great sigh of relief among almost all of the prisoners. Now we would know what the Japanese intended to do with us. Speculation didn't stop there—it increased. Everyone had his own opinion and voiced it. The Japanese seemed a little excited too. They just wanted to get rid of us. I'm sure they were a little afraid for the *Nitta Maru* itself. Imagine what a submarine or a well-directed torpedo could do. There seemed to be no other ships in sight. The *Nitta Maru* had made a special trip to Wake and now it wanted to get out of there as quickly as possible.

During the weeks after the surrender of the atoll to the Japanese, the Japanese had been going through the records of all of the men on Wake. Then on the 11th we learned their plans for each of us. They had decided that many of the prisoners had training in the various trades of construction that were still needed to make Wake a very formidable military outpost in the Pacific. There were construction materials there on the island to build almost anything they wanted, and so why not make use of the prisoners' construction talents? It was a great idea for them and so, as they went over the construction records of the men, they selected those they wanted to keep on Wake and those they were going to send to Japan. I was a reinforcing steel worker and my trade was one they wanted to keep. But for some reason I was not selected to stay.

Many of the men had mixed feelings about leaving. Some wanted to stay, others felt that this might be the only chance to get away

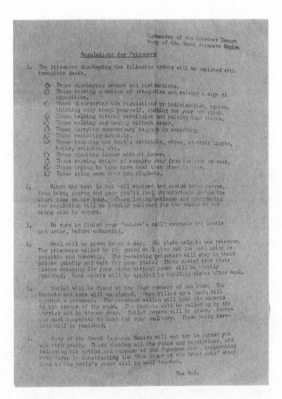

Photograph of original document given the POWs prior to boarding the Nitta Maru

from Wake. Then there were a few who just knew that they were going to be repatriated by a friendly government. Boy, were they in for some kind of a surprise. To put away any hopes of repatriation, the Japanese gave every man who was going on the *Nitta Maru* a list of printed rules for the journey to Japan. It read:

Regulations for Prisoners

1. The prisoners disobeying the following orders will be punished with immediate death.

    a. Those disobeying orders and instructions.

    b. Those showing a motion of antagonism and raising a sign of opposition.

    c. Those disordering the regulations by individualism, egoism, thinking only about yourself, rushing for your own goods.

    d. Those talking without permission and raising loud voices.

    e. Those walking and moving without order.

    f. Those carrying unnecessary baggage in embarking.

    g. Those resisting mutually.

    h. Those touching the boat's materials, wires, electric lights, tools, switches, etc.

    i. Those climbing ladder without order.

    j. Those showing action of running away from the room or boat.

    k. Those trying to take more meal than given to them.

    l. Those using more than two blankets.

2. Since the boat is not well equiped and the inside being narrow, food being scarce and poor you'll feel uncomfortable during the short time on the boat. Those losing patience and disordering the regulation will be heavily punished for the reason of not being able to escort.

3. Be sure to finish your "nature's call" evacuate the bowels and urine, before embarking.

4. Meal will be given twice a day. One plate only to one prisoner. The prisoners called by the guard will give out the meal quick as possible and honestly. The remaining prisoners will stay in their places quietly and wait for your plate. Those moving from their places reaching for your plate without order will be heavily punished. Same orders will be applied in handling plates after meal.

5. *Toilet will be fixed at the four corners of the room. (Ours had two cans.) When filled up a guard will appoint a prisoner. The prisoner called will take the buckets to the corner of the room. The buckets will be pulled up by the derrick and be thrown away. Toilet papers will be given. Everyone must cooperate to make the room sanitary. Those being careless will be punished.*

6. *Navy of the Great Japanese Empire will not try to punish you all with death. Those obeying all the rules and regulations, and believing the action and purpose of the Japanese Navy, cooperating with Japan in constructing the "New order of the Great Asia" which lead to the world's peace will be well treated.*

The End.

At about six o'clock, the morning of the 12th, we were up with the sun and ready to board the *Nitta Maru*. Because the *Nitta Maru* was anchored about a quarter of a mile off shore, the Japanese used our own barges and small boats to take the prisoners out to the transport. When we arrived at the transport, there was a barge anchored to the side of the boat. The idea was to jump from the landing boat we had boarded on Wake to the deck of the barge. Then we were supposed to jump from the barge into a doorway on the side of the boat. Sounds easy, doesn't it? But it was difficult to jump from a barge that was bobbing in the waves. When the barge rose high on a current surge, a number of men threw their bags inside and jumped at the same time into the ship. The barge would then pull back about five or six feet from the side of the *Nitta Maru* and waited for the next surge. Then when the barge slammed into the side of the boat again, another group would jump into the hold.

I was the last of my group and when it was my turn to board the barge, it had already pulled away from the side of the *Nitta Maru* about six feet. When the barge pulled away from the boat, I saw it drop about a foot. I took one look at the distance of the barge from the boat and thought, "I can't make this jump." I knew if I couldn't make the jump and fell between the barge and boat, I would be crushed. But the Japanese marine inside the boat pointed his rifle at me and yelled something. He wasn't smiling and he motioned for me to jump. I had no choice, so I threw my little bundle into the doorway of the ship, and wondered if I could dive under the barge. Then in an instant, I thought about the vicious barracudas, which were plentiful around Wake. I backed up and ran toward the ship's iron door. I jumped as hard as I could. I missed but managed to grab the threshold of the boat's doorway. I couldn't pull myself up as my feet kept slipping on the side of the boat. By this time, the barge was starting to come back and within seconds would bang into the side of the *Nitta Maru*. I felt someone grab my shirt from behind and haul me into the boat. As I turned over on my side and looked up, I was stunned, in near disbelief. The man who pulled me onto the boat and saved my life was the same Japanese marine who had previously ordered me to jump. There is untold kindness even in war, and this young enemy marine, without word, saved my life.

After this escape from near death, I was herded to a steel bulkhead door and stopped by the threshold. I waited a few seconds to get my eyes adjusted. There was a steel ladder that went straight down. I couldn't see how far. As I descended the ladder, it seemed as though I had gone about seventy feet when my feet hit the bottom of the steel deck. Turning around I saw that this deck, which was the bottom of the ship, was really a hold that was used for hauling bulk cargo. Looking around, I saw that this hold was already filled with a lot of prisoners. We were on the very bottom of the ship. There was a flat area right above the keel where men sat shoulder-to-shoulder. On each side, the sides of the ship gradually sloped up. I worked my way over to this area looking for a place to sit. Finally I heard a voice say, "Hey Bill, come over here." Peering ahead I saw my friends Oscar Ray, Chalas Loveland, and Mac McCurry. (I later learned that my brother Jack had boarded with a different group and was on the other side of the hold.) They were all sitting on a metal slope. This steel slope was just the bottom of the ship where

From barges we boarded the Nitta Maru, *a former NYK luxury liner. Lining up in the companion way, we were searched from head to foot. Eyeglasses were ripped of the faces of those who wore them and dashed to the deck.*

the keel was located. About every six or eight feet, there was a rib of steel about three inches high running lengthwise with the boat.

As I sat down next to my friends, I noticed that I had to brace myself a little because of the slight slope. I noticed that over a period of time as my knees would gradually relax, I would find myself in a crouched position. I didn't make any complaints. I felt like I was just lucky to be alive. I could put up with the discomfort, but I did wonder how the men in their fifties or sixties would make out. How long would they last under these conditions?

About thirty feet over our heads, there was a single light hanging on a long electric wire from the deck above. It had a small globe in it, about forty watts. This was all the light we had. On each side of the hold, there was a five-gallon can without a top. There was a hole about three inches from the top on each side of the can. A heavy wire loop was bent and shoved through the holes on each side, forming a handle. These were our toilets for the journey to "wherever" land.

There we were, sitting on the very bottom of that great luxury liner called the *Nitta Maru*. I bet that first-class passengers who once occupied the suites above us could never have imagined such a terrible situation on their luxury cruiser.

The only access to the cargo area was the never-ending ladder we descended. At the top of that steel ladder was a small landing and a bulkhead door. When it was slammed shut, we were sealed in the hold. As I looked around in the dim light, I couldn't help but wonder what was coming next. I figured there were about 1,180 civilians and Marines on the *Nitta Maru*. With that figure in mind, I would say we had about 250 men in our hold. About twenty feet above was another deck, which held a similar number of civilians and Military. There was another hold next to us just like ours with two decks. I figured the Japanese were sailing with about twelve hundred prisoners. That meant that approximately 350 men, plus or minus, were still on Wake. I also thought, "We're going to Japan. They are going to stay on Wake and who knows how they will make out." Really, it was anybody's guess. I later found out that everyone, except for ninety-eight men that the Japanese wanted to keep to run things on Wake, were shipped out.

As I looked around the hold, I could see that we were really in a death coffin made of steel. There was no way out if we were torpedoed, shelled, or bombed. All the Japanese would have to do to contain us was slam shut the steel bulkhead door above us. In our hold there was little ventilation and the only way we could know if it was morning or night was by our morning and evening inspections by our captors.

There was such a contrast between our emotions and those of our enemy. They were so pumped up about their victory over us on Wake. They had beaten us and taken the island. Never mind the loss of ten of theirs to one of ours.

The night of January 12, 1942 was one we will never forget. At about five o'clock in the evening the steel door of the bulkhead, about seventy feet above us, banged open. A sailor came swiftly down the ladder. When he reached the bottom, he banged his baton against the ladder, then turned and screamed at us in Japanese. Soon more sailors were climbing down the ladder. We didn't know what they were yelling about. The first soldier then motioned for everybody to kneel facing the ladder. To emphasize his command, he had the other sailors jump into the prisoners, beating us and swinging their clubs at us. Then they just stopped and soon it was deathly quiet. Then we heard a clicking on the ladder and a Japanese officer came into view. As he descended the ladder, we just waited. After he reached the bottom, he turned and looked at us in contempt. His eyes said more than words. If you ever saw hate, it was in that man's eyes. He spoke to us for a few minutes, his voice getting louder. We were kneeling on the cold deck facing him as he gave commands. If anyone moved a muscle or didn't pay attention while he spoke, he would be ordered to stand and a soldier would beat him unmercifully with a three-foot club. As this inspection was taking place, the sailors walked around inspecting every prisoner for what they were wearing, not their clothes, but their rings and watches. We knew a few words of Japanese by now: *ima* (now), *hai* (yes), *domo arigato* (thank you), and *isoide* (hurry). But sometimes they spoke so quickly that we had to respond, "*Wakarimasen*" (I don't understand).

After the inspection, the officer climbed the ladder and was gone. This left us with the sailors. The officer had already spoken to the prisoners above us and we understood what they had all gone through. Then, when the door closed up above, the sailors pounced on us like animals that were starving. It shortly became apparent that they were going to steal our valuables. Many of the men just handed over anything of value they had. Those that were hiding anything from those thieves, if discovered, were beaten unmercifully. It put fear into everyone that had anything of value. There was a guy next to me who had an Ingersoll watch and a Schaefer pen and pencil set. He said he was going to give it to the Japanese when they came by. I told him not to, but he said, "No way. I'm going to give my watch and pen and pencil set to the next guy that comes by." I then offered, "If you'll give them to me, I'll take the chance of getting them out of here. But if I don't get caught, I'm going to keep them." He said, "That's okay with me," and handed them to me. I wasn't caught.

Right after this thieving inspection by the Royal Imperial Navy, we were given a pickled fish about five or six inches long, served with a pickle. We were told that the pickled fish was to be split between two people. Now this was the first fish I had ever seen that was all head and tail, nothing in between. We broke the fish in half. I was sharing this pickled wonder with Oscar Ray, which meant he got the half with the head and I got the tail. There were some of the men that said they wouldn't eat the fish, but not Oscar or me. Mac and Chal shared our thoughts. We also had two cups of water each day, and in the morning we were given a bowl of barley cereal that was watered down. If we didn't eat everything that we were given, although it wasn't much, our death would come much sooner. There was no way we could live very long under such conditions of terrible food, stale water, unclean sanitation, beatings, and a cold, slanted, steel deck on which to lie down. There was a little steel angle that ran lengthwise with the hold. We braced our feet against this railing and dozed off. As our legs would relax, our bodies moved into a crouched position. Then, after awhile our legs would be in pain until we straightened up again.

All night the *Nitta Maru* moved without an escort and at full speed. About eighteen inches away, we could hear the rush of the water against the steel sides of our hold as we sped on in the darkness of a very hostile night. All we could do was hold on, pray, and hope that we would survive to see the next day. We were living a real nightmare. Where was our Navy and where was theirs? We knew for certain by then that we weren't headed for friendly territory.

I suppose that prisoners of war throughout all the pages of history suffered as we did then. Yes, and many of them, like us, never knew what the next day would bring. Our case was also desperate. In just a few days the men would start getting sick and soon there would be deaths in our own hold. We were a mixed group whose ages ranged from the early twenties to middle age and above, and all of us were being stressed to our limits. The single little electric light that burned night and day in our hold gave a dim view of the faces of each man peering around, all not believing what they were seeing and experiencing.

Those were no conditions for privacy. If you had to go to the can, you just worked your way to the five-gallon can, pulled your pants down, and let it go. All of this was done in front of everyone. There was no privacy at all, and no one seemed to care.

When a toilet can was full, at a specified time, someone would haul it over to the only ladder in the hold. Soon a rope with a hook would come down. The hook was then placed onto the wire handle of the bucket. With a jerk on the rope, the bucket was on its way up to the top of the hold. When it arrived at the top, someone took hold of the bucket and it was taken out. We were all fascinated while we intently watched the whole process through the dim light. We had a guy in our group that seemed to be fascinated with the hauling of the waste. He took it upon himself to see that all of the waste was hauled out properly. He would stand right underneath each bucket as it was being hauled seventy feet up to a guy who would then unhook it and hand it to someone else to take it outside.

About the third day out, when it came time to haul out the waste, the buckets, as usual, were hauled over to the ladder. I, like everyone, watched this evacuation with some anxiety, as they did have to go a long way to be safely taken out. Besides, what else was there to do or watch? When the buckets got over to the ladder that day, the rope was lowered as usual. The first bucket went up, was dumped, and the empty bucket came down. Then the second bucket was hooked and ready to be hauled up. When it got to the top of the ladder, however, the guy who was taking the hook off of this bucket made a misjudgment while he was transferring the bucket to his other hand after releasing the hook. Somehow, when he tried to grab the bucket of waste, he missed the wire handle. It was too late. The bucket went straight down the same hole from which it had just been hauled. It didn't hit a thing as it went whistling down from the top to the bottom.

When all of this happened the guy at the bottom of the ladder said in a loud voice, "Here it comes!" then quickly stepped aside. The bucket hit the deck with a sickening crunch. Because it was full, it seemed to explode when it hit the bottom. In slow motion the waste seemed to melt together and then disperse in a cloud all over the hold. I don't believe there were many in our group that didn't get some of that sewage on them. We never smelled the same after that.

During these depressing and discouraging days, Mac, Chal, Oscar, and I tried to make the best of our situation. We tried to entertain each other with stories from our lives, history, and current events. Where are we going? What will become of us? It wasn't encouraging, to say the least. One day Oscar, who was a scriptorian and also a member of my church, said, "Would you like to learn the Articles of Faith?" I said, "Sure, why not. What are they?" He then repeated the articles defining the beliefs of our church and I learned them very quickly. When I knew them all verbatim, he said, "You don't know it Bill, but you just graduated from Primary." ["Primary" is the term for Sunday School for children in Bill's church.]

I thought about this and how much I had missed by not going to church. I think I could count on one hand all the church meetings I had ever attended. For some reason our family just didn't go to church. We moved from place to place. There were seven of us in the family and there was no work because of the depression. I was sent from Los Angeles, California to Ogden, Utah, to live with my mother's sister, Lucille Baker, when I turned fifteen. My uncle was not a church-goer.

The depression of the 1930s was tough on many families in the United States. Before the depression our family had lived in Ogden. My father was very successful financially and we lived among the rich and successful. The stock market, however, wiped out everything we had. My father kept saying, "Don't worry, everything is going to be okay." Then he died. He was only fifty.

While living with Uncle Charley and Aunt Lucille, none of us attended any church. The year went by and I had picked up smoking and drinking and other bad habits. And of all places, there in the bottom of a prison ship where life was so uncertain and very precarious, my friend Oscar Ray taught me the Articles of Faith. Then he taught me the Beatitudes. Oscar was brilliant and had a fantastic memory. He could quote almost whole chapters of scripture and knew many church hymns. I was hungry to hear what he had to say. Oscar helped change my life in the bottom of the *Nitta Maru* and I will always be grateful to him for that.

So day after day the Japanese came down the ladder for inspection, and we were forced to kneel and listen to the officer who was in charge of the inspection as he would harangue us, curse us, and insult us. If you moved, he would be sure that you were beaten. The air in our hold was sickening. The food was awful. We were gradually starving to death. Our clothes smelled so foul I could never describe the awful odor. Many were rapidly losing their strength. This, of course, took its toll on the older men. Many were discouraged and thought that the Japanese were just going to let us die. After five days of traveling to an unknown destination, the engines suddenly stopped and we learned that we had arrived in Yokohama, Japan. Yokohama is the main seaport for Tokyo. "Now," we thought, "maybe we will get out of this hell ship." Nothing changed for us, however, we just sat in silence and waited. Two days later, the *Nitta Maru* trembled again. The screws revved up and we were on our way, unsure of where we would end up.

We learned later that a small number of men had gotten off the boat at Yokohama. On the ninth day of our journey, two days out of Yokohama, in the early morning, three Navy sailors and two Marine sergeants from VMF-211, who were on the deck above us, were called out and interviewed by the Japanese. When they came back to the hold from this interview, they were really shaken up emotionally and

We experienced sixteen days of hell in the hold of the Nitta Maru, *not only enduring severe beatings and starvation, but transitioning from sub-tropical weather to freezing January temperatures within forty-eight hours. The shock was terrific.*

seemed frightened. They had been accused of lying about their Naval experience and other crimes, which they knew nothing about. A few hours later, they were summoned out again. They never came back. We learned later that when they were called out the second time, they were told to bring their belongings, as they would not be returning.

After WWII, at a war crimes trial in Yohohama in 1947, the truth finally came out when a member of Japan's Imperial Navy, Tsumori Misaka, who was the *Nitta Maru*'s second purser, testified about what really happened to the three Navy sailors and two Marine sergeants from the Marine VMF-211. He reported, "When I heard the announcement to go up on the deck to witness the execution, I accepted willingly in anticipation of seeing the men executed. I had never before that time seen any human-being killed."

Continuing his account, Misaka said, "There were approximately 150 spectators, including members of the ship's crew and Guard Detachment standing around in a sort of semi-circle. . . . The first time I saw the American victims they were blindfolded. I think their hands were tied at their backs. At the time of the execution I was standing on . . . the same deck on which the executions were carried out. I was approximately 20 feet away from the box upon which Saito stood [and] . . . approximately 15 feet away from where the five American Prisoners of War stood." Misaka remembered that Saito stood about five feet from the prisoners.

Saito stood on a box and holding a paper in both hands (in his right hand he also held his sword) he read aloud the death warrant. Misaka reported, "I recall the following message was read by Saito to the five Prisoners of War in front of him in Japanese and was substantially as follows: 'You have killed many Japanese soldiers on Wake Island in battle. You have done those things and caused death to the Japanese soldiers. Since you have done it, it is a custom in the Japanese way to revenge ourselves. For what you have done you are now going to be killed in payment for the blood you caused from the Japanese soldiers you killed and you are now going to be killed for revenge. You are here as representatives of your American soldiers. . . . You can now pray to be happy in the next world—in heaven.'" (How strange that he would talk about how happy they would be in heaven.) Misaka said he did not believe that the Americans knew that they were going to be executed, let alone why they would be killed, as the warrant was read in Japanese and not translated into English.

After the death warrant was read, each of the victims was made to kneel by the guards. An executioner with a drawn Samurai sword stood beside each prisoner and the execution began. Misaka later recalled, "After the executions had been completed and the bodies had been disposed of, the spectators dispersed themselves and went to their respective quarters. I and some other crew members returned to our quarters and finished our meals. Some of the crew members ate their food. I tasted the food but could not relish it after having seen such gruesome sights."

There were war crime trials after the war in which four of those who were executioners received life sentences. Captain Toshio Saito heard about the trial and disappeared from sight. He was never caught. I would like to say that Captain Toshio Saito was not alone in this execution. He must have had permission from a higher source. All of the Japanese on the *Nitta Maru* must have known what Saito was going to do. It was not a secret. The captain of the *Nitta Maru* knew and gave full permission for the atrocity to take place—all in the spirit of Bushido. [Bushido means "the way of the warrior," the Sumurai warrior, a Japanese code of moral conduct.] When you look at the Japanese culture and history, you realize that the Japanese come from a very different background and belief system.

On January 24, 1942, the *Nitta Maru* entered the delta of the great Yangtze River in China. Moving slowly up the Yangtze, it took the split into the Whangpoo, a tributary of the Yangtze, and anchored at the Port of Woosung. The engines shut down and everything became quiet in our hold.

Arrival at Woosung POW Camp, China

Suddenly the steel hatch door in our hold seventy feet above us banged open and the men on the deck above us were told to move out. This took a few minutes. Then we were told to climb the ladder and move out. This may sound like a small thing, but we suddenly realized that we were not as strong and agile as we were when we left Wake. Many of the men stumbled as they moved to the steel ladder. Then climbing the ladder was quite difficult. It was a slow process, but we had no choice. When I reached the deck right above us, we were told to wait a minute. I glanced around, noting that this deck, which had housed the prisoners above us for the previous twelve days, was now empty. There were about a half dozen guards from Captain Saito's command sitting around and yelling at the prisoners who were seated. They laughed and yelled and pointed and punched at us. We knew that they were taunting us to say something—but no one did.

I learned later that one of the Marines in the group before us talked back to them and they beat him unmercifully. How dumb of the Marine. Nothing is gained by showing bravery when you are under the jurisdiction of an enemy who would love to kill you. I learned this lesson early in my captivity.

After a short wait, we were told to climb the ladder to the bulkhead door and disembark the ship. Climbing the ladder again was a little difficult because the Ingersoll watch and the Schaefer pen and pencil, which I had in my shoe, were rubbing my ankles. After reaching the bulkhead door, a guard pointed to a long passageway running the length of the boat. I took off down that passage running. Then I noticed that there were stateroom doors open on either side of the passageway and in each doorway was a Japanese sailor armed with a club. As we ran down that passageway, those sailors would try to strike us with their clubs. I ran as fast as I could and I don't remember getting hit. Others were not so lucky and received multiple blows.

The passageway then wound to the left to a gangplank that reached from ship to shore. The weather was bitter cold, accompanied by a light, drizzling rain. We had been in the tropics and now we were in a polar land. We all shivered from this near-freezing rain. As I started down the gangplank, however, the sun broke loose from the storm cloud in all of its blazing glory. Because I had been in the hold for twelve days, just a little bit of sun was most welcome, though I was temporarily blinded by the glare. Upon reaching the bottom of the gangplank, I stepped onto the wharf. I was weak and unsteady; for once again I had sea legs.

The Japanese had us all line up shoulder-to-shoulder, first a front rank and then a rear rank. A Japanese officer then gave us a short talk. When he was finished, we turned and started to walk toward our future home, the Woosung Prison Camp, which was about seven or eight miles from the dock. Before we left the docks, I was able to transfer my Schaefer pen and pencil set and my Ingersoll watch to my pants pocket. I never would have made it to camp if they were rubbing against my foot or ankle.

Some of the Chinese people were watching us as we walked by them in this freezing rain. Most of them were dressed in a cloth-buttoned shirt jacket and a pair of one-sized pants that were just wrapped around their waist and tied. Large Cooley hats seemed to float on top of the heads that they protected from rain and sunshine. All they wore on their feet were thong slippers or cloth sandals. Perhaps the most memorable part of this walk along the Woosung docks on this wintry day in Shanghai was passing a small group of Chinese and seeing a Cooley standing in a partial puddle of water. When I looked down at his feet, he was actually standing in a little depression of water and ice. I noticed that his feet were bare and that ice was right around his toes. I thought at that time, "If this Chinese Cooley is living like this under these conditions, what will happen to us now? What will our living conditions be like? Will we get any better food? Will we have any doctors around when we get sick?"

We came in view of our future home. The barracks were long camouflaged buildings that had been used by the Japanese for cavalry units in the past. There was a steel electrified fence that ran around the whole compound. I was told it carried 2,300 volts, enough to kill anyone who was trying to escape.

After we walked through the electrified gates, we were marched to a flat area and lined up. The commandant of the camp stood upon a raised platform. His name was Colonel Yuse (pronounced "you see"). He was about five feet one. The size of his boots made him stand out in the most notable way; they were highly polished and came up over his knees. There was no way his feet could have filled those boots. The boots were long, probably a size fourteen or fifteen. He looked so ridiculous that we had a hard time controlling our laughter.

Then another Japanese man jumped up beside him. He wore civilian clothes, but what really set him apart was his hat. It was a regular felt hat, but the brim in front was pinned to the hat in a ridiculous manner. It was difficult to take him seriously when he looked at us in that hat. When we listened to him, we only saw a college student wanting to be recognized. His nickname from then on was "Joe College."

Joe was the interpreter for Colonel Yuse. His English was terrible, but we were able to understand what Colonel Yuse told him. I'm sure he elaborated on almost everything the colonel said, for this was his time to be noticed and he really enjoyed his position.

Colonel Yuse spoke in the freezing, intermittent rain for about half an hour and Joe interpreted. We were asked, "Why did you surrender? Don't you know that you were supposed to die for your country? You are cowards. Why didn't you die? You are a disgrace to your country. Now you will obey and do what I tell you to do. If you disobey, you will be punished. The emperor has granted you your lives. You are now prisoners of the Greater East Asia Company Prosperity Sphere and you will be allowed to live if you obey all orders." We listened to "Joe College" as he interpreted Yuse's commands. When he was finished, we were assigned to the barracks.

"Room and Board" as a Japanese POW in China

This prisoner compound was composed of seven barracks-type buildings, forty-five feet wide and two hundred feet long. There was a wash rack and a "benjo" (toilet) for each barracks. These barracks were surrounded by a 2,300-volt fence. Outside of the barracks there were numerous other buildings, which included a galley, hospital, library, and Japanese barracks. Then around the whole camp was another 2,300-volt fence. Outside, on each corner of the compound, were four raised guard towers with machine guns.

I was assigned to Barracks 4. When I walked into my section with Oscar Ray, Chal Loveland, and Mac McCurry, I saw that the living situation was going to be quite crowded. My brother Jack was assigned to Barracks 3. The barracks I was in had eight sections. Each section was rectangular—about eighteen feet wide and forty-five feet long. There was a continuous six-foot aisle that ran down the length of the barracks. Each section of the barracks was divided in half by a six-foot wide aisle. Then, each section was split by another aisle, running perpendicularly. On each side of this opening in each section was a notched railing about four feet off the floor. Then above this four-foot railing there was a single board with five-inch wooden pins sticking out. On each side of each section there was a place to store rifles when not in use. In each half section separated by the aisle there were two raised platforms about eighteen feet long, six feet six inches deep and eighteen inches above the floor.

An aisle divided each sub-section. There were four eighteen-inch raised platforms, two on each side of the divided section. In each half section, between the two raised eighteen-inch platforms, there was a table about six feet long and on each side were benches to sit on. The platform on each side of the section, where we were

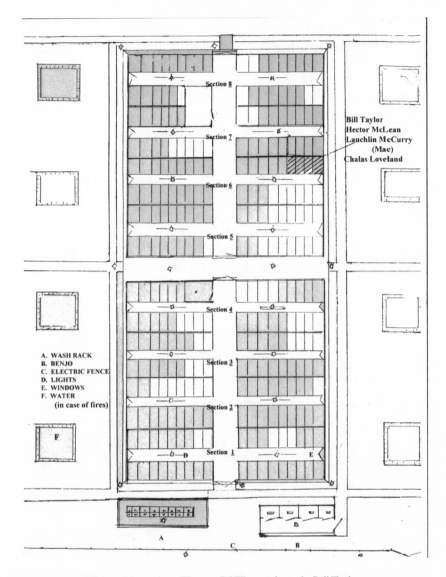

Bill Taylor
Hector McLean
Lauchlin McCurry
(Mac)
Chalas Loveland

A. WASH RACK
B. BENJO
C. ELECTRIC FENCE
D. LIGHTS
E. WINDOWS
F. WATER
   (in case of fires)

Map of barracks at Woosung POW camp drawn by Bill Taylor

going to spend the rest of our prison life, was eighteen feet wide and six feet six inches deep. There were four of these platforms in each section, two on each side of the aisle. Those two half sections were also separated by six feet and a table. A single electric light of about forty watts hung down from the wooden ceiling. The globe had a green shade covering its dim light. All of the platforms butted into a solid wall on each side of the section. In a sense this separated us from the next section. There were two windows about three feet wide by four feet high on each half section. These windows could be locked or kept open. The most desired spot in the barracks was next to the window.

Each man had an area thirty-four inches wide by six feet six inches long on this raised platform. There also was a shelf on the wall where you could store a few items as well as a thin strip of wood with a hook on which to hang your mess kit. Under the platform was a small space to store a few things.

The Japanese supplied us with cotton ticks (a cloth bag shaped like a sleeping bag), which we then filled with straw. They also gave us four blankets, which supplied us with some comfort. They were so thin, however, that if you held them up to the light, you could see through them. It was so cold that any warmth you could get was most appreciated. The warmth, however, usually wouldn't come. The weather in Shanghai was a damp cold that could plummet down to 30 degrees Fahrenheit.

We were shown our benjo, or outhouse. It was something else. When I first went to the benjo, I almost threw up. It was a little framed building and was supposed to take care of almost 250 men. The building was about eight feet wide and fifteen feet long. When you walked on the wooden path leading to it, if it was raining, the path would sink into the mud. It opened with a swinging door and was lit by a dim electric light. On the left side was a sloping metal urinal trough, about ten feet long. On the right-hand side were the "toilets." They hardly resembled toilets for they were merely four little enclosures that were two steps above the floor. As you pushed open the swinging door to the toilet, the only thing you saw was a hole in the floor about ten inches wide and fourteen or fifteen inches long, nothing else. There was nothing to hang onto except a little wooden rod that was nailed into the wall ahead of you.

As your eyes became adjusted when you took your pants down

and looked down the hole in the floor, you could see where every-thing was going. If you weren't sick before, than at that point you were really being tested. About four feet down sat a large earthen container and as your eyes became more adjusted you could detect movement. As you peered in for an even closer look, you could see rats trying to feed on the waste. These were the largest rats I had ever seen and they were everywhere. We made cages to trap them and once we caught one that was twenty-two inches long, including the tail. They were very smart and we could hear them in the walls and under the floor. Some nights, it seemed that they even played soccer in the attic above us! Occasionally, it was so cold during the winter that the rats would come down and crawl up between us.

Because the weather was so cold, there were times when some of the men wouldn't take their shoes off when they came back from the outhouse; they simply only had energy to get back into their sacks. I cannot criticize them at all, because if you are really ill, you just don't have the will, desire, or strength to do otherwise. This became a real problem to many, especially if you had to run back and forth to the benjo continually. There was a wash rack next to our barracks and the benjo. You could wash with this water, but you would never dare drink it because of pollution. We did use this water to wash our clothing. But drying the clothes was very difficult because of the cold, rainy weather in Woosung.

The first night in the Woosung prison is one I will never forget. After we were assigned to our barracks, the Japanese fed us with hot, cooked rice and curry with meat. It was then that we were is-sued our mess kit: a bowl, a spoon, and a cup. We ate this meal like it would be the only meal we would ever get. This was a gesture of kindness from the Japanese. They did not have to do this, but they did, and the next day they did it again. Some of the men ate so quickly and furiously that they got sick and had to throw it all up. On the third day, the Japanese saw the men throw away some of their rice. That was it. From then on for the duration of our POW

Photograph of original benjo, 1945

experience, our meals were much different.

I should mention that on the day after we arrived in Woosung, the Japanese issued us Military clothing: a pair of pants, jackets, shoes, socks, and underwear. The shoes were hobnailed and much of the clothing was too small to wear, though it did help us a lot. The climate was bitter cold and many of the men got sick. For a short period of time the Japanese let us have portable wood heaters. But when the Japanese found some of the men taking out part of the wood trusses in the attics, they became very angry and took all of the stoves away. Then they made the men who had removed the attic wood carry the stove around the compound with a sign that said, "I stole the wood and the stove made me guilty."

Mac McCurry, Chalas Loveland, Oscar Ray and I lived in a space eight feet wide by six feet six inches deep. Each of us had a two-and-a-half-foot wide by six-foot long straw tick. This was a very tight fit, fifteen square feet—that was it. We lived together this way for three and a half years. We shared stories and talked to each other. There was hardly anything we didn't know about each other's lives. We were like brothers, and in all of those POW years we never had a serious argument. McCurry was a tough little American Irishman, rather short with red hair, with a great sense of humor and a quick temper. In a way, he was like a pit bull. There was also a big, mean carpenter in our section named Butch. He was continually creating trouble and one day he centered his dislike on me, for no reason, and wanted to fight. Finally, after one of his comments, I stood up to face him knowing that I was going to be clobbered. Suddenly, I was shoved aside by little Mac. The carpenter said, "I've got no beef with you, Mac, and I don't want to hurt you." Mac said, "Butch, Bill and I are friends and you are a no good, trouble-making SOB." The carpenter, looking Mac in the eyes, had a problem and said, "Listen Mac, don't push me or you and I are going to have it out now and if I have to, I'll beat you up too. How are you ever going to fight me?" Mac didn't budge an inch and he didn't back up at all. Instead, he picked up a hard wooden club from under his bunk that was three inches wide and about three and a half feet long. He had it in both hands and was in a crouched position. He then said, with a look of cold fury in his eyes, "This is my equalizer, Butch, you come at me and I'll break your leg." Everyone was looking at Mac who had a real killer look in his eyes. Butch, seeing it too, then said, "Okay Mac, no problem, let's forget it." I was relieved and Mac just laughed and sat down next to me. Butch never bothered me or anyone else in the section after that. A year later he was shipped out to Japan.

It was so cold inside our barracks that you could see your breath. But there was nothing we could do about it. We needed food and clothing desperately, anything to keep us warm. It rained constantly and then froze. After every meal, in order to keep warm, the men would pace up and down the six-foot wide aisle that separated the sections, exhaling icy breath in clouds as they walked. We were quite the motley crew, for no one was dressed the same. The thing that people would probably notice about us first was our hodgepodge of footwear. Hobnailed Japanese shoes, tennis shoes, dress shoes, Marine issue shoes, slippers, and "go-aheads." Men in camp made many of the "go-ahead" slippers. I had a pair of go-aheads that I had made out of wood. They were very crude, just a couple of

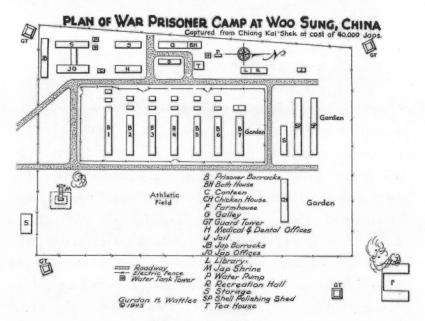

Map of Woosung POW camp

boards about ten inches long, rounded in front, with a leather strap over each one. I could slip my feet into the straps and walk quite well. These slippers were very useful because if I had to go to the benjo at night, all I had to do was slip out from under my blankets, step into my slippers and go. When I returned, I just slipped out of my slippers and into my "Russian sleeping bag."

There was a guy in the section next to us who taught us how to make a Russian sleeping bag out of the four blankets we had been issued. It made the most out of your blankets to keep you extra warm. To assemble it, you take one blanket, No. 1, and lay it out flat on the platform we used for beds. Then you take another blanket, No. 2, and lay it on the left half of blanket No. 1. Then you take blanket No. 3 and lay it only on the right half of blanket No. 2. Then you take blanket No. 4 and lay it on the left half of blanket No. 3. When this is done, you fold blanket No. 3 over blanket No. 4. Then you fold blanket No. 2 over No. 3 and No. 4. After blanket No. 2, No. 3, and No. 4 are in place, you fold blanket No. 1 over No. 2, No. 3, and No. 4. Blanket No. 1 is then the top and bottom of all the blankets. You then tie No. 1 to itself on the side. Four ties keep all blankets in place. Then you take a rope and tie all of the blankets together six inches up from the bottom as tight as you can. There you have a Russian sleeping bag.

After about a week in Woosung, we went to work. We heard the Japanese wake-up bugle at half past six in the morning. Then we hurriedly got up, folded our blankets, placed them next to the wall, washed at the wash rack, and headed back to the section for inspection at seven o'clock. A Japanese officer accompanied by four guards made the daily inspection. They would bang open the door to the barracks. Then two of the enlisted Japanese would walk in front of the officer and two would walk behind. Our section leader at the beginning was a fifty-plus-year-old carpenter by the name of Joe Williams. Joe would stand in the center of the section and yell *kiotski* (attention). Everyone in the section would stand in front of his sleeping pad as silence filled the whole section. Saluting the Japanese officer of the day, the men would then count off with *ichi* (one), *ni* (two), *san* (three) . . . until all of the men in our section had been accounted for. At this time, we had thirty-eight men or *san ju hachi* in our section. After the count, the officer would say, *yasumi* (rest). After our section had inspection, the Japanese moved to the next section and then the next until all eight sections in our barrack were accounted for.

Breakfast was then brought into the barracks in five-gallon wooden buckets. The men sat on the end of their ticks (bunks) with their feet on the floor. Each man had a soup bowl, a cup, and a spoon, all of which came in a small cloth bag with a string to tighten it up. Then the guy with the hot cereal in a five-gallon can started serving a full cup of cereal to each man as he sat on the end of his tick. The cereal was not bad. Most of the time it was rice or wheat. We also had hot tea, which wasn't really tea. Some said it was an inferior grade of tea while others said it was merely made from willow leaves. It was, however, boiling hot and that was good. Our drinking water had to be pre-boiled. Everything we put in our mouths in China, for that matter, had to be cooked or boiled. At noon we would receive a small biscuit about three by four by three inches high. If the men were out working, the biscuit was placed on the platform or mattress.

Then at about half past five, the evening meals were brought over to the barracks in the five-gallon wooden buckets. Every man would be sitting on the edge of his bunk with his bowl in his hand. When the guys came into our barracks, they would all gather together by the swinging entry door. There they would dip and measure to be sure each section got its share of the soup, which, if we were lucky, contained either beans, soybeans, rice, or potatoes. The nice thing about the meals at night was that they were hot. But we were always hungry and we were slowly losing weight.

Sometimes the meal was quite good and other times it was just a few vegetables in hot water. That's when the extra rice I had saved came in handy. The server had a long dipper and could twist around to serve up whatever combination from the bucket he chose. There were always those guys who couldn't be satisfied and who thought they were being cheated, but I think the server did a fine job of dishing out the food fairly.

After the evening meal, the men would walk up and down the aisle that separated the sections. There would be two lines of traffic, one going and one coming. All this was to keep us a little warm. When you walked after a meal, you could actually feel the warmth circulate through your system.

At the same time, though, we were gradually becoming weaker. The question lingered as to how long it would be before we would die from starvation. All I knew was, "Never give up." Most of us were young, nineteen to twenty-five years of age, and so we could take a lot of punishment—and we did. Everybody suffered, especially the men in their fifties and sixties.

I remember one time when the food was being distributed in my section and the server had gotten near the end of the line. Dipping down in the basket and swishing it around, he finally brought up something that I'm sure he thought was a large bone, but it was a dead rat. When this happened, the guy getting served yelled, "Oh, no!" Everything stopped in the section. It became very quiet. Most of the men were well into their dinner. Some men couldn't eat a thing more. Others left the section to heave out what they had eaten. I ate everything in the bowl. If you stop eating, then you will die much sooner.

Occasionally the call would go out through the barracks that there was burnt rice coming. You get burnt rice for several reasons: not enough water, too much fire, too long of cooking, et cetera. When the rice is cooked right, it comes out moist and ready to eat. But sometimes there is a brown shield of rice sticking to the side of the rice vessel. It has to be scraped out. We soon discovered that this rice

We were always weary, hungry and cold. We welcomed the occasional cup of steaming hot tea. Many of us took to pacing the floor of the barracks to keep warm.

was a real delicacy. It couldn't be served to the men as a substitute for a meal, but occasionally a basket of rice would be assigned to our section. We really enjoyed this burnt rice when we could get it. I bought it quite often. I remember that one day some of it fell out of a bucket into the mud and a guy was trying to pick it up and out of the mud. You've got to be really hungry to do that.

It seemed as though we were always lacking something when we ate. We ate the food that was given us, but we also noticed in our soup that over a period of time we were getting more water and fewer solids. So you can see that with this kind of a diet, you were going to gradually lose weight. Food was on our minds continually.

We often talked about what we wanted to do when the war was over. Many of the men said they were going to become chefs when they got home. They even made crude little menus of what they would cook. Then they would discuss how they would cook it, et cetera. Well all that talk only created an intolerable appetite, which affected their minds and bodies. With some of the men, it went too far. For instance, I remember finding one man drooling in thought over food. I was not like this.

We never knew what was going to happen from one moment to another, so we just went through each day as it came. I personally figured that one of three things would happen sooner or later. One, the Japanese would surrender. But from the looks of things, the Japanese certainly were not going to surrender. Two, our forces would rescue us. In that event almost every man would be killed. Three, when things got really tough and the Japanese knew that they were going to lose the war; they would just take us out and kill us all. That would then release them from watching over us. So you can see that the chances for us to get out alive were almost nonexistent.

I might mention that occasionally we would have unexpected visits from these "Jeeps." (I don't know why we called them "Jeeps." Someone said the nickname was taken from the comic strip *Little Abner*.) Whenever we had one of these visits, someone would yell out "Jeeps!" and everyone would know the Japanese were coming in. Some men that were very ill and many of the older men would just stay on their ticks. The Japanese just didn't bother them. I don't recall any of the older men getting a beating.

January of 1942 was a tough month for all of us. It snowed and rained every day. There was a water tower in our camp that was about twenty-five feet high and completely covered with ice. I wondered why it just didn't fall over. We'd have rain and then freezing spells.

After about ten days in Woosung, I became very ill. My stomach wouldn't stay quiet and I became very nauseated. Even though there was no thermometer handy, I knew that I had a high fever. My bowels were out of control. It was one trip after another to the filthy benjo day and night. It was just a short distance away, but it was through wet snow or cold rain.

There was no medicine in our camp. For about two months our only doctor was Navy Lieutenant Gustav Mason Kahn, who also had been taken prisoner on Wake. The only medication anyone got at this time was a handful of charcoal. This was supposed to stop the bowels from running. Did it? Well, not for me. One night, as I was curled up in my sack, I got this tremendous urge to go to the benjo. Wiggling out of my sack and slipping into a pair of carpenter overalls, I bolted toward the benjo. Just as I reached the door outside of our barracks, I just couldn't contain myself and my clothing became a mess. I pushed the outside door open against a wind that carried snow mixed with rain. It was dark, bitter cold, and windy outside. The only light came from one of the lights that lit up the compound that separated the two electric fences. I squirmed out of my clothes until I was naked, then rolled up my clothes and laid them by the barracks door and walked bare-footed about thirty feet to the hooded light that was next to the 2,300-volt fence that surrounded our barrack compound.

Standing under the light was a Japanese sentry. He was dressed for the cold weather with a hood over his head. As I approached him, stumbling through the half-frozen mud, he just stood looking at the crazy naked man approaching him. When I got about five feet from him, the only thing that separated us was the electric fence and the electric light from above. I said in Japanese *"Heitai San, Watashi wa byoki des,"* which means, "Mr. Soldier, I am sick." He replied *"Anata no kichigai,"* which means, "You are crazy." I explained that I had been to the benjo, but I needed to wash. He said to go to the wash rack and wash off the filth. This I did while fighting the icy rain. Then I went back into the cold barracks and my tick. I climbed, shivering, into the blankets and tried to rest. Finally, I went to sleep. When the bugle blew in the morning, I got up hurriedly, ran outside to get my clothes and they were gone. They had been stolen during the night. I was able to get more clothes in the morning, which then consisted of another pair of carpenter overalls, a green knit shirt, and shoes—accessorized with my Ingersoll watch and my Schaefer pen and pencil set.

That experience was one of the low points of my entire life as a POW. But I was young and determined that I was going to get well—and I did. Prayer plays a major part in getting through difficult times. What a wonderful thing it is when you can talk to the Lord with no strings attached and know that everything you want to say and discuss is being heard.

Chapter Eight

CIGARETTE CURRENCY AND A
CHANGE OF CAMPS

T he marines from Northern China were stationed in Peking and Tientsin, China, before the war. They were the embassy guard and when the war started, they surrendered to the Japanese without a shot, thinking they would be repatriated. Well, they weren't repatriated, but they were allowed to keep all of the money they had, which had been used for salaries and maintenance, as well as all of their belongings—clothing, bedding, and personal effects. As a result, when they arrived in Woosung, they were in great shape with their money, clothes, and bedding, which they shared with no one. There was little love lost between the Northern China Marines and the Wake Island Marines and civilians. That's why the Japanese set up their own commissary. They were going to steal everything from the Northern China Marines—legally. Why they just didn't come into camp and take what they wanted was because of the close proximity to the International Red Cross, stationed just a few miles away in Shanghai. This was lucky for us because the Red Cross helped sustain us throughout the war.

My section leader, Joe Williams, was a smart carpenter. One of his responsibilities was to make the Japanese Commissary available as a place to sell things to the prisoners, which he did. But he also figured out how to steal from the Japanese while working.

One day he got caught red-handed stealing from the Japanese. That very night, he was taken to the officers' quarters where he was beaten over and over. He returned to our section later that night, but he died of internal injuries three days later. Nothing was said about it and nothing was done about it. It was just a reminder to watch what you do and to be careful not to get caught.

Right after Joe Williams was gone, I was made the new leader of Barracks 4, Section 6, Honcho 1. I became known to the Japanese as "yon-roku-ichi" or 4-6-1. That was the number I had all through the war. My duties were to see that all of the men in the section were ready for morning and evening inspections.

The Japanese issued us ten cigarettes twice a week. For ten cigarettes you could buy a man's ration of rice. I didn't smoke; I hadn't lit up since my promise to the Lord while on Wake. At the time I made that promise, I wasn't aware of how soon that promise would prove a blessing. That one decision I made on Wake that night later saved my life while I was in the Woosung and Kiangwan Prison Camps. It's strange how we receive blessings. There would be those who would say, "You're cuckoo" for my talk about blessings. But in all of my years as a POW, I never stopped thanking the Lord for all He did for me.

It was so cold during January and February and we had no source of heat. There were days, however, when you could stand outside with your back to the barracks on the east side, if you weren't working and the weather was clear, and you would get a little comfort from the sun shining down on you.

Cigarettes and How They Saved My Life

It was during the early spring of 1942 that I decided to try to gather more cigarettes, for they were the medium of exchange in our camp. You could buy almost anything with cigarettes. Each package of twenty cigarettes sold for ten yen. So in my efforts to gather more riches, I sold my Ingersoll watch and Schaeffer pen and pencil set to a North China Marine for ten dollars gold or ten dollars American money. Then I exchanged this ten dollars gold for forty Japanese yen. The ratio was one dollar US for four Japanese yen. So after the trade, I had forty Japanese yen.

You could buy a package of twenty Atkatuke cigarettes for one yen, so now I had enough money to buy forty packages of cigarettes, which would then give me eighty extra cups of rice. I thought about this for a few days and decided to gamble and try to buy cigarettes right from the Japanese. It was a risky thing to do because if you got caught, it would mean a long time in the brig, beatings, or torture, and in extreme cases, death.

I had given this much thought and decided that I needed better food. Peanut butter was at the top of the list, then candy, then canned vegetables. It would be risky and the price was high. For a large jar of peanut butter, the cost was one hundred yen, so you can see that I needed a lot of money to buy enough food to really eat well.

I had money, so I soon wondered, "What would be better than to trade with the enemy?" I knew a little Japanese and there was a Japanese soldier that was on duty every other day or so down at the northeast corner of the compound. One afternoon, about one week after I had received my forty Japanese yen, I walked out to the northeast corner of the barracks. I looked across the hot electric fence of 2,400 volts at the Japanese sentry who was standing not more than seventy feet away. We just stood there looking at each other for a few minutes. Then I said in Japanese, "Heitai san, Watashi wa kane mochi des anata wa tobako arimaska." (Mr. Soldier, I have quite a bit of money. Do you have cigarettes?) Then I told him my number.

It was very quiet. He said nothing and so after a few minutes I turned and went back into the barracks thinking, "Well I tried, and nothing happened." Then one dark night about eleven thirty the door on our barracks banged open. Everyone awakened and we listened to the hob-nailed shoes as they came thumping down the hallway. We all thought, "Who are they after tonight?" As we listened, the *thump, thump, thump* stopped right at my sack, I felt a tap on my feet and a voice in Japanese say *"Anata wa, yon roku ichi, kuru.* (You, 4-6-1, come). I immediately slid out of my Russian sleeping bag, put on my carpenter overalls, shirt, and go-aheads and followed him down through the barracks. Just before going outside, we came to a room on the left side of the hall. We entered, and the soldier turned on the small light hanging from the ceiling on a cord. He then leaned his rifle in the corner of the room. Turning around and facing me, he started dropping package after package of Atkatuke cigarettes on the floor. While he was doing this, I realized that he was the Japanese sentry I had seen a few days earlier at the corner of the compound.

He was small, about five-feet four-inches tall and had a beard. He did not smile. He dropped package after package of cigarettes on the floor, and finally there were twenty-five packages on the floor. Then he held out his hand and said, *"Ni ju go yen,"* which meant that he wanted twenty-five yen for the twenty-five packages. I told him no, explaining that one package of twenty cigarettes in camp cost a yen. I couldn't risk my life for nothing when there was no profit. He looked at me and again said, "Ni ju go yen" (twenty-five). I told him that I could only give him ten yen for the twenty-five packages, and so it went back and forth for a few minutes like a couple of Las Vegas Jews. I finally told him that I would only give ten yen and that was it, then I turned to walk out of the room. At this point I think he realized that I wasn't going to give in. He said, *"Matsu, ju yen"* (Wait, it is all right). I gave him ten yen, picked up the twenty-five packages, opened the door, and went back to my sack. The last I heard was the *clack, clack, clack,* of his hob-nailed shoes as he opened the door and went out of the barracks. When the door closed behind him and I was safe in my sack, Chal and Mac, almost whispered in unison, "What in hell is going on?" "I'll tell you in the morning," I answered.

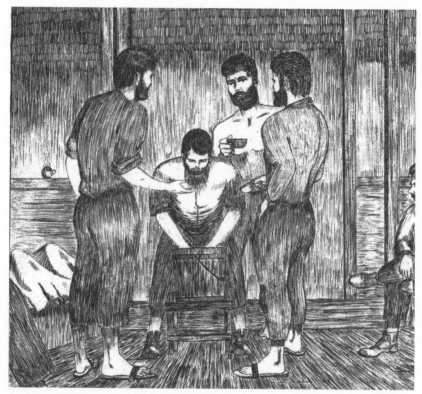

Each prisoner was given only a teacup full of rice. Food was always the main topic of conversation. We talked about what kind of food we used to have and what we could do with the same food now.

The next morning I sold my twenty-five packages of cigarettes for twenty-five yen, making fifteen yen in fifteen minutes. I now had fifty-five yen—a good trade. After this little episode with the sentry, I realized that if I kept on trading with the Japanese, I would eventually get caught. So what would be the next step to a better life?

I had money now, enough to buy at least 110 cups of rice. I knew I wasn't going to trade with the Japanese sentry again or anyone else who could get me in trouble. As I considered this, I thought, "Someday I might get robbed of what little I had in cigarettes and money." Then, one day as I was discussing the duration of the war with one of my friends, the conversation slipped to cigarettes and how long the Japanese were going to give us our ration of ten cigarettes. I said, "There are many guys that think the war will be over in three months.

Well, I think it will take longer and we don't know how long the Japanese are going to continue to give us our ration, so this is what I'll do. I'll give you thirteen packages of cigarettes right now, but in return I want your Japanese ration for the duration of the war. Now if the Japanese stop giving us cigarettes, then I lose, but if the war goes on and on, then I will profit." "Well," my friend said, "I think you are going to lose on this one, Bill." Anyway, I gave him the thirteen packages of Atkatuke cigarettes. I made the same deal with another guy. So I now had, including my own ration, three rations of cigarettes (thirty cigarettes) twice a week. As there were twenty cigarettes in a package, every week my income was three packages.

With the cigarette deal closed, I had established a steady income for myself. The trade and my stash of cigarettes and cash was no secret to others, so my next step was how to get rid of the money and cigarettes before I was robbed.

When we first arrived to Kiangwan in December of 1942, I built a wooden drawer safe under my bunk. This cash drawer made out of wood was four inches wide, three inches thick, and twelve inches long. I installed it at night under my sack and platform. It operated on five levers attached to the front of the safe. By pulling a combination of levers, I could open the safe. Here I kept some but not all of my money. I also kept it full of packages of cigarettes.

There I was in a position to buy and sell cigarettes. After I purchased food from the Japanese Commissary, which put me on the road to better health, some of the first things I bought were three wool blankets, a pair of almost new issue shoes (hitting above the ankle), a belt, and an almost new pair of trousers from the Northern China Marines, which I still have to this day. I might mention that these later purchases were done in the summer of 1942. It was so easy to buy the above, as the Northern China Marines thought they were going to be repatriated. Well, they weren't repatriated. They served full time.

The Move to Kiangwan POW Camp

We moved to Kiangwan, about ten miles from Woosung, on December 6, 1942. The Pacific war had been going for about a year at that point. The Kiangwan camp was much more secured than Woosung was. The only thing that kept us all in Woosung was the two 2,300-volt electric fences. A number of Military and civilians had tried to escape from Woosung and all had been caught, so the Japanese built the inescapable prisoner compound at Kiangwan. A Japanese soldier had also been killed by a hidden sniper outside of the Woosung Camp. The Kiangwan Prison Camp was an improvement, especially in medical care, thanks to Dr. Yoshihiro Shindo. Mac McCurry, Chalas Loveland, and I were still together. We also had Butch, the carpenter, who had given me such a bad time. It so happened that because I was the section leader, I was in the first row where the section leader was assigned. Mac and Chalas were now on the east side, one space from the wall. Being next to the wall was the best place you could be because you had some privacy there. It ended up that Butch the carpenter who threatened to beat me up, had the bunk next to the wall. He was next to Chalas and Mac. That was a no-good situation. Butch didn't want Mac next to him and Chalas didn't want to be anywhere near Butch.

By that time I was pretty well off, having a good supply of money and cigarettes. Butch was broke and smoked profusely. So after we moved into our new section, I approached Butch and asked him if he wanted to trade places with me. We argued about the price and finally I was able to trade bunks for about a carton of cigarettes. Not long after our trade, Butch was transferred to Japan. I was glad to see him go. I guess he was a good person underneath, but in our section he was not very well liked.

So now I had one of the best places in the section, right next to a window. I had a certain amount of privacy. Plus, I had money and cigarettes and I was able to buy extra food. Bread was delivered in small loaves in the afternoon. The guy that delivered the bread

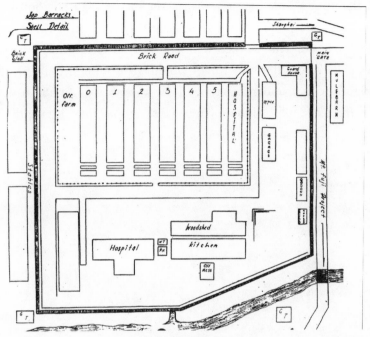

Map of Kiangwan POW camp

would put it on the bottom of each man's tick or the edge of the wooden platform in front of the sack. This was a little scary for the edge of the platform was dusty and the tick mattresses in almost all cases were dirty. Now this bread was delivered to our section in the afternoon and so for two hours or more it was left in front of each man's bunk with no protection from the multitude of flies that were continually buzzing around the section. So when you got off work and walked into your section, the first thing you saw was this little loaf of bread with flies on it. Most of the men, being hungry, would just pick up their food and gobble it down. I was no different than the rest, except I did go out to the wash rack and clean my hands and arms, then go back to my bunk and eat. I hated the way the bread was handled.

So then I got an idea. Why not make a hood? So I got a hold of some wire, with a twelve- or fourteen-inch gauge, and made myself a wire hood that was about twelve by twelve by eight inches.

I then put a little handle about three inches long on top of that. I scrounged around and found some mosquito netting that I attached to the hood. This worked well, and each afternoon when the bread was delivered, the bread man would lift the hood I had made and place the loaf under the hood. That way when I came in from work or from a walk, I didn't have to worry about flies. I gave the bread man a few cigarettes once in a while.

Chapter Nine

SURVIVING THE POW LIFE

Before the war, Shanghai was really a city of mixed nationalities. It was a city of different cultures, ideas, languages, dress, likes, and dislikes. There were many embassies that included all of the major countries of the world and they all had their own languages (though English was the most common language spoken). When the war started and the Japanese gained complete control of the city, almost all of the embassies closed.

When the embassies shut their doors, they also closed their libraries. Both the British and American Embassies had libraries. But what was going to be done with those collections of books? The problem was solved easily as the books were allocated to the prisoners of war located in Kiangwan. The Japanese approved the idea and the books were shipped to our prison camp in Kiangwan. There were about three thousand books in all.

What a wonderful contribution to our camp. A library was set up for us, which was open from three o'clock in the afternoon until eight o'clock in the evening every day except Sunday, in an empty building in the camp. It was a wonderful break for all of the men in camp because we could choose from a selection of books covering mathematics, grammar, history, economics, as well as novels written by Mark Twain, William Shakespeare, Robert Louis Stevenson, Zane Grey, Alexandre Dumas, Kenneth Robert, and other greats. In short, the library was a lifesaver for many men who didn't know what the next day would bring. I checked out book after book during those years in camp. I even began to recognize which publishing houses published certain types of books. Reading so many books greatly increased my vocabulary. I took a course in English grammar from one of the library books and passed it.

Sitting in my quarters next to the window, I got another idea. I wondered if the Japanese would care if I put a little folding table just below the window that was at the bottom of my bunk. I would try to make it as inconspicuous as possible. I would make the top of the desk out of an eighteen-square-inch piece of paneling with a bordering one-inch trim around the outside and two hinges on the part that would fasten to the wall below the window. When this was done, I mounted the table about two inches below the window. Then I fastened a little two-square-inch wooden brace on a hinge underneath the table on the front. When this was all done, all I had to do was raise my table up to a level position, push the two square inches out, and anchor it in a little clip below the window.

It worked perfectly. There I could sit on the end of my bunk and raise my table up to a comfortable level. I just folded it down when I wasn't there. It was a great place to eat, read, or write. It was also a perfect place for my bread to be placed when I wasn't there. The surface was always clean and my little hood fit right on the table. In all of the time that I was a POW, no one ever bothered me about that little table—not even the Japanese. As I looked back on all of the things that had happened to me since I made the promise to the Lord way back on Wake, I realized I was being blessed.

We never knew when the Japanese would choose to make a visit to the barracks, day or night. At first when they came bursting in, some of the guys were punished for various reasons. When we did have those unexpected visits, someone would send out a warning of their arrival by yelling, "Shake your blankets!" The guy in the next section who heard it would yell, "Shake your blankets!" and so it would go all the way through the barracks. The "Japs" would ask, "Why you shake the blankets?" No one gave a straight answer and the "Japs" never caught on.

I learned early on to do exactly what the Japanese wanted us to do. From January 1942, when we arrived in Woosung, to about the middle of April 1942, the biggest problems were cold and rainy weather, lack of food and clothing, flies, rats, and disease. We got along with the Japanese in most cases. There were some beatings and punishments of various kinds, but we weathered through them. By this time, we weren't calling them Japanese "Japs," but rather, "Jeeps." The weather was starting to break and many thought the war was going to be over quickly.

Isamu Ishihara

By April and May of 1942 the war was actually just getting started. During May, a new interpreter came to Woosung. His name was Isamu Ishihara. He was about five feet six and weighed about 130 pounds. He spoke excellent English and conducted himself as an officer, which of course he was not. He wore broad-rimmed glasses and dressed as if he were the most important man in our camp. I suppose the most striking thing about Ishihara was his coal black eyes. He seldom smiled and when he talked to you there was a look in his eyes that said, "You're an American; you think you're better than I am. Well, I'm going to show you that you are not superior to me." The thought that came to you was "Don't lie to this guy because he already knows the truth about what he is asking." If he had you in for questioning, you stood at attention, unless he told you to sit down. He carried a quirt, which was a riding whip with a leather lash attached to a short handle, and he would snap it against his leather leggings from time to time as he talked.

It was nothing for him to stop you or anyone else and ask a few questions while you were walking by. If the answers were what he wanted to hear, he would let you go. If he for one minute thought you were lying, then he would slap you while screaming, "Why do you lie to me? Don't you know that I know if you are telling the truth or not?" After the tirade, Ishi often would say, "Why didn't you die on Otori Shima (the new name for Wake Island, meaning Bird Island)? You should have died fighting for your country. You have no honor. You are nothing and now you are a disgraced prisoner of war of the Greater East Asia Company Prosperity Sphere, and you will do what I tell you to do." By this time he had usually worked himself into a rage. Now if you stood at attention very quietly with your hands at your side, looking straight ahead, Ishi would glare at you, then in most cases would turn to the next guy or just walk away. He only used his quirt if everything got out of hand.

Ishi questioned me about the money that my brother Jack had given me just before he was sent to Japan in December of 1943. He ordered a soldier to bring me to a little shack near the project. When I walked in, Ishi was sitting at a desk writing. There were two other chairs in front of the desk and a small window behind it.

He continued to write and I just stood at attention. After a few moments, he looked up and said, "Did you ever trade with the Chinese?" (The Chinese he referred to were the benjo people who came into camp to take out the poop every other day. We called them "the Honey-Bucket boys." He was also referring to "Chinese Charlie," who was doing business with the Japanese, but trading with the Americans on the side.) This was a no-no. No trading with the Chinese. That was classified as espionage and the penalty could be death. I said, "No, I haven't." At that point I was a little concerned that he was going to ask me if I had ever traded with or received money from the Japanese. But fortunately he didn't. He then asked, "Did you ever receive any money from anybody?" I thought about that for a split second, then answered, "Yes, I did receive one hundred CRBs from my brother Jack, who is in Tokyo." Ishi asked, "And where did your brother, Jack, get this money?" I said, "I really don't know. I didn't even think about it." He then asked me if I had ever met Charlie. I said, "No, I haven't." Ishi stared at me for a minute or so, then motioned for me to leave.

I was convinced that he knew all about my brother Jack's dealings with Charlie. However, he couldn't do anything about it because Jack was in Tokyo. Not long after that, we heard that Charlie had been punished severely by the Japanese. I was glad he didn't ask me about the Japanese sentry. I don't think Ishi knew about my trading with the Japanese. To have stopped trading with the Japanese when I did was a blessing. I am sure that if I had continued trading, I would have been punished severely. Because of this incident with Charlie, Ishi decided to have his own inquisition. By that time we were calling Ishihara the "Beast of the East."

Another incident that I didn't see was the day Marine Platoon Sergeant Bernie Kitner, a well-muscled section leader in Barracks 2, took on Ishihara. It seems someone in the section had done something to upset Ishi, so at inspection time in the evening, Ishi showed up with four Japanese soldiers. Everybody was called to attention. The section leader Bernie was in the middle of the aisle separating the section. While talking to Bernie and accusing him of something one of the men in his section had done, Ishi became vocally abusive. Bernie just stood at attention looking straight ahead. Finally Ishi became more agitated and began slapping and cursing Bernie, telling him that he was a no-good white SOB. When Ishi could get no reaction from Bernie, he lost control and began slapping him harder. Finally Bernie had had enough. In a split second he reared back and smacked Ishi flat onto his back. Ishi was so stunned and enraged that he ordered his sergeant of the guard to beat him up. And that's just what they did. They beat Bernie with rifle butts, fists, boots, and Ishi even beat him unmercifully about the head, neck, and arms with the back side of his sword. Bernie was unable to defend himself. After about thirty minutes of this and just as Bernie started to lose consciousness, Ishi called his men off. He then spat on Bernie, kicked him in his testicles, and called him a "white American son of a bitch." A few minutes later he congratulated Bernie on being able to take the beating they gave him. After that Bernie spent time in the brig without food. He showed great courage for standing up to Ishi, but I thought he was a fool for hitting him. It was a wonder he didn't get shot.

Ishi had made life miserable for almost all of the prisoners. Among the cruel things he did was keep from us any mail that came from our loved ones back in the states. As the years went by, we endured the antics of Ishihara. Then one day the situation became more intense when the "Jeeps" discovered that there was more money in the camp than they thought. So after many months, they figured out that we were trading dollars for the Chinese yuan. In other words, we had a money market behind the backs of the Japanese. When the word got to the "Beast of the East," he became infuriated and started his own inquisition. He first called in Mickey, a British seaman, one evening and he didn't return that night. The next day he called in a couple more guys, one Army officer and one Marine. After he had questioned them, they were put in the guardhouse with no communication with anyone in camp. In the late evening, Ishi personally called in Joe Stowe, a Wake Island Marine.

By this time we knew that someone was really getting worked over. We heard screams coming from Ishi's office and it went on for hours. When the inquisition was over, the victim was taken to the guardhouse and was told that he was to have no communication with any of the people that were taking food to the men who had been tortured. We finally got word from those who had been tortured. The message was simple, "Ishi knows everything." After that, bit-by-bit, more information came out of the guardhouse.

Then came the news about what kind of torture the men were going through. It was called the "water cure." There were a few men in camp that knew what the water cure was. When a man walked into the room, he was told to strip down to his underwear, then lie down on a board that was tilted at one end about one foot off the floor. His feet would be tied to the upper part of the board with his head on the lower end. His hands would be tied above his head and around the board. When this was done, he was forced to drink water. When he had drunk all he could, his mouth was forced open and slowly more water was added. After the man vomited, then Ishi interrogated him again. If he didn't say what Ishi wanted him to, the process would begin again until he got the information he wanted. If a man passed out, the torturers would wait until the victim came to before they started the process all over again. I don't know of any men that have not yielded to this torture. I can also tell you that under torture anybody will eventually tell what the torturers want to know. If a person is subjected to torture, he will be much better off if he just tells the truth. If he doesn't and instead lies during the interrogation, then lies to cover up the lies, eventually as the torture continues over a period of time, he can't remember the lies. This goes on for hours and eventually he will tell the truth over and over again. While going through the torture, his body becomes weaker and weaker until he passes out, is revived, then is tortured again. This can go on for hours and even days. In the meantime, the physical damage to his body and mind can become so brutal that he may never recover physically or mentally.

Even men who have not been tortured but who have simply endured an extended period of imprisonment eventually decline mentally and even physically. They may not realize it during imprisonment, but they still have likely developed post-traumatic stress disorder (PTSD). There are so many terrible tortures that have been invented and used over thousands of years and it would not be helpful to discuss it in any more detail. But I think that if anybody goes through what we went through during those years in prison camp, they can't help but have PTSD for the rest of their lives.

All of the former prisoners of war that I know have it. PTSD is displayed in various ways, sometimes in violent ways. The amazing thing about PTSD is that many POWs who have it don't recognize what has happened to them. I believe that most people who have been in combat for a long period of time develop stress, but may not realize that they are suffering from symptoms of PTSD.

I have recognized PTSD in myself. Take, for example, these experiences: I'm in the kitchen wiping dishes and I drop a dish. I pick it up and it slides out of my hand again. As I pick it up again, it slides along the floor before I can get a hold of it. By that time I want to pick it up and throw it against the wall. I want to destroy it forever. If I'm alone, I might cuss the plate. Or when I am putting on pants, I get agitated as I struggle to get my foot into the right leg. After a short time, I want to scream and eventually throw the pants into the corner of the closet. Or I am outside in the garden digging around a rock. I want the rock to move. It moves a little, but eventually it won't even budge. Eventually I end up throwing the shovel away.

A person who has PTSD has to watch what they say and do. If they know they are suffering from PTSD, they should be on guard for outbursts and know how to cool down. When these attacks happen to me and my temper blows up, my wife just quiets down and says nothing. When I recognize what's going on, I just turn around and go into my den, close the door, and wait. In about five minutes or less all of the anger disperses and I return to my wonderful wife and give her a hug. She is marvelous and always hugs me back. Every man who has PTSD should be married to someone like my wife Barbara.

Morisako (Mortimer Snerd), the Mail, and My Miracle

Ishihara was the number one interpreter in Woosung and Kiangwan. He spoke excellent English. The other interpreter was Morisako whom we nicknamed "Mortimer Snerd." The reason we called him Mortimer Snerd was because he was infatuated with Hollywood, the movie stars, the glitter, and anything connected to the film industry.

He knew that many of us lived in or near Hollywood. Morisako also wasn't a very handsome man. He was about five feet two. His front teeth protruded and when he spoke it was with a heavy lisp. He wore dark glasses most of the time, and when he walked it was more of an amble. And he always had his hands in the side pockets of his coat.

I got along with Morisako very well and I treated him with respect. Somebody in camp started calling him "Mortimer Snerd" and soon everybody was calling him "Mortimer." He asked one of the

ASTARITA

Morisako, better known as "Mortimer Snerd," No. 2 Interpreter. He was a funny sort of fellow who had a mania for taking personal pictures from prisoners' incoming mail.

prisoners, "Why you call me Mortimer Snerd?" The guy didn't know what to say but finally said in desperation, "Mortimer Snerd is a very famous actor in Hollywood, and because you're a lot like him, we just started calling you Mortimer." So Morisako thought that his nickname was great. Time went on and while we joked about it in private, we hoped that Morisako wouldn't find out who Mortimer Snerd really was—nothing more than a fabricated dummy that sat on the lap of the famous ventriloquist Edgar Bergen. Bergen and his dummy Mortimer were in high demand throughout the movie industry in the late 1930s into the 1940s.

Time went on in Kiangwan prison. Then late one afternoon Mortimer came flying out of the officers' barracks and he was terribly mad and upset. He questioned a number of prisoners and wanted to know who it was that had named him Mortimer. Of course everyone was innocent. Nobody knew anything about how that most embarrassing name had come about. He said, "I have been good to you and now you have made me lose face." Many of us felt bad for him, but there was nothing we could do about it.

Later we learned why Mortimer became so angry. He was the one who went through and censored any mail that came into camp. One day a mail delivery came from Shanghai that contained a Hollywood movie magazine. Out of curiosity he started to thumb through it page after page, enjoying every minute, until he came to several pages in which several pictures of Edgar Bergen and his dummy Mortimer Snerd were featured. That's when Morisako flipped his lid. From that day on it became more unpleasant for all of us. I had never had a problem with Mortimer. I would always address him as Mr. Morisako and saluted him sharply when I met him. This eventually paid off for me.

As I mentioned before, a library was brought in from Shanghai. Many did not take advantage of this blessing, but just sat and stared and worried. I did not. I lived with what we had and hoped that someday it would end. I told myself, "I am going to live and look forward to the day that I will be free again." After about two years, I felt that I needed a Book of Mormon. I missed the passages of scripture that had been so uplifting to me. I needed something that would bolster me, and that would also be a reference for anyone who asked me about my religion.

During the three and a half years I was a prisoner, the Japanese would occasionally permit us to write home. The letters were simple and short. If you tried to convey any kind of negative message about the camp to anyone back home, the Japanese censor Morisako ("Mortimer Snerd") would just throw your letter away. I got along with Morisako and I think all my letters went through. I now have several of the letters that I wrote to my mother while I was a POW. In the summer of 1943 I decided to write to my brother Dick and ask him for a Book of Mormon, though I really doubted that anything like that would ever make it through the Japanese censors. It could even take as long as a year from the time you wrote to get a response to your letter. If you did get a letter back, it would often only say, "I'm looking forward to seeing you again. The family is fine. Take care of yourself. We love you."

After I had written Dick, I prayed about my letter and then waited. Something unusual happened; my letter must have flown to the mainland. My brother Dick received it and immediately purchased a leather-bound copy of a Book of Mormon. He wrote on the first blank page dated August 23, 1943: "To my brother William L. Taylor, Barrack 4, Section 6, Shanghai War Prisoners Camp, Shanghai, China. At your request, search the treasures of knowledge deeply and learn to love your fellow men and may God bless you. Richard J. Taylor." Then he added, "Through the grace of the Japanese Government."

The book arrived at the Kiangwan Prison Camp the first week in February 1944 and was sent to the Japanese interpreter's office. I was told one late afternoon to report to Morisako's office as soon as possible. I had just come in from a work detail, so I quickly took off my clothes, washed as well as I could, dressed, and hurried over to Morisako's office. As I walked in, Morisako was writing at a desk. He didn't even look up. In the meantime, I just stood at attention. Then I noticed a book on his desk. It was the Book of Mormon that I had asked my Brother Dick to send to me about four months earlier.

After about a minute, Mortimer looked up and just stared at me through his large horn- rimmed glasses. He was inscrutable. He didn't laugh or smile. He just stared at me with black eyes. Finally he said, "yasumi" (rest). I relaxed a little, and then he picked up the book, held it in his hand, and said, "Tayror (there are no *l*'s in the Japanese language), what is this book? It looks like the Bible, but then it isn't. What do you say it is?"

I said, "It's a lot like the Bible, but it's different." Morisako didn't bat an eye as he thumbed through the pages, then said, "There are too many pages for me to read, must be about nine hundred pages, and I don't understand what they mean. I am to read and approve everything, which I cannot do. What do you suggest, Tayror?"

I really didn't know what to say and then finally I said, "Morisako san, I know it might be hard for you to understand and read this book, but it's easy for me to understand. With your permission, I would like to come up here every afternoon and we can read it together." Morisako just sat immovable as I spoke. Then he picked up the book and thumbed through it again. As he was doing this, I prayed in my heart that he would relent and give it to me. I knew that if I didn't get the book, then it would be lost. You must remember that I had always treated Morisako with the utmost courtesy and respect. Boy, did that pay off. I always saluted him when I passed him on the road or in the barracks and I felt that he liked me, for I liked him.

Finally Morisako said, "I have not got time to read this book, therefore I will censor it as having been read." And he picked up his seal, stamped the book, and handed it to me, saying with a wave of his hand, "You may go." I bowed and as I turned and walked out the door, I noticed that Morisako was already busy with something else.

Now with this wonderful book of scripture in my hand, I really had something to read when I got off from my work details. I could wash, unfold my little tabletop that was at the bottom of my sack, open up that precious book, ponder its contents, look out of my window and completely lose myself. This dedication and blessing is a result of that promise I made to the Lord years before while on Wake.

We had a civilian named Al Boutell who was struggling mentally. I felt sorry for him. He walked around the camp road that separated the outside wall, which had a 2,300-volt barbed wire fence on top of it, from the electric fence that went around our barracks. There was a dirt road that ran between the two electrical fences. Some of the men liked to walk between the fences that went all around the barracks. One day Boutell was walking around the fence when he met Morisako. They were about thirty yards away when Boutell saw Morisako coming toward him. Boutell snapped to attention and as Morisako was about to pass him said, "Good afternoon Mortimer." Morisako stopped walking, screamed at Boutell and said, "What is my name?" Well, Boutell didn't know that Morisako had found out about "Mortimer Snerd." Boutell was standing at attention at that point and Morisako was screaming his head off. Morisako yelled at Boutell, "What is my real name?" By this time Boutell was frightened and Morisako was screaming in his face at a distance of not more than two feet. Boutell then blurted out, "Mr. Snerd." Then Morisako said, "What is my full name," and then Al Boutell blurted out, "Mr. Mortimer Snerd." Morisako was so angry by then that he started to slap Boutell. Then it dawned on Morisako that the guy actually didn't know his real name, so he just turned and walked away. Al Boutell never did know why he had upset Morisako so badly. When the war was over and everyone was going home by boat from Yokohama, Al Boutell committed suicide by jumping over the stern of the freighter he was on. It was a very sad ending to a very nice guy.

Disease and Illness in the POW Camps

From the icy day on January 23, 1942 when we disembarked at the Huangpu River Dock until the end of the war, everyone held their breath for the hidden enemy to everyone—Japanese and POW alike. These were the unseen enemies: malaria, dysentery, cholera, typhoid, tetanus, and other diseases. All of us talked about them and hoped that they wouldn't hit our camp.

After being in Woosung for about a week, we heard that Asiatic cholera, a painful intestinal epidemic, was raging in Shanghai and that thousands of Chinese, Japanese, and others were infected. It was so bad that thousands who had this terrible disease were just dying on the streets in Shanghai. You can imagine what would happen if a cholera epidemic spread itself in our camp. I really don't know how they would have contained it. It's a miracle that this terrible disease didn't find itself in our camp.

We had other diseases to worry about too. One was dysentery, a most painful intestinal disorder accompanied by intestinal inflammation, diarrhea, and bloody mucous. I will never forget Ned Nye sitting naked on his sack with a towel under him. He was in intense intestinal pain. Everyone liked Ned Nye, but there was nothing we could do to help. Eventually Ned got some medicine from Dr. Yoshihiro Shindo and the dysentery gradually went away. Without help, Ned Nye would have died. We all knew that Ned's illness could well have happened to any one of us.

I guess the biggest health threat to us, especially in the summertime, was malaria, the biggest killer in the world. Malaria is transported to the body by the Anopheles mosquito and is found mostly in the tropics and semi-tropics. It is very painful and if not treated quickly with quinine, the infected person would die within a week or two.

All of the sections in all of the barracks had huge mosquito nets that covered each side of each half section. When the mosquitoes showed up during the middle of April, the mosquito nets were brought out. We strung the nets from one end of the sleeping platform we were on, covering all eight bunks. When the nets were up and hung, we had a rectangular tube that was five feet high on two sides by about sixteen feet long. Separating these two side panels of net was a top piece of net that was about six feet six inches wide by sixteen feet long. Each end was also covered with netting. This netting then covered the entire sleeping platform from one end to the other. All of the sacks were also covered. Getting in and out of our sacks with the netting wasn't a problem because we simply pulled open the netting, crawled inside, and then turned and tacked the mosquito netting under our sack. This setup worked quite well, aside from the disturbing sound the mosquitoes made at night. They came in swarms attempting to attack the bloody meals therein. Without those nets, I probably wouldn't be writing this today.

If we had to go to the benjo at night, we had to make it very quick and short because the mosquitoes liked to gather there. When you went inside, a hundred mosquitoes would swarm out of the hole straight for you. There were also rats busy down below.

Chances were that at some point an Anopheles mosquito would sink his blood-carrying stinger into you. And it eventually happened to me. When you get malaria, it is accompanied by a high temperature of more than 104 degrees, which lingers for about twenty-four to forty-eight hours. You lie absolutely naked, removing anything that would retain heat, on your back on top of a rubberized sheet that is draped across a rickety bed, and you sweat a continuous stream of water from every pore in your body. Your temperature peaks between 104 and 105 degrees and you drift in and out of consciousness. This goes on for about twenty-four hours. Then your body quiets down and you relax for about a day. You are not as strong as you were before you came down with the fever. After about twenty-four hours of feeling better, you start getting chills. At first you can handle chills but then they get stronger and stronger. Your teeth begin to rattle and your body just bounces up and down on the bed. A piece of wood or heavy cloth is also given to you to put between your rattling teeth in order to prevent fracturing from the heavy banging.

The chills go on hour after hour. You strain your body from one end to the other. After hours of this torture, the chills stop and you lie there exhausted and amazed that you are still alive. Twenty-four to forty-eight hours later, the process starts all over again. If you don't get medical help by that point, your chance of surviving goes way down and it's only another week or so before you die. The only medicine available that we had was quinine. Quinine is extracted from cinchona bark, and then compressed. It is a common remedy for malaria. The quinine that I took was in pill form.

Isn't medicine wonderful? I wonder when this cinchona bark was discovered. Just think of the lives it has saved over the years all around the world. Malaria has been the cause of numerous deaths. I know that I wouldn't be writing today if Dr. Shindo hadn't gotten the medicine for me when I was a POW. I contracted malaria twice. The first time was a shocker. The second was just as intense, but this time I got quinine sooner. There were many prisoner-of-war camps under Japanese control and the treatment you received in any one of these camps depended on who was in charge. All I can tell you is that because we had Dr. Shindo, lives were saved.

Dr. Shindo was tall for a Japanese man. He was about six foot two, slender, and he walked with a slight slouch forward with both hands in his pockets. With Dr. Shindo, we had access to medicine for dysentery, diarrhea, typhus, and cholera. Not only was he a good doctor, but he was also concerned about all of the prisoners who relied upon him for their health. Dr. Shindo was also unique in that he didn't seem to make distinctions based on skin color.

I know that because of the respect we all had for Dr. Shindo and because of the way he treated us, he eventually became somewhat suspect by the Japanese hierarchy and was told to not treat us as well as he had been. So, in a sense, our good doctor was put in a bind. His duty was to serve the emperor and to hate and kill the enemy. It's a common principle for all nations that are engaged in war. But Dr. Shindo had also been taught to help people that were sick and injured. Overall, I think Dr. Shindo handled his position very well. He helped us tremendously and yet tried to stay within the bounds that his superiors demanded of him. Without Dr. Shindo's help, many of the POWs would never have survived the war.

Radios in Camp Bringing News of the War

When we first came to camp in Woosung, the Japanese gave us small radios that broadcast the local news. The US news wasn't uplifting. The Japanese were running over all of the US opposition. Nothing,

Captain and Doctor Yoshihiro Shindo

it seemed, could stop them. In the Philippines, the cities of Manila and Corregidor came under a devastating attack. Before the war, it was assumed that Corregidor could not be conquered. But the Japanese ran over Corregidor and Manila in just a few short months.

Singapore was also lost. Everyone thought Singapore would repel the Japanese and that the Royal British Navy would stop the invaders. But it didn't happen that way. The Japanese just landed on the narrow isthmus above Singapore and then moved south on land. The Japanese took down some British warships, including Britain's unsinkable *Prince of Wales*. Just north of Singapore were Malaysia, Indonesia, Burma, and Thailand. South and somewhat east of Singapore were Java, Sumatra, and Borneo, and farther east was New Guinea. All were lost to Japan just a few months after the war began.

Why did the Japanese overrun all of those countries at the beginning of the war? They felt compelled to do so. The United States had cut off most of their oil in July of 1941. The Japanese economy, like every other industrial nation on the face of the planet, had to have oil. Without oil, the Japanese industry, like ours, would come to a halt. Instead of a very progressive nation, it would have had a strangled economy.

I don't believe that the United States would have cut off oil to Japan if Japan had not been so aggressive militarily in the years preceding World War II. The Japanese had been an invading force in Korea for many years. Japan had fought Russia in Manchuria and had invaded China in the early 1930s. Japan was feared by all of its neighbors because they did not stop their aggressive wars. After all, they had won every war they had been involved in since the early 1930s—why stop?

Their desire to conquer was born from a feeling of necessity. Japan is really just a group of large islands off the coast of Korea, China, and Russia. Japan has a very limited supply of its own oil, iron, food, et cetera, so they thought that if they conquered Manchuria, Korea, and China, they would have everything they needed to become a mighty nation. The danger in this kind of thinking is that aggression never stops until it is overcome.

With the radios we were able to get the Japanese side of the war. The Japanese had run roughshod over everybody they had attacked, establishing their empire called the Greater East Asia Company Prosperity Sphere.

In June of 1942, we discovered that the Japanese had been badly beaten at a huge naval battle near Midway Island. This was good news for the United States because we were starved for a victory of any kind. When the United States began winning battles, the Japanese came into the barracks and took away all of the radios. They didn't give us a reason for this and we didn't ask. Then in October 1942, we learned that the Marines had landed on the island of Guadalcanal in the South Pacific. The object of the US invasion of Guadalcanal was to protect Australia from the Japanese onslaught. Success in Guadalcanal was in a way one of the turning points of the Pacific War.

However, you can see that the Japanese in less than nine months, from December of 1941 to September of 1942, had managed to control almost all of Southeast Asia, including Burma, Thailand, Malaysia, Sumatra, Singapore, Borneo, Celebes, two-thirds of New Guinea, Solomon Islands, Marshall and Gilbert Islands, Wake, Guam, and even the Aleutian Islands at the tip of Alaska. They also had control of the coasts of China, Korea, and Manchuria. Yes, the Japanese had really been moving. I think they thought that nothing could stop them in their conquest.

Possible Escape Plans

From the first day we disembarked at Woosung to the time I escaped, I contemplated my chances of escape. I studied the four twenty-five-foot guard towers on each corner of the prison compound. They were always manned by a Japanese soldier equipped with a twenty-five-caliber machine gun and a very strong searchlight. These four guard towers were just outside the eight-foot block wall that surrounded the compound. On top of this masonry wall the Japanese had placed a five-foot electric fence that carried 2,300 volts of electricity. The full barrier then was about thirteen feet high. Another electric fence that was five feet high and carried 2,300 volts of electricity surrounded the barracks inside the compound. So to escape from inside the camp, you had to get past a five-foot, 2,300-volt fence that enclosed the barracks, an eight-foot masonry wall with an additional electric fence, and four manned towers armed with machine guns.

We had several prisoners attempt to escape from our compound in Woosung and Kiangwan and they all failed. One attempted to escape by digging under the masonry wall. He was caught. On April 13th some other prisoners in Woosung tried to escape before the masonry wall was formed. The attempt was led by Commander Winfield Scott Cunningham, US Navy; Lieutenant Commander Wooley, US Navy; Lieutenant Commander C.O. Smith, commanding officer of the USS Wake (a river gunboat serving on the Yangtze River); Dan Teters, who was in charge of construction on Wake Island; and Lie, a Chinese servant of Smith. Their objective was to wait until evening inspection, then meet at the outside electric fence. They met after roll call at the electric fence and soon they were able to crawl under the outside electric fence. The Chinese boy told Captain Smith to stay away from the river, but they didn't and got caught in a dense fog. Early the next morning they surrendered to the Wang Ching-wei puppet troops of the Japanese. The Japanese handcuffed them, then brought them through the barracks.

The Japanese wanted to show everyone that no one could escape from them. One of these attempts, however, happened to prove humorous for all the prisoners. On that particular occasion, the Japanese took some of the clothing that some escapees had been wearing. They then took the dogs and the clothing to the eight-foot masonry wall where the men had escaped. When they got to the wall, they let the dogs smell the clothing of the guys who had escaped. They then turned the dogs loose expecting them to howl and chase down the escapees. Well they did howl all right, but they then promptly headed straight for the kitchen. Very embarrassing for the Japanese, and we all got a good laugh, which we desperately needed.

Everybody had ideas about escaping. I remember talking about it one day while I was on a detail with Tony Wallace. We had just sat down for the meager lunch that we had brought with us and the conversation had turned to the possibility of making a successful escape from the Japanese. We both agreed it would be impossible to escape. Why? Well, there was the language barrier and the need for food and water. And who would you be willing to trust? If you did receive help from anyone, there was always the question that they would just turn you over to the Japanese Army. Then there was the question of which direction to go before you would meet anyone who would really be willing to help you. We came to the conclusion that you would never make it unless you had outside help. But where would you get someone to really help you, someone who would be risking certain torture and death if discovered? Then again, what good would it be for anyone to help someone they didn't know, let alone a white person? This alone would probably do you in. Also there would be a reward given to anyone who turned you in to the Japanese. Whoever helped you would be risking their life and the lives of their family members.

Then Tony and I started to talk about what it would take to make an escape successful. We came to the conclusion that the best chance a person would at a successful escape would be from a moving train or boat. We figured that if the train was not moving too fast and if there was a way to jump out during the night (plus a few other "ifs"), a person might have a chance to escape. It all depended, however, on the chance that the person was not injured and was able to contact friendly forces.

In short, everything had to fall into place at the right time. Incidentally, the reason the train had to be a moving train, bus, or ship, was because if the Japanese didn't know where you jumped then you probably wouldn't have to worry about dogs or soldiers. You would have an advantage to start with. For example, if the train was traveling at thirty-five miles an hour, you could have a seven- or eight-hour jump on the Japanese before they even recognized you were gone. You could be two hundred and fifty miles apart before they began chasing you. Dogs wouldn't help them so you would just have to worry about whom you met after that, assuming you weren't injured from the fall. All of these ideas we came up with were just something to think about. We knew that you had to have the help of the Almighty, a bit of courage, and the intense desire to be free.

Sir Mark Young

I think at this time I should tell you a little about Sir Mark Young, the former governor general of Hong Kong and the highest-ranking officer in the camp. Captured at the beginning of the war when the Japanese took Hong Kong, Sir Mark Young was sent to the Woosung Prison Camp near Shanghai. Sir Mark was just the kind of a man you would expect the British to send to represent the empire in Hong Kong. Tall, about six feet two, slim and trim, with graying hair and a small mustache. His speech was a distinct clipped English that had a marked touch of authority. And when he spoke, you listened. His gray-blue eyes really commanded attention. He was, by definition, a leader.

At the camp he was given a large room with a shower and a private toilet. He was offered better food than anyone else in camp. When his first meal was served to him, Sir Mark said, "I know that the rest of the prisoners are not getting this type of food, so hereafter, consider me as one of them and I will eat what they eat." Now that was a revelation to all of the POWs because we didn't know that we weren't getting the same kind of food that the officers were getting. The officers had their own garden and raised vegetables that they shared among themselves. (According to Captain John White's book, *United States Marines North China*, The officers had beefsteak tomatoes, all kinds of beans; string, pole, soya, and lima. In September, they would also have beets, potatoes, and sweet potatoes. They valued turnips, rutabaga, kohlrabi, daikon [Japanese radish], okra, and egg plant, which grew large and profuse. It sounded great, but we never saw or ate anything from that garden.)

Right after the five escapees were caught, Colonel Yuse, the Japanese commanding officer in Woosung, called Colonel Ashurst and Major Brown into his office. He thrust a typed agreement in front of them that promised that no one in camp would attempt to escape. Colonel Ashurst and Major Brown refused to sign, whereupon Colonel Yuse went into a rage and said, "If you don't sign, we will start killing the prisoners and we will continue killing until you do sign." Finally, after Colonel Ashurst and Major Brown had huddled and talked it over, Colonel Ashurst turned to Yuse and said, "We will sign if you will permit me to write above my signature that I signed under the threat of death for myself and those under my jurisdiction."

Yuse was thrilled when his interpreter told him what Colonel Ashurst had said, so the paper was signed with Colonel Ashurst's written protest above his signature. Yuse then broke out a bottle of whiskey and wanted to celebrate. Colonel Ashurst refused Yuse's toast and told Yuse he had no control over the British and that his signature did not include the British. Eventually the British did sign, however, because the Japanese forced them to by cutting their food ration nearly in half. After a few weeks of slow starvation and an increase in illness, Sir Mark Young also signed under his objection to the condition on which he had been compelled to sign.

Now after all of the threats by the Japanese and the signing by Colonel Ashurst and Sir Mark Young, I concluded that it didn't make any difference whether we signed or not. It was a save-your-face thing for the Japanese and we went along with it. I never did sign and no one ever insisted that I sign. Sir Mark Young stayed in our camp for about four months, then he was moved out. It was rumored that he was taken to Formosa [now Taiwan], an island off the coast of central China.

It was rumored that the Military was getting paid. I didn't pay much attention to this because I never saw any of the money. Years after the war was over, I saw a paper from the Liaison and Research Branch American Prisoner of War Information Bureau, written by Captain James I. Norwood and Captain Emily L. Shek, dated July 31, 1946. From this document, I quote, "Second Lieutenant was paid 70.83 yen, first lieutenant: 85 yen, major: 170 yen, lieutenant colonel: 23 yen, captain: 122.50 yen, colonel: 312.50 yen. Sixty yen was deducted for room and board. Enlisted men, 15 yen a day." I didn't personally know anybody who received money from the Japanese; I know I never did. The Marines, at least the officers I believe, received money and they cultivated a garden too.

But I made out very well on my own. Before a year had passed I had bought a pair of Marine shoes, Marine wool blankets, and some Marine clothes. I had a phonograph, a stack of records, money, and the best place in the barracks to sleep. In all, I did very well while in both Woosung and Kiangwan Prison Camps.

Chapter Ten

CREATIVE WORK DETAIL
AND THE CHINESE CULTURE

O ne of the most impossible and dumbest orders that the
Japanese ever gave us came after we had been in Woosung
a few weeks. The order came from Colonel Yuse: "All
prisoners of war are ordered to catch forty flies a day." Forty flies
a day for each man? You have got to be kidding. I suppose we had
about 1,200 eligible men to trap forty flies a day. That amounts to
48,000 flies each day. Now if every man available had to catch forty
flies each day for just five days, we would be catching about 240,000
flies a week.

We had to provide our own containers, so we used a rough
brown paper that was used for everything—toilet paper, food wrap,
towels, et cetera. The Japanese were supposed to count the flies we
caught each day. But it was impossible to really catch forty flies for
days on end. The Japanese counted all the flies the first day. The second day went slower. On the third day some of the men saved their
flies from the previous day, scattering some of the freshly killed
flies on top of the old ones. The project was a huge failure. Nobody
wanted to do it and after the second day the Japanese couldn't keep
track of the flies and the men who caught them. It was laughable

and so impossible for anyone to meet the goal. I actually never caught more than five or six flies.

The "Honey Bucket" Boys

Three times a week, the "Honey-Bucket boys" would come into the compound to clean out the benjo. They approached from the outside where the sewage containers were and brought out a long bamboo pole, about seven feet long. Attached to the end of the pole was a large wooden cup about seven inches wide by six inches deep. They would then stick the cup under the swinging cover of the benjo that had been opened and secured. They would then shove the cup down into the human waste and haul it out and dump it into one of the two five-gallon buckets they carried on a yoke that went across their shoulders. On each end of the yoke was a hook that fastened into the two five-gallon buckets.

There were usually about ten Honey-Bucket boys, each of whom filled and carried away two five-gallon buckets. When they were ready to leave, each of the Honey-Bucket boys shouldered his yoke and on a given signal picked up the two five-gallon wooden buckets, which must have weighed about ninety pounds. Then one of the peasants would start to chant in a rhythm, "Hunga he, hunga ho, hunga he, hunga ho, ho, ho, ho." They would repeat the chant as they went down the road. This was not as silly as it sounded because this rhythm allowed the buckets to swing up and down easing the load on their shoulders. I noticed that the legs on these guys were all muscle. As they left the benjo, they all paraded right by my window—smell and all. It seemed to me that they always planned their departure to coincide with my mealtime. "Hunga he, hunga ho"—oh boy.

It was so interesting and educational to see how our own human waste was recycled and put to good use. When the Honey-Bucket boys left our compound they went right to the nearest truck available, or in most cases to the closest canal that ran all over the area.

The "Honey Bucket" Boys

When they got to the canal, there was a flat-bottomed boat that was about thirty-five feet long and nine feet wide. On one end of this boat was a small helm that controlled the motor and electrical system of the boat. The gunwale, the boat's railing, that ran around the boat was very low, not more than eight inches to one foot above the water of the canal. At the top of the gunwale there was a two-inch thick by two-foot board fastened to the gunwale that was used as a walkway. I think the depth of the boat was about three to four feet, which was rather shallow for a boat, but you have to realize that this was a canal, not a stream or river. These canals were very dirty and muddy. I don't believe anything deeper than five inches could be seen from the surface of the water. Flies formed a cloud above the boats, which were usually run by two men.

When the waste was brought alongside the flat-bottomed boat, a plank was laid from the edge of the boat to the shore. The Honey-Bucket boys then quickly unloaded by hand, one bucket at a time. Even though twenty five-gallon buckets only amounted to about a hundred gallons of human waste, it was able to fertilize a large area when mixed with water and sprayed across the soil. (This fertilizer has been used since the beginning of time over most of the world, especially in Asia where the dense population doesn't have the benefit of modern fertilizers.) A flat-bottomed boat that was ten feet wide by thirty feet long by four feet deep could carry about nine hundred cubic feet of high-priced sewage. When the sewage was mixed with water and sprayed on the newly planted ground, the results were spectacular.

One of the guys in camp got a hold of a small tomato plant. He planted it outside at the end of one of the barracks, mixed up his own waste with a little water, and fertilized his plant. Would you believe that within two months that tomato plant had grown over eight feet tall and produced large, beautiful tomatoes? I don't know what happened to the tomatoes when they ripened. I didn't get any myself, but over the years during the war and after when I was in China, I'm sure that I ate vegetables that were fertilized by someone's sewage.

If you had money, yen, yuan, or American dollars, you could buy cigarettes or even canned food. I had money, cigarettes, and generally was better off than most of the other guys in my section of the barracks, or for that matter, throughout camp. I didn't exploit what I had. For me, the improvement from nothing to something was very gradual: better and more food, Marine clothing, Marine shoes, and medicine, which included quinine for malaria, dysentery, sulfa quinidine, and others. I also had Marine wool blankets, Marine trousers, soap, a toothbrush, razor blades, writing materials—a pencil and pens—in short, I made out very well.

During those three and a half years as a POW, I had it as good as anyone in my position could have. Beyond Butch, I didn't even have a fight, and I had only a few arguments. Our section was really quite peaceful. I was the section leader, 4-6-1, and if there was a dispute, it was always settled peacefully. This doesn't mean it was easy, because it wasn't. We never knew when and if we were all going to be killed, beaten, or starved to death. If the war had gone on much longer, nearly everyone would have been killed or would have starved to death.

One day while I was walking back to camp late in the afternoon after a hard day's work at Fuji mountain, I saw a Chinese peasant about a hundred yards ahead with a wheelbarrow waiting to get on the road. As I drew abreast of him, I looked down in his old dilapidated wheelbarrow to see what he was carrying. You can understand how surprised I was when I saw that the wheelbarrow was full of paper money, all of which was yuan, the money the Japanese and Chinese used in Shanghai. This was a shock to me. There was a lot of money in the wheelbarrow, but nobody was trying to steal it. This observation has generated in me some profound thoughts about our own currency and where it was headed. Inflation was on my mind and I wondered what the American dollar would be worth in the future.

The Mt. Fuji Project

About a week after we were settled in Kiangwan, we were assigned to a new work project. It was called "Mt. Fuji." It was from the passion and brainstorming of Ishmu Ishihara. Ishihara said he wanted to build a playground where the ancient sports of Japan would be taught. These ancient Japanese sports had endured through the centuries. They included jujitsu and karate, among others. Ishi said, "You will be proud of what you are going to build and everybody is going to work very hard to get Mt. Fuji built." Everyone was required to work—Marines, civilians, and other POWs who had been brought into camp.

The Japanese brought in narrow-gauge tracks and small rail carts that held about two yards of dirt. We were assigned to move twenty loads a day. Two men filled the carts and two other men pushed each cart up the ramp for dumping. At first a ramp wasn't needed but as Fuji started to rise, it took more strength to push the cart up the ramp. The carts were undoubtedly from some kind of a mining operation. They

One of the largest details was the Mt. Fuji Project. The big stick was Ishihara (above) better known as the "Screaming Skull." A wild and vicious fanatic, he was head interpreter of the Shanghai camp. Hated by all, he would think nothing of smashing one in the adams apple with his riding crop or beating up our officers. In the background is his pet project, "Mt. Fuji."

were quite sturdy and were easy to dump. All you had to do was lift one side of the cart out of the holes holding it to the bed and dump it.

Now this sounds like just a simple job. With four men to a cart and twenty loads a day, and it was easy—*at first*. But then Mt. Fuji started to grow and we learned that it was going to be a lot bigger than we originally thought. In fact, the finished project was going to measure about two hundred feet long by one hundred feet wide and approximately thirty feet high, in the form of a triangle.

The dirt came from the flat ground in front of our Mt. Fuji. We ran into problems with digging up this dirt because hundreds of square miles around Shanghai formed a delta, the soil of which had been deposited by the Yangtze River over thousands of years, so the water table was only a few feet underground. As we dug out the dirt in front of our Mt. Fuji, we could only go down about four or five feet until we hit the water table. After hitting the water table, we would have to move to another spot and continue to dig. We had to be careful how we dug. Over a period of time, we had a shallow lake.

After a few weeks, Ishi said, "Tomorrow is a holiday. You are doing twenty loads a day, so when you finish twenty loads tomorrow, you can go back to the barracks." The next day the men were all finished by noon. Ishi smiled and said, "You've done a great job today." With that, some of the men thought Ishi wasn't such a bad guy after all. But the next day, Ishi raised the workload to twenty-five carts a day. And the week after that, it was raised to thirty loads a day. As our Mt. Fuji grew taller, it also became steeper. Many guys tried to think of different ways of getting out of the strenuous work of pushing the carts up the steep incline. Some would fill a cart up, take it up the mount, and then not dump it. And some pushed up empty carts. But all got caught. And every time they got caught, two extra loads were added on. It was hard work and we were terribly underfed.

When the mountain was finally finished, all of us were relieved. But the work wasn't over. Now Ishi wanted more, smaller, little eight-foot-high triangle mounds about thirty feet long that ran parallel to Mt. Fuji. When this happened, it caught the attention of the Marines who then recognized that Mt. Fuji was going to be used as a rifle range. It took us eighteen months of hard labor to build Ishi's rifle range. Ishi was delighted that he had fooled us.

But in the end, it really didn't make any difference whether we knew if Mt. Fuji was going to be used as a rifle range or a park for little children to play in. When it came down to push and shove, the

Japanese could make us do anything they wanted. In almost any POW camp the Japanese controlled, you did what they wanted you to do. You didn't argue about anything. If you did argue about this or that, the Japanese would torture or kill you. We did complain among ourselves, but we were very careful not to complain to the Japanese.

When the "Mt. Fuji" was finished, Ishi said that we ought to have a party to celebrate the success of the project. We were to be given an extra ration of food and a holiday for the whole camp with no work details for that day. We sang popular songs changing some of the words to fit our situation. One of the songs we sang was the "Chattanooga Choo Choo," which told how Mr. Morrison of Morrison & Knudsen Construction Co. would greet us at the dock with lots of money. "Anchors Aweigh" was another hit. But the biggest hit of all was a composition written by Dar Dodds. The title of this song was "Yasumi" and was written to the tune, "There's a Gold Mine in the Sky." The quartet of guys who sang this song to the whole camp were Dar Dodds, myself, and two other guys from Barracks 3. It was a tremendous hit all through the camp and was sung individually and in groups for many weeks after the Fuji celebration was over.

The lyrics went something like this:

Verse 1

There's a mountain in the sky far away
Where we took up forty loads every day
With a front day every one day out of nine
While the flags down run a short load while there's time

Chorus

Yasumi, Yasumi (Rest, Rest)
To our children we will sit and we'll say
That we sat there and watched those cars roll by
While we built Mt. Fujiyama to the sky

Verse 2

On this mountain every day we had to toil

As we pushed up every load of virgin soil

And we did our best on rice and tasty stew

(Boy did it taste)

We were members of a tough and rugged crew

Chorus

Verse 3

We went to work each bleak and dreary morn

When we heard the bugler blow his little horn

But there came a day we gave a heavy sigh

We had built Mt. Fujiyama to the sky

Chorus

Verse 4

In appreciation for all the work we'd done

We were given a track and field meet just for fun

And because we worked with "eager" every day

We would all get a pack of Akatukis for our pay

(Akatuki cigarettes, twenty to a pack)

Chorus

One day we were assigned to work in a cemetery that had been used for many years, maybe centuries, by the local Chinese. It was about a mile from our camp. It seemed that the Japanese wanted to use this cemetery as a playground for the surrounding area. The Japanese ordered us to clean it up as best we could. That included filling in the holes, leveling the ground, and cleaning up the weeds.

I was one of those assigned to work in the cemetery. We had been warned to keep an eye out for poisonous vipers. I didn't think too much of that warning until one day when I was digging in a burial hole. When I looked at the place where my spade had sliced the dirt away, I saw that I had exposed a tube of viper eggs that were just ready to hatch. It was a little spooky to see all of the viper eggs, each with an unborn viper inside. I just stood there and stared at what I had uncovered about four feet from my face. After staring at these eggs, I suddenly looked down at my feet and was relieved that there were no vipers where I was standing. Needless to say, I was a little concerned and upset, so I smashed my shovel against the tube holding the eggs. When I did this, I was amazed at what I saw. These vipers were already formed and it looked as though they were ready to break their eggs and come out. I probably should not have killed them because the vipers likely took care of a large number of cockroaches, mice, and a multitude of other small pests and insects.

We started out in early 1942 with thirty-eight men in the section. Over a period of three years we lost about twelve men who were transferred to Japan to work on the docks, mines, machine shops, and other projects where they were needed. The rest of us were left at Kiangwan and were used at various places when the Japanese needed help.

Every time we went out on an assignment to work I would look around and think, "Would this be a good place to escape?" And in every case the answer would be "No." Now if you had a contact outside of the camp that would help you, if you could get out undetected, that would make it more possible to be successful. But the odds of finding anyone willing to take the risk to help you escape after you got out of the camp would be almost nonexistent. And if you were able to get away undetected, it wouldn't be long before you would meet a person or group who would offer to help but then promptly send someone to get the Japanese. Another huge drawback would be the language barrier. It is very difficult to communicate with someone who speaks a foreign language and it creates suspicion or distrust right off the bat.

Your chances for a successful escape would increase if you were in an area where the Chinese guerrillas were operating and you were able to come into contact with them. But, the greatest chance for escape, I believed, would be in an attempt from a moving vehicle, car, bus, or boat. If you did escape, it would have to be from a moving vehicle in a place where no dogs could find you. It must be something a person in his right mind would not attempt, something the Japanese would not think possible. All the time I was a POW, I would think how this could be accomplished successfully. But I didn't think the opportunity would ever come to me.

On many of the projects we had, our group would walk or ride in a truck if it were a long distance. Kiangwan and Woosung were both outside and northwest of Shanghai and we usually traveled by farms that produced much of the vegetables for Shanghai and the surrounding area. The farmers who cultivated the fields and did most of the work were Chinese women. There were no farm machines that could turn over the dirt in those days in China, so the Chinese women did all of the hard labor by hand. It was a community effort and the women, usually about six to ten of them, would line up sideways to each other facing the rows to be cultivated. Using a steel prong or hoe that had forks about six inches long and eight inches wide, the women would force the steel fork into the ground, then pull back and turn the dirt over, uprooting the weeds. They seemed to be in a cadence as they worked forward in the field. The Chinese farmers also used heavy plows that were pulled by wide-horned water buffaloes. But it was the women peasants who did all of the cultivating of the rows after the plants started to grow.

Binding of Feet of Chinese Women

If you looked closely, you could see that these peasants walked, or I should say hobbled, in a strange way. They all had tiny feet no more than three to four inches long and they walked as if they were on stilts because they didn't have very good balance. One day I was able to get closer to one of these peasant farmers and I saw that her feet looked as though they had a large bandage around them. I became more curious and asked one of the Chinese guys from San Francisco who had been captured on Wake about these bandaged feet. He said that her feet had been bound since she was a little child less than three years old and that as she grew older the feet of this little child were not allowed to grow. So when she reached maturity, her feet would be the same size as when she was a small child. He said that the bones in the toes had been broken and forced backward under the foot to prevent further growth. I then asked when and where did this awful practice originate. He said the practice had been going on in China for more than a thousand years and that it had started when a Chinese emperor admired his concubines' very small feet. For centuries thereafter, bound feet were considered a sign of beauty. Now that is a tragedy beyond belief.

What pain these women must have gone through all of their lives just to please some stupid Emperor. He should have had *his* feet bound! I remember watching these women peasants walk with bundles on their heads as they were compelled to work on hot days with the sun beating down on their heads. How cruel.

The Jiangwan Race Track Project

Another place I worked was the Jiangwan Race Track just northwest of Shanghai. I only worked there a few times, but those few times were quite memorable. The Japanese had a large automotive repair garage between the racetrack and the Jiangwan Air Field. Because gasoline was a rare commodity, large cans of grain alcohol were used for various jobs in the compound and for fuel in most of their trucks.

It didn't take the men very long to learn that this alcohol could give them a high within just a few minutes. They even learned that if you were very careful, you could bring a small amount back to the barracks for later consumption. They were creative in the containers they used to bring the booze into camp. Some wore a small rubber inner tube around their waist, some used small bottles, and others used a short 3-inch wide bamboo sleeve with a small bamboo cup over the end to keep it from spilling.

Getting booze into camp was becoming more difficult. The Japanese were getting suspicious that alcohol was getting into camp, but they didn't know where it was coming from. I decided to try and bring some of the booze back into camp because if I were successful, I could sell it in various barracks. I saw no problem doing this, so the next time our detail was called to go to the stadium, I decided to bring a bamboo container back with me. A few days later, my detail was called up to go to the racetrack. I was wearing a Japanese Army jacket with large sleeves. My empty bamboo container fit comfortably under my left side, so I went to the garage just before we were to take the bus back to Kiangwan and got my bamboo container filled. Then I put it under my jacket and boarded the bus for the ride back to the barracks. There were about fifty men in my group. Once we had passed into the prison compound, the bus suddenly stopped and everyone was ordered to quickly exit the bus. We were then told to get into three lines facing the guardhouse with each line about three feet apart. I was in the middle line. A Japanese officer then announced that we would all be searched for alcohol.

I thought to myself, "These Japanese are going to search me and find the booze and then they will probably beat me and throw me in the brig." I started sweating as they came closer to search me. Out of desperation, I unbuttoned my jacket and got my right arm out of the sleeve. I then just left my left arm covered with the container of booze in it hanging on my left shoulder. The Japanese guard soon stood in front of me. I spread my arms. He searched me from the shoes to my head and other than a feel on the jacket, never bothered my left arm and coat, which was covering the booze. Nobody got caught, then the soldiers stood in front of us and the O.D. (Officer of the Day) said, "Yasumi."

Wow, did we take off for the barracks! By the time we were about one hundred feet away from the Japanese inspection party, we were strung out and really moving. Then suddenly someone dropped a container of alcohol. The Japanese officer saw it fall and started jumping up and down yelling at us to stop. We didn't stop but ran as fast as we could into the barracks. He knew that he couldn't catch us and that was the end of the search.

Once I successfully got the booze into camp, I suddenly didn't want anything to do with it. I realized that it was something that could have really gotten me into trouble, so I flushed it down the drain where we washed, feeling a little foolish about what I had done. It suddenly dawned on me what kind of consequences I would have faced if I had been caught. Isn't it interesting how a little thing can suddenly turn into a big problem? Although some risks turn out to be very helpful, sometimes little risks can be disastrous. It turned out that this alcohol made several of the men go blind for a period of time. If someone had gotten a hold of my flask of alcohol and then went blind or got seriously ill, I would have felt terrible.

We arrived to work at the Jiangwan Racetrack one cloudless morning. Planes were landing and taking off from the nearby Jiangwan Airfield, which was only about four miles north of where we were working. At about eleven o'clock that morning, I happened to look up and see a large Japanese transport aircraft coming in for a landing at the airport. It was low, no more than one thousand feet off the deck. I didn't think anything about it until a few seconds later when I heard a blast of machine gunfire coming from the vicinity of the transport aircraft. I looked more closely and saw that the gunfire was coming from a North American P-51 Mustang fighter that was sweeping by the transport. As I stood mesmerized, the P-51 made a 360-degree turn and came in from the rear, firing continually. The Japanese transport couldn't do anything about this attack. I looked over at the transport to see that it was already on fire. The second attack only doubled the flames. You could see that this aircraft was going down. It was all ablaze. By that time, the Japanese aircraft was almost right above us. Then suddenly I saw soldier after soldier without parachutes jumping out of the doomed transport—some were on fire. Then the flaming aircraft was gone from view, leaving a trail of smoke behind it. This all suddenly happened within one minute. We were all standing looking up in a cloudless sky. Japanese soldiers, our guards, prisoners of war—for a small moment, we were all as one. I thought, "What a cruel way for anyone to go." After watching all of this, we were very somber and almost everyone was thinking, "This is war. War is so cruel and precarious. What will the next few hours, days, months, or years be like?"

Electrical Storm

One day while on assignment at the Jiangwan Stadium, which is just a short distance from the Jiangwan Airport, a strange thing I had only heard about happened to us. We had been working at different buildings and grounds around the stadium. There had been a rumbling of thunder off in the distance northward and a few sprinkles of rain where we were working. The day was drawing to a close. At about four-thirty that afternoon, the guards told us to gather all of the tools together and wash them so they would be clean for whoever would use them next. We did what was requested and then gathered near a small building where the prison truck would pick us up.

Numbering about forty men, we gathered together and waited with increasing anxiety as we saw the storm approaching. The lightning and thunder was becoming more and more ominous. Suddenly there was a pause in the thunder while the black clouds became darker and more threatening. It seemed that everything stood still for a few seconds. There was a feeling that something was going to happen, but we had no idea what it would be. Suddenly off to our right, a huge bolt of lightning struck the barbed wire fence. This fence was about two hundred feet long and joined the main fence that ran around the stadium. Then a huge bolt of lightning struck the fence leading down toward us. It was accompanied simultaneously by a tremendous crack of sound that almost broke our eardrums.

Looking up to where the lightning had struck, we saw a brilliant huge ball of fire about the size of a basketball sitting on the top of the barbed wire fence. It was just sitting there throwing off pieces of pure electricity. We were stunned as we looked at this fireball, wondering what would happen next. The ball of fire just sat there for a few seconds as if it were waiting for a further command. At this point it looked to be about twelve to fifteen inches in diameter and very alive. Then, as if it were given a secret command, this ball of electricity started to roll towards us along the top of the highest strand of barbed wire. It was moving down the fence slowly at first, then it started picking up speed as it moved toward us. As it traveled, when it came to a fence post, it jumped over the post and continued toward us.

Stunned, we just watched this electric fireball that seemed to know exactly where it was going. I thought, "This fireball has a mind of its own." Nobody moved. It was as if we were all rooted to the ground. When the fireball reached the end of the fence near us, it exploded with a huge deafening bang and lit up everything around us in an unbelievable white glow. We all felt like we had witnessed something very few men ever had. It was a while before this stunned feeling wore off. On the way back it seemed like we were all a little quieter and more somber than usual.

The Shell Detail

After we had been in the Kiangwan Prison Camp for about a year and a half, Ishihara announced that we were going to work on a new project. Ishihara ordered 180 men, including myself, for this particular labor group that would work on this project situated right next to our walled-in compound. We lined up and walked through the main gate and electrical fences then headed left around the stonewall onto a dirt road that led to the rear of our compound. When we had walked on the outside of the wall almost halfway around our compound, we came to a large wooden building that had been

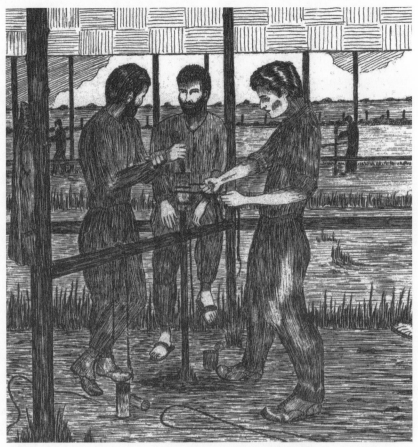

One of the pet projects of the Japanese was the shell polishing detail. This work was despised by all the men. After polishing each shell, we would bang it up as much as possible before turning it in.

used in the past as a stable for horses as well as housing for the men. We were told to halt. Soon Colonel Otero, the commandant of the camp, and Ishihara made their appearance. Ishi stepped upon a little wooden platform. Colonel Otero was right beside him. Ishi began to speak and Otero started nodding his head at everything Ishi was saying. Colonel Otero may have understood Ishi, but I didn't think so. After about five minutes of a tireless tirade against us and our nation and a demeaning speech questioning our honor for not being killed in the battle for Wake, he finally got to the point of why we were here that day and what we were going to do.

Ishi said that this project would be called the shell detail, and that we were to polish all of the used artillery shells that had been brought to our camp so that they could be used again. This was an assignment of which nobody wanted part. The officers told the Japanese flat out that they didn't want to have anything to do with that new project. The Japanese relented to that right away, as if they knew exactly what the officers would say. The officers were then excused to work in the garden and the enlisted men and civilians were ordered to do the job. Our officers were greatly relieved. And we began work on the shell detail. The Japanese were smart in the way they handled the situation. They got what they wanted and the officers felt that they got what they wanted. But in reality, the Japanese could have said to everyone, "You will polish these shells or you will be beaten and some will die."

In fact, when you are prisoners of war, if the enemy wants you to do anything, against any protest you might have, they can force you to do it. What you do as a prisoner of war all depends on where you are, who captures you, and who is running the show. The secret of being able to stay alive is in doing what the enemy wants you to do while he is in control. There are ways to placate the enemy and still live for another day when the tables will be turned. But there is always the unwritten law that says you would never betray your country or your comrades, even if it costs you your life.

To polish these shells, we started with shells that were about the size of three-inch artillery shells and put them on a post that was wrapped in a course material, something like burlap. Then we would polish the outside by rubbing an abrasive cloth around it. Eventually, the outside would glisten. We cleaned the inside of the shell by looping a rope around the outside and rolling it back and forth. Every once in a while we would take the shell to a large water pond just outside of the building where we were working. There we would wash the shell, then bring it back, and repeat the cleaning process.

We really hated the fact that we were cleaning artillery shells.

After working three or four days, however, we discovered a way that we could sabotage the project. After I took my shell to the large pond to clean it, half of the time I came back empty-handed. I got into the habit of leaving the shells in the muddy, dirty pond about eight to ten feet offshore. We also started bending the shells a little. But the worst thing we did to these shells was strip the firing caps threads so they were irreparable. The Japanese soldiers guarding didn't count the shells. And they never inspected them. They were completely engrossed in themselves. Polishing the shells was a laughable project. No one seemed to care what went on. The project was a complete flop for the Japanese. But for us, the project couldn't have been better.

If a man got sick out on this shell detail, he could ask to be sent to the sick bay. The sick bay would then send him to the hospital for treatment. The detail usually left about one o'clock in the afternoon. As I was a section leader, one day I was asked to escort the men to sick bay and the hospital inside the camp. After lunch the seven or eight of us in the detail got together in a group and waited for the two Japanese guards to escort us in. For some reason the guards didn't show up. We waited for about half an hour and then the Japanese sergeant in charge of the detail told me to take the men into the hospital without an armed guard. I didn't think much about going without a guard because we were right next to the camp and just outside the walls.

Well we started down the dirt road that would take us to the front entrance of the prison camp. When we were about halfway to the entrance, we met Lieutenant Akiyama, the officer of the day. He wore a red and white sash that indicated his position as officer of the day. We all lined up at the side of the dirt road to let him pass. When he was about to pass us he stopped and walked over to me and asked in Japanese, "Dochira e irasshaimasa-ka?" (Where are you going)? I told him the hospital. He asked where the guards were and I replied, "Wakarirmasen" (I don't know). I could see that Lieutenant Akiyama was getting mad. Finally he motioned for us to keep on going. I saluted him and we were on our way.

After I took the men to the hospital, we proceeded back to the shell detail without any guards. When I walked into the area where the men were working, I saw the Japanese Sergeant Oyama sitting at a desk that was positioned so he could see the men work. When he saw me, he screamed at me to come over to his desk. As I hurriedly walked over towards him, I noticed that it had become very quiet in the building. All of the prisoners had stopped working. There was tension in the air and I could feel that something was going to happen. Sergeant Oyama was sitting as I approached his desk. I asked Heavenly Father to help me. When I was about two feet from him, he jumped up out of his chair and started screaming in Japanese for me to stop, which I did. He was speaking and yelling so fast that I couldn't understand a word he was saying. Suddenly, he turned around and grabbed his rifle out of the rifle rack behind him. It was a bolt-action twenty-seven-caliber rifle. He pulled the bolt back, then shoved it forward and cocked it.

He slammed the rifle down on the desk about twelve inches from my gut and continued to yell at me, only not as loudly. I glanced down and noticed his finger on the trigger. As I was standing there looking him in the eye, a strange thing happened. I noticed his left eye had a lot of puss in it. He suddenly stopped yelling and just stood there with his right hand wrapped around the rifle and his finger on the trigger. I didn't move a muscle as I continued to look him in the eye. Strangely, I didn't panic; there was nothing I could do about the situation. He had a little smile on his face as he pulled the trigger. It made a loud noise, but no bullet came out. He was trying to scare me, but I stood firm and didn't flinch. This made him look foolish. He was embarrassed and told me that I was wanted in the back of the building. During this emotional time, one of the Japanese soldiers who were watching us motioned for me to follow him, which I did.

We wound our way to the back of this large building and finally came to two double doors. The guard opened the doors for me and I walked into a large classroom type of room that was about thirty feet wide and fifty feet long with windows on both sides. In the middle of this room, there were two rows of benches about six feet apart. Sitting on these benches, with eight on each row, were about sixteen soldiers carrying no weapons. They were just sitting there with their hands resting on their spread legs. Then I noticed the Japanese sergeant standing at the end of the two rows of soldiers. He motioned for me to come forward.

I started to walk around the seated men, but then he yelled for me to come up the center between the two rows of benches. I thought, "They're going to knock me around and try to get me to fall. And if I fall, well, that's when the kicking will start." By this time they were standing waiting for me, so instead of walking slow, I went up the aisle between them very quickly. That caught them off guard, and I was able to pass through them in about three seconds. Then I was standing before the sergeant who had told me earlier to take the men to sick bay without a Japanese escort. I noticed that his face looked as though he had been beaten and he didn't have on any belt to hold a revolver or sword. He was stripped down. When I stood in front of him, he motioned for me to turn sideways and then he also turned sideways so that the two rows of soldiers could see us both.

After I was in position, he started out with a long tirade of what I had done wrong. He gradually worked himself up into a frenzy. Then he started slapping my face—first left, then right, over and over again. I tried to ride with his slapping back and forth. I was really getting knocked around, but I tried not to fall. My ears were now ringing with every blow. If he had hit me with his fists, I would have been long gone. This beating went on for at least five minutes. Looking at him, I could see that he was sweating a stream. Finally he stopped, looked at me, and motioned for me to leave. I was so lucky that I wasn't hurt badly. I think I got a blessing on this one.

I might mention that after this shell detail experience, whenever I saw this Japanese sergeant in the compound, he would look at me then turn around and go the other way. I'm sure he thought that if I ever met him after this was all over, that I would kill him. No way. I would actually try to become his friend. I made it a policy to never carry a grudge. A war is a war and when it is over, we need to forgive and forget.

Chapter Eleven

THE WAR'S DEVELOPMENTS
AND KEEPING OUR SANITY

W e had a guy on our shell detail whose name was Joe. One afternoon as we were about to go back to the barracks, I noticed that Joe was sitting outside the entrance. I said "Come on Joe, we are going home." Joe didn't move and just continued talking to himself. I got a little closer and then I could hear what he was mumbling. He was repeating over and over, "Blood, blood, it's blood." I got Joe up and with a little help from some of the guys we were able to get him back to camp. We immediately took him over to the hospital.

We didn't see Joe for about two weeks, then one afternoon I saw Joe walking around the compound between the two electric fences. He was kind of bent forward and his feet were facing inside on every step as if he were pigeon-toed. He also didn't swing his arms from front to back but held them forward and moved them from left to right as he walked. The doctors examined Joe, confined him to a room in Barracks 5, and left him by himself. It was the opinion of the medical team we had in camp and Dr. Yoshihiro Shindo, that Joe was insane and that there wasn't any positive treatment available for him. We started to call him "Crazy Joe." The Japanese, on the other hand, then treated Joe with great respect because of his condition. They even gave him better food from time to time and all the cigarettes he wanted. He also had a room to himself, although it was locked up tight at night.

About six years after the war was over I was working on a big bridge that spanned a highway in Sacramento, California. The bridge was a reinforced steel concrete span that was about thirty feet above the road. Under the bridge there was a sidewalk. As I was looking down I noticed a guy that looked a lot like Crazy Joe approaching us on the sidewalk. I looked more closely, then yelled out, "Hey Joe." He looked up at me and smiled. I shouted, "Joe, stay where you are, I'll be right down." I ran down the nearby ramp and hurried over to where "Crazy Joe" was standing. As I approached him I realized that he was no longer crazy. We moved off to the side of the walk and found a place to sit down. Joe looked great. There was nothing wrong with this guy. We started talking and I noticed that he was as rational and unrestricted in his speech as anyone you would meet.

Finally I said, "Joe it is so good to see you. You were a different person the last time I saw you. You were out of it. Everybody was sorry for you in our camp. What happened to change that?" Then I blurted out, "We thought you were insane. Were you?" Joe just leaned back and laughed, "You know Bill, I was never insane, not even for one minute. It was a game for me. And I fooled everyone, even the doctors." He continued, "I figured if I really could make the doctors and everyone else believe I was insane and incurable, they might send me back to the United States on one of those ships like the *Conte Verde*, which was scheduled to repatriate Americans and English from Shanghai. I also thought they might send me to one of the camps near Shanghai that was composed of civilians." Then he reasoned, "Any way you look at it, I was better off than anyone else. Interesting, isn't it? Even the Japanese treated me with great respect; they gave me anything I wanted. But, they did lock me up at night."

"Well, Joe," I asked, "Didn't anything bug you? Weren't you lonesome being by yourself year after year with no one to talk to?"

"Nothing bothered me," he said, "until they confined that crazy North China Marine to my room. That marine was really cuckoo. He was really gone mentally. He scared the living hell out of me. Occasionally, during the night, I would look over to his bed, which was about twelve feet away from me on the opposite side of the room. Every time I looked over to where he was, especially during the night, I could see him resting his head on his propped up arm staring at me. I can still imagine clearly today. Actually, it was this piercing stare that almost drove me insane." I laughed and then he grinned at me and said, "You know Bill, I had everybody fooled." We talked for a few more minutes and then said goodbye. I liked "Crazy Joe." He had his plan and I had mine, and others had theirs—maybe Crazy Joe's plan had been the best of all.

Red Cross Boxes

We were very fortunate to be in a prison camp near Shanghai. The International Red Cross had a major headquarters in Shanghai and every once in a while a party from their organization would visit our camp. The Japanese would lie about how they treated us. The Red Cross agent knew they were lying and reminded them that prisoners of war were to be treated according to the Geneva Convention rules and laws.

The Red Cross brought a large quantity of packages to our camp at Kiangwan. I think we unloaded nine to eleven thousand boxes of food from the Red Cross. We received our first box about Christmas time. Each POW received a box that contained a couple of cans of corned beef, a couple of cans of Spam (or something like Spam), a large box of raisins, a small can of cheese, two or three high-protein chocolate bars, a can of coffee, a can of powdered milk, and a small can of butter. There were also four to six packages of American cigarettes. We really appreciated these boxes of food. I always traded my coffee and cigarettes for chocolate bars.

In the beginning we were given a box about every two or three months. The boxes came at the right time and helped us with the meager food we were getting from the Japanese. Everyone seemed to eat the food from the Red Cross boxes almost immediately. Some of the men opened their boxes and promptly ate everything in them. In a number of cases, once the food hit their stomachs, they became ill and threw up what they had just eaten. I strung my meager rations out to last about a week. The Red Cross boxes helped us psychologically and physically, but we needed ten times more than we received to really make a difference in our eroding health.

Making Preparations

One day when we were in Woosung, the Japanese decided to build deep holes to fill up with three feet of water up to a foot below ground level. We were to dig two holes for each barrack, each hole being twenty feet wide, twenty feet long, and four feet deep. We had seven barracks, so we excavated fourteen pits that would later be filled with water. The Japanese said that these water holes were being built in case there was a fire in the barracks. As the barracks were wooden, we thought it was a good idea. The Japanese however, did not mention that the reasoning was that someday we might be bombed by one of our own planes.

Late one night a plane flew over our camp. Sirens and searchlights went crazy, but nothing more happened. Then one afternoon a flight of B-29s flew over Kiangwan about thirty thousand feet high, and then they were gone. Another day, the airports in Shanghai were hit. And then one day about noon, a P-51 flew right around our compound. I was standing near the entrance to our camp when I saw the P-51. It was low, about five hundred feet above us. The pilot's aircraft was turned sideways and his wings were perpendicular to the ground as he circled around our barracks. You could see the pilot's face as he buzzed around the compound. He was only there about ten seconds and then he was gone. The guys in camp were waving to him, but whether the pilot knew who we were or not was questionable. If he had known, I think he would have flown over our camp again and wiggled his wings.

The Winter of 1943–44

The winter of 1943–1944 was a bitter one with snow and freezing rain. We huddled and walked the corridor between sections in the barracks to keep us warm, for there was no means of heating. The water tower was frozen from the top to the bottom. If you were sick, you went to the hospital where there was some heat. It was full of sick people, though, so most men ended up returning to their section, covering up with blankets, and trying to get warm. There were work details, but even the Japanese didn't want to stay out in the bitter weather.

On one winter detail, as we were walking down a dirt road, I will never forget the terrible scene we saw as we approached a group of Japanese soldiers huddled around a wood fire. They were heating water in a large bucket. About ten feet from them there was a Chinese peasant standing stark naked in a wooden tub about a foot high. His arms and hands were tied to a wooden post behind him. He was standing in this tub shivering and shaking. Suddenly one of the soldiers took hold of the bucket they were heating over the fire. It evidently was very hot. Then he hurriedly walked over to the bound Chinese peasant and dumped the scalding hot water on him. The peasant screamed and screamed and the Japanese soldier laughed and went back to his friends. We all felt so sorry for the torture this poor Chinese man was being put through. We were on this work detail for several more days and saw the same horrible torture each day. On the fourth day, there were only four Japanese soldiers huddling around a fire—the peasant was gone.

The Italians

At the beginning of World War II, the Italians, being pro-Fascist, joined the triumvirate with Japan and Germany. The prime minister and dic-

ASTARITA

While marching off to work one cold morning, we saw some Japanese soldiers torturing a Chinese peasant. They roped the poor man to a post and poured hot water over his naked body. Then they tied a broken bottle around his neck. The hot water treatment was given on especially cold days.

tator of Italy at that time was Benito Mussolini. Mussolini and his entire regime held onto power by force, intimidation, and especially fear. Mussolini gave the impression that his soldiers were undefeatable and that Italy was truly a great world power. Hitler must have also thought so in the beginning. But as the war progressed, Mussolini seemed to be more of a paper-dictator that Hitler had to hold up.

When Italy surrendered to the Allied forces on September 3, 1943, the Japanese in the Far East demanded that the pro-Fascist Italians would not be imprisoned. Those Italians who declared themselves anti-Fascist, however, were immediately interned. Some of the Italian marines that were anti-Fascist arrived in Kiangwan in November 1943. There were twenty-four of them and they were assigned to Barracks 4, Section 8—just two sections from mine.

When they arrived, I went to their section and we got acquainted. One thing they could do was sing, which they did every night. At first I was a little annoyed, but then I realized that this was their way of life. And their singing wasn't that bad. In fact, I thought they were very good. Everything they sang was classical, mostly from operas. I didn't know the names of the operas, nor the songs they sang, but sometimes I recognized the music. After a few weeks of the Italians' singing, I began to appreciate their musical ability greatly.

The leader of the twenty-eight Italians was a man by the name of Pasqual. We got to know each other quite well. He spoke broken English and was very interested in everything American. I asked him why his men had denounced the regime of Benito Mussolini. He told me that being an Italian marine did not inspire in him pride or allegiance to the regime of Mussolini.

I have thought about Pasqual and his marine buddies and have come to the conclusion that the reason Italy had capitulated in Africa and in Italy itself was because of the weakness in their desire to fight. I believe that this reflects a dictator's cruelty to his own people. When it came time to fight, the Italians didn't have the will to fight and simply gave up. The Italian government under Mussolini, even with all the show of a great and courageous military machine, was like a shiny red apple that looked great from the outside but was wormy and rotten inside. It collapsed from within. When this happened, Hitler had to come into Italy and take over all of the fighting.

Before the war's end, Mussolini was captured by a mob before he could get to Germany. The group then hung his dead body in Milan for the public to witness.

Playing Cards

We had only been in Woosung Camp a couple of months when the men discovered that by meticulously cutting up small pieces of cardboard they could make a fifty-two-card deck. And thus began the gambling—poker, draw, blackjack, twenty-one, and stud. But these homemade cards only lasted a few days. When the North China Marines came into camp, a couple of the things they brought with them were decks of cards and money. It didn't take us very long to get a few decks in our barracks. Then the "Japs" put decks of cards in their canteen, which was located between the two hot electric fences. The US playing cards filtered down from the North China Marines and it didn't take long for some of those to make it to our barracks. With the good old US playing cards, the gambling began in earnest. I didn't get involved, but many did and they bet on cigarettes, food, even on their clothes and future IOUs.

At the same time, the card game of bridge began to make an appearance. I liked bridge and was successful in playing it. It was 98 percent luck, but some of the guys were really good. One of them was my friend Tony Wallace. Tony was a whiz at bridge, but he could only break even playing. Finally, Tony told me one day, "Bill, you are the luckiest guy I know. Now what I would suggest to you, my friend, is that we become partners playing contract bridge. If we do, I'm sure we can become the best bridge players in the camp and we will make a lot of money."

It sounded like a good idea, so we started playing bridge for money. Would you believe that we never won—not even once! Laughing, we both said, "Let's give this up." I rather suspect that we had professional gamblers that went to Wake with the idea of making a lot of money from the workers. I'm sure they could have taken a lot of money from the unsuspecting.

Chapter Twelve

SURVIVAL AND INGENUITY

My brother Jack and I were separated during much of our time on Wake Island. Although we boarded separately, we were in the same hold for twelve days on the *Nitta Maru* and were together in the prison camp at Woosung. But we were separated at Kiangwan when I became the section leader of Section 6 in Barracks 4 and Jack became the second man in charge in Barracks 3.

Jack often headed up work parties of two hundred or more civilians. Sometime during the month of August in 1943, Jack was in charge of a large group of men. There were about two hundred men from Barracks 3 and 4 in his work party. I was in charge of about twenty men and we were assigned to a different work project. My detail left Kiangwan about eight hours earlier that day. When we arrived back from our work detail, it was four o'clock. The minute we unloaded in Kiangwan, a guy from Barracks 3 hurried over to where I was standing and said, "Bill, your brother Jack had the living hell beat out of him today by Squeaky." Squeaky was the Japanese NCO (noncommissioned officer) in charge of Jack's detail that day.

That morning when the men in Jack's detail reached the large ditch they were to clean, they unloaded from the trucks and spread out along the ditch. The day was cold and the weather was very cloudy. A few drops of rain came down on them. The Japanese built a fire near the ditch and gathered around the flames to warm themselves. A few others were on sentry duty to watch the prisoners. Hardly any work was being done. Squeaky had been at the fire with some of the Japanese and decided to check out the prisoners. When he saw the men just standing around, he started throwing rocks at them. As he did so, a few of the men began to cackle like chickens and soon nearly everyone was cackling like chickens. At first Squeaky did not catch on to what the cackling was about. Then suddenly it dawned on him that the men were making fun of him because they had seen him abuse a chicken the day before. When he realized that he had been exposed for that deed, he became furious and unmanageable.

Squeaky saw Jack, who was in charge of the POWs, and started up the ditch toward him. On his way he picked up a pick, knocked out the handle, and readied a club that looked like a baseball bat. He made Jack stand at attention then proceeded to work him over from head to toe in front of the men. Nothing was spared in his cruelty to Jack. By this time the men in the ditch became restless and started to come out to protect Jack. But the guards immediately leveled their rifles and machine guns on them. When Squeaky saw this, he promptly stopped beating Jack and an uneasy peace was restored. In another minute, though, a lot of men could have died.

The order was given to return to Kiangwan and soon they were all back in camp. But the damage was done. When I saw Jack at the hospital, he was almost unrecognizable. Blood was seeping out from his eyes, ears, nose, and mouth. He was black and blue all over. His head had swollen so much that his ears were almost hidden. He told me that every joint in his body ached and that he was having a terrible time breathing. His nose was broken in several places and his arms and elbows were so sore that he had difficulty raising them. Jack's eyes were irreparably damaged. He had a wrinkled membrane of the retina resulting in double vision and no depth perception.

Jack reported to the top-ranking Marine officer, Colonel Ashurst. Colonel Ashurst immediately met with Colonel Yuse, the Japanese camp commandant. He, in turn, ordered the whole camp to turn out and stand at attention as we all watched Squeaky get worked over by a Japanese officer.

After the war was over and he had returned home to the United States, Jack told me the following: In November of 1943, he went to Tokyo, supposedly to write propaganda for the Japanese. But he refused to write for them. He was told that if he would write propaganda for the Japanese, he could have a good place to live, good food, women, and all the luxuries that go with doing what they wanted. After a few weeks of Jack's refusal to write for them, the Japanese tortured him to get him to write. For example, they would burn his legs with cigarettes while interrogating him. Finally, one rainy night he was given a shovel, told to dig a hole, and the Japanese would bury him. A couple of hours later he was told to refill the hole, then he was brought inside. Through all of this Jack didn't budge. So in March of 1944, the Japanese finally sent him to the notorious Sumidagawa Prison Camp located in Tokyo. In Sumidagawa he was housed in a huge warehouse in the middle of the largest railroad yard in Japan. Most of the POWs in Sumidagawa Prison were pilots and crews who had been shot down by the Japanese. Everyone in this camp was worked to the bone unmercifully. The POWs there were beaten and starved, having little or no medical help. While Jack was in Sumidagawa, his health teetered between life and death.

The prisoners were forced to shovel coal, loading and unloading trucks and railroad cars. The men had to clean out ships after unloading. Jack said they had to work in the bottom of the holds in filthy, ankle-deep water. The nights were horrible, for hoards of lice and bedbugs filled the camp. The prisoners' raw bodies were covered with bites. Jack's ankles and feet became swollen. He told me that he was so malnourished that when he would push his finger in his lower leg and pull it away he could see that the hole where his finger had been before it slowly filled up. As a result of this malnourishment, Jack's teeth became loose. In one year he had to have another POW remove five of his teeth with pliers.

The bombings by US B-29s became almost unbearable. At midnight on March 10, 1945, US bombers dropped more bombs in Tokyo than were dropped in any other air raid in World War II, including Europe. The Japanese say that more than one hundred thousand people were killed in that single raid.

Jack said it was unbelievable that all of the POWs were not killed. When Jack finally got out of prison camp, he had a fourteen-inch waist and weighed seventy-eight pounds.

From those agonizing years in prison camp, Jack bore terrible scars. He continued to suffer from uncontrollable stress, eyesight problems, wet and dry beriberi, arthritis, frostbite (he slept, as I do even today, with his feet out of the bed covers), tingling in the feet, pellagra, anxiety disorders, severe post-traumatic stress disorder, and peripheral neuropathy. And on top of all those ailments, his nose had been broken four times by war's end. Jack told me that if the war had lasted just a few more months, he would never have made it.

For some reason, Jack never sought compensation for his service-connected disabilities. Finally, in June of 1995, I took him to Seattle to determine whether he could qualify for the service-connected disability benefits. It took some time and a number of examinations, but in May of 1996 he did receive 100 percent disability, three months before he died. Jack, to me, represents the character of a fine man who never realized he had so many problems, or so many friends. Jack died August 5, 1996, in Thousand Oaks, California.

A Shave and a Haircut

Isn't it interesting how you manage to survive even when common sense tells you that it is not possible? Let me give you a simple illustration of this. I had a Gillette razor blade that was used for shaving. After using it a few times, it became very dull and quite useless. Someone said that a razor blade could be sharpened by rubbing it on the smooth inside part of a drinking glass. I thought the trick would be too good to be true, but I decided to give it a try. So I got a small drinking glass and put a little water in the bottom of the glass to act as a lubricant. Then I put the blade flat against the glass and held it there with my forefinger. After getting the blade in place, I pushed the blade gently against the glass and moved it back and forth about ten or twelve times. Then I turned the blade over and repeated the process again. After removing the blade from the glass, I put it in my razor, lathered my face, and shaved. I couldn't believe the results. The blade worked perfectly. Now, the most remarkable thing was that I used this same blade for at least six months. I've wondered about that method of sharpening over the years. For it to work right, the glass you use as a sharpener has to be flawless. And you need to sharpen both sides of the blade, making sure not to press too hard. Now why hasn't Gillette advertised that you can sharpen your old blades?

Another hygiene question you face as a POW: "How do you take care of your teeth when you're in prison camp?" The answer is that you don't, unless you can get a toothbrush and toothpaste. But there was very little sugar, so tooth decay was slower. When the Red Cross boxes came into camp in 1942, each box had a toothbrush. We had soap, but no toothpaste. I used soap in place of toothpaste at first—it was better than nothing. But what I really needed was an abrasive. I began using salt, mixing it up in my hand with a couple of drops of water and applying it to my toothbrush. I brushed with that simple concoction morning and night. It worked quite well for three and a half years. In fact, I have all of my teeth today except for two molars that were pulled out a couple of years ago.

The Japanese let us use a room in Barracks 3 as a barbershop. You could get a haircut for two cigarettes. Nearly everyone, including myself, used the barbershop. I found that the shorter your hair was, the easier it was to control, wash, and keep lice or fleas away. It always felt good for us to get our heads shaved.

John "Shorty" Martin

We had a guy in Barracks 4, Section 1, by the name of John Martin. He was well liked and because he wasn't very tall everyone called him "Shorty" Martin. Shorty loved to gamble. He was very good at poker and won consistently. I asked Tony Wallace what he thought of Shorty and his uncanny ability to consistently win at poker. Tony said that he thought Shorty was a professional gambler. Tony said, "Guys like Shorty follow construction jobs all over the world, especially when the men are isolated in camps for long periods of time. They also work at whatever trade they have signed up for, but that's for the small money. The big money comes in when the day is over and it's time to relax." So in the long run, Shorty would make three or four times as much as the guy across from him. Salary didn't mean much. In gambling there was much more money to be made. If he hadn't have become a POW, Shorty probably would have shipped out from Wake after his nine months was over with plenty of money.

Shorty Martin was not only a very good gambler, but he also liked to drink. There wasn't any liquor in camp, so he decided to make his own. When the Red Cross boxes were given out from time to time, they all contained a small box of raisins. Shorty traded the contents of his entire Red Cross box (except for the raisins) for raisins from others in the barracks. Then he got a hold of a lot of sugar and filled a container with water, sugar, and raisins. He stored this container under his bunk. It was in the summertime and the temperature was up in the nineties. Shorty kept his fermenting brew covered. This turned out to be a mistake. Time went on and Shorty's brew really started to ferment. One Sunday when everything was quiet, about three o'clock in the afternoon, there was a tremendous explosion in the barracks. It caused quite the excitement. The Japanese came running into our compound. They searched everywhere but found nothing. They left after a couple hours and we took a sigh of relief.

The cause of the explosion was Shorty Martin's raisin brew. It had blown up, creating a huge mess around his bunk. Shorty lost his whole batch of booze. We all laughed at the sad ending to his home-made brew. What a Sunday afternoon! A lot of guys had hoped that the explosion meant that Uncle had arrived. We wished.

Wagers in Camp

During those prison days we knew that eventually the war would end. But how it would end was always in question. So much of the time, especially at night, we pondered, worried, and hoped that we would make it through. We didn't trust the Japanese. They could be very nice at times, but at the drop of a hat we could have all been killed. The difference between their culture and ours was like the contrast between night and day. The men would spend much of the time speculating about the future. A lot of bets were made concerning how long the war would last.

You may wonder what someone would use for money in a prison camp. Well, it's amazing what a person who loves to gamble will come up with: cigarettes, food, and IOUs for money to be paid after the war. Now that may seem ridiculous, but let me tell you about a bet I made with a friend of mine while I was a POW in the Kiang-wan Prison Camp near Shanghai. I made a wager with John Allen on an election, which I won. The winner was to get his money after the war was over. Well the war ended and everybody went home. Years went by and then in December of 1981, thirty-six years after the war was over, I received a Christmas letter from John. In it he said he was sorry it had taken so long to get in touch with me and how he learned through his daughter, who was also living in Maui, that I was also living in Maui. Enclosed in his Christmas letter to me was a check for twenty-five dollars made out December 14, 1981.

Also enclosed was another unopened envelope addressed to William Taylor and dated December 14, 1946. It had been returned to John unopened with the stamped notation on the envelope reading, "moved, left no address." It had been addressed to a home my grandfather James Douglas had owned in the early forties and where my mother had been receiving her mail in 1941. Grandfather had died in 1943 while I was a prisoner in China. When John Allen had received his first letter back, he didn't open it. He just filed it away. He never opened the first letter addressed to me but enclosed it with his Christmas greeting of 1981. I opened the sealed letter and found another card and another check for twenty-five dollars dated December 14, 1946. I still have both Christmas cards and checks. To me they show the integrity of a bet that was fulfilled after so many years.

Chapter Thirteen

NEWS AND GRIM REALIZATIONS

There had been word around camp that Japan had lost the Naval Battle of Midway. We were not supposed to have any idea about what was happening in the war because the Japanese had taken away our radios. But a few of us were able to get information thanks to our friend Lieutenant John Kinney, a Marine pilot captured on Wake. He foresaw that the Japanese would take the radios away when the war news started to report anything negative for the Japanese.

John was an electrical engineer, having graduated from the University of Washington before he joined the Marine Corps. He had remarkably repaired some of our damaged airplanes while we were defending Wake. Anything electrical or mechanical was right down his alley. John Kinney was the man that was called upon to fix anything that went wrong and to get it running. John was one of a kind and was never given enough credit for his part as a fighter pilot on Wake at the beginning of the war. John was way ahead of the Japanese and he knew that it was just a matter of time before all radios would be taken away. When the radios were removed, he built a radio from scratch. So, all through the war John received the news, sharing it with only one or two close friends. The Japanese searched high and low for John's radio, but never did find it.

During all the years in prison camp, all we could do was wonder and wait to see what the Japanese were going to do with us. We knew with a surety that if they were ordered to kill us, they would do it without hesitation. We also knew that they would never surrender. They had never surrendered in the history of their nation. It was fight to the finish. If the Americans invaded our camp, we would all die. So the only option left to us was escape. No one had ever successfully escaped from our camp. So, in a sense, our camp at Kiangwan was inescapable.

We would roll the possibility over and over in our minds and finally come to the conclusions that escape from Kiangwan could not happen. Then the days, weeks, months, and years just rolled by. You lie on your bunk and count the boards in the ceiling. And you read the books in the library. It's amazing what a good book will do for morale in a situation such as ours. But when you close up your book that you've borrowed from the prison library, reality swamps you. People who have experienced what we went through as POWs have a difficult time adjusting then and for the rest of their lives.

Water

We had a wash rack in front of every barrack that contained twelve sinks with faucets. We washed everything we had with those faucets. The water looked nice and clear and came from a deep well. But we didn't use this water for drinking purposes or for anything that was going in the body unless the water was boiled because it was polluted. The whole land area of Shanghai is a delta. For hundreds of square miles around Shanghai the water table is only three to five feet underground, which means that if you dig three, four, or five feet down in the ground, you are going to reach the water table.

The great Yangtze River is one of the longest and oldest rivers in the world. It starts in Tibet and winds its way eastward for about

3,500 miles until it reaches the east coast of China, near Shanghai. As it nears the eastern coast, the Huangpu River and other tributaries join it. The Yangtze, along with the Huangpu and other rivers, form what is known as a "delta," a huge triangular piece of land. All of these rivers have deposits of free soil they have carried with them for hundreds or even thousands of miles. When they reach the delta and the ocean, the fine particles of soil are deposited, forming rich farmland. The delta that has been formed by the Yangtze, Huangpu, and other tributaries is one of the richest and largest farming areas in the entire world.

Almost anything will grow on that wonderful delta land in China. Thousands of Chinese farmers grow their crops there. As a result of the high population, factories have sprouted up everywhere, which then add to the pollution. Collected human waste is diluted with water and is sprayed back on the land, acting as fertilizer for the next crop. Nothing is purified. You take your life in your hands if you drink water from the wells. I understand that wells provide water from deep underground and yield water that is not so contaminated.

The water that we got out of our taps came from a deep well and was much cleaner. We used it to wash clothing, our dirty food bowls, and to brush our teeth, but we didn't drink it. As I said before, our drinking water usually came to us as tea, which tasted more like leaves. We were sometimes given simply boiled water for drinking. During the years, I thought about the water and where you would get it if you were able to escape. Who would give you uncontaminated water and help you along the way at the risk of losing their life and maybe their entire family?

Grim Realization

We knew that the war was moving closer to us. Bombers were flying over Shanghai on their way to Japan. The Japanese were very close-mouthed then about the way the war was developing. On July 5, 1944 there was a heavy bombing at a military base near Shanghai.

In the meantime, life just went on in our prison camp. We all wondered what would happen when things got really rough. If the Japanese were going to fight to the end, then they would massacre all prisoners under their control. I didn't think that the United States was going to negotiate any peace with Japan. We were going to have to go into the very heart of Japan to win and that alone would probably cost the United States over two hundred thousand men. These are the thoughts and the kind of talk that almost everyone had during the years of captivity.

Day followed day, week followed week, and month and years that seemed endless gradually passed on. Our POW camp back in early 1942 was a camp of military men, including men from the Army, Navy, and Air Force. We had British Military from Hong Kong and Italian Military from North China and Shanghai. In January of 1944 Kiangwan was made up of US Marines and a few Army and Navy personnel, but mostly civilians. As the years went by many of the POWs, mostly civilians, were sent to Japan. Suddenly our sections in the barracks were half empty.

When these POWs first starting leaving for Japan we wondered about their fate, but only for a short time. We soon found out that these prisoners shipped to Japan were being forced into hard labor. That made all of us who were still in Kiangwan nervous. We realized that being sent to Japan to work would be very difficult and that once there, all thoughts of escape would be forgotten and set aside. The work that those sent to Japan would have to do would be brutal, the food would be very bad, and life expectancy would be shortened to almost nothing—months or one or two years. They would be beaten, whipped, starved, and worked for endless hours. They slept with bedbugs, lice, and filth, and were plagued by many diseases.

We hated the idea of going to Japan to help their war effort. It did not appeal to any of us, but what could we do about it? We were doomed, it seemed. The outlook was grim. It would take a miracle to escape. Many had tried over the years and all had been caught.

Once we were in Japan, all would be lost, for even if you escaped, you would quickly be caught and punished. As the years went by, over and over again, year in and year out, I wondered about escaping. If caught, there would be beatings and maybe even death, but I realized that the alternatives were also not very good. Being a prisoner of war in Japan eventually would bring on a lingering death. I came to the conclusion that the answer was to make a successful escape as soon as possible. It would require perfect timing, luck, and a resolve to not turn back. But how?

December of 1944 passed quietly in the night. There was no Christmas celebration, only a small electric bulb with a green shade that hung down about three feet from the wooden ceiling. Everyone in the barrack seemed quiet, nervous, and preoccupied. My heart went out to those who had families. You could see the pain on the faces and you could almost read their thoughts. I think the young guys were wondering about their wives and family. Many young husbands thought, "I wonder what my wife would be doing tonight." And the older ones with families probably thought, "I wonder if my kids will know me when I come home—if I'm lucky enough to get home."

Chal, Mac, and I were not married, and so the separation wasn't as hard on us. But we knew down deep that it was going to get worse for everyone before it got better. It was freezing cold in our section. We had no heat and very little food. At a time like that, we needed extra food to prevent a quicker death.

Radio Station Detail

About the middle of February 1945, John Burroughs, who was in charge of Barracks 4, assigned my Section 6 to a Japanese controlled radio station about ten miles away from our camp in Kiangwan. There were about twenty men in our detail and we traveled by trucks. When we arrived at the radio station, a Major Sakamoto and Japanese guards met us. Our assignment was to make a large anti-tank ditch around the radio station. About the second day of our assignment, Major Sakamoto asked if any of the men played tennis. No one raised his hand, so I told Major Sakamoto that I had played a lot of tennis before the war. He immediately became very interested, and so we played a few sets. After a couple days of working and tennis, our food improved and the guys didn't have to work so many hours. After about a week of playing tennis, the major started talking to me about the war. I didn't have very much to say because it didn't make any sense to me to argue about anything with him, especially the war. I could feel that he wasn't very happy with the way the war was going, so I would talk about other topics that were more pleasant. Major Sakamoto felt good about our conversations and in time we became *tomodachi* (friends). As a result, my crew was given good food—ample rice and some meat—and their workload became less burdensome.

I mentioned to the men on our detail, "Keep quiet and if someone questions you about your work and how it is going when we get back into camp, all you say is that this is one detail where you have had to work hard." We never bragged about how we were being treated.

Then one day the major said, "Soon you all will be shipped out either by boat or train, probably by prison train, going north, at least to Peking."

Chapter Fourteen

A MOVE AND A CHANCE
FOR ESCAPE

As early as February 1945, we had an idea that the Japanese were planning on moving us from Shanghai. Every year about December or January, the Japanese brought in American Flyers—those shot down while flying over China. These men were usually immediately released to mingle with the other men in camp. But the flying men brought into camp in December 1944 and January of 1945 were isolated from us in an adjoining barrack and separated from us by two stout barbed wire fences. We were able to talk to these men, however, and soon learned all they knew about the outside. Thanks to Captain Donald Burch of Louisville, Kentucky and Sergeant Donald Watts of Marian, Ohio, I was able to get valuable information that was later used to help me in my break. Captain Burch would crawl through the two fences after taps at night and tell me about conditions in China and chances of an escape. This was always a little risky because if the Japanese caught us talking together, it would be trouble.

From a Chinese friend of mine, Quock Ching Yuen, I was able to get a pointy-talky card. A pointy-talky was nothing more than a piece of paper with questions written in Chinese and English.

For example, one question in Chinese was, "Can you get me boiled water?" Under this was written the same in English. Another was, "Can you take me to an American Air Base?" At the bottom of the paper were written these two questions in both languages: "Can you do this?" and "Can you not do this?" So by pointing to a question that was written in Chinese and English, and then pointing to one of the two questions at the bottom of the page, one could ask the Chinese he came in contact with almost anything he needed. Besides my pointy-talky card, I had a map of China. I also had sulfa quinidine for diarrhea, iodine to purify my water, and a canteen that the Japanese had issued to each one of us. It came in a package and was supposed to last us until we arrived at our destination in North China. We also had a good supply of Red Cross food. So, I was fairly well prepared to escape if and when the time arrived.

At first we thought the Japanese were going to send us to Japan by water, but for some reason they changed their minds. It was a good thing for us that they did because traveling on the water at that time would have been suicide—no one is safe on the water during a war. On May 4, 1945, 101 men were picked out from the camp and sent ahead to Fung Tai in North China. They left early in the morning from the Kiangwan railroad station.

Freight Cars

On May 7th, John Burroughs, my adjutant in Barracks 4, asked me to take a party of men down to the train the next day and see that the freight cars allotted to our barracks were cleaned out. On the morning of May 8th, about twenty of us left from Barracks 4, along with the same amount of men from the other barracks. When we reached the Kiangwan railroad yards, we went to work cleaning up the cars, which were filthy, with a depth of two or three inches of fresh horse manure. All day long we worked on cleaning out the cars. As we worked, Japanese guards strung barbed wire between the doors and over the windows. During the day, I had a chance to wander from car to car, stopping every once in a while to talk to someone. While meandering around, I managed to steal a pair of pliers from one of the cars. I didn't know if I would ever be able to use them, but I thought if anything should happen while in route, I would at least have something to help me get out of the car quickly. What scared us the most was a bombing or strafing attack from one of our own planes, as they had no way of knowing that we were in those cars.

On May 9th, everybody, about nine hundred men, got up about four o'clock in the morning and by five o'clock, we had evacuated camp. We marched down to the Kiangwan railroad yards and boarded our separate cars. In each car there were fifty men, twenty-five on each side. You might say that the car was divided into thirds—one-third for us, one-third for the "Japs," and one-third for our fellow prisoners in the other end of the car. We had four windows in our car, two in each end. The windows were directly across from one another. Each window had two bars about eight inches apart with barbed wire strung across all of these. The window on my side, for some reason, only had one bar. Barbed wire was strung across the car from door to door. This left a clear place in the center of the car for our guards. There were four guards in every car. They were separated from us by the barbed wire, and each guard had 150 rounds of ammunition, along with their rifles and other weapons. The POWs in the car were terribly cramped. We had to sit side-by-side, many hours at a stretch. We were able to lie down for only two hours at a time, as there was only room for five men to lie down at once. It was quite uncomfortable. Two hours out of ten isn't very much rest. For toilets, we had two five-gallon cans, one in each end of the car.

About noon of the 9th we pulled out for Nanking. It was such a relief to be moving after sitting around in the car on that hot Shanghai morning that we didn't mind being cramped. Our Japanese interpreters had told us that if anything happened while we were en route that we were not to try to break out or run away or we would be shot. We were also told that if anyone attempted to escape and was caught, he would be immediately shot or stabbed to death. All the rest of the day we traveled, pulling into Nanking early in the morning of the 10th. At Nanking, we got off the train and waited in a small park near the depot while the train was being ferried across the river. After resting for a couple of hours at the park, we were marched down to the banks of the Yangtze and crammed onto a small river ferry, 450 at a time. The trip across the river took about twenty minutes. Reaching the other side, we were hustled up to the railroad yards and there we waited for an engine to come and hook onto our train. Finally we boarded the train and about six o'clock that evening we were again on our way.

The POWs were herded into freight cars in Shanghai, China, after leaving the Kiangwan Prison Camp. The cars, which were approximately thirty-two feet long and eight feet wide, were crammed full of prisoners.

For food, we had hard tack, which we had baked in our bakery at camp, and the last supplies from our Red Cross boxes we received early in March of 1945. These boxes were supposed to last us at least a week on the road so we wouldn't need to stop to cook rice.

Resolve to Escape

Early on the morning of May 11th, five officer friends of mine escaped. The Japanese didn't tell us this, but we knew something had happened because they got so excited and kept a close watch on us all the rest of the night, counting us every ten or fifteen minutes. That morning we stopped at Soochow. I volunteered to get water and learned from Lieutenant Murray Lee Lewis that five officers had escaped the night before. While walking back to the car, I resolved to escape that night, if at all possible. This would be my only chance.

I talked with McCurry and Chal, asking if they would go with me. They both told me, "It won't work, Bill. It's dark out there; you'll get caught and shot. Even if you do make it out of the window, jumping while the train is moving so fast and not knowing what you'll hit when you smack the ground—it's just too risky. And remember, Bill, there are four guards in the car only ten feet away. This is a no-no." But I was determined and knew that it was now or never; this was going to be as good as it would get as far as opportunities for escape. I also knew it could cost me my life, but I couldn't let the opportunity slip by. Besides, surprise was the key for any success.

We stayed at Soochow all day. During the day there was an occasion to get more water, so I volunteered again. This time I asked a friend, Jack Hernandez, if he would accompany me to get water. On our way I glanced over my shoulder to make sure that we would not be overheard, then I asked Jack if he would like to try an escape with me. He said he would, so we both agreed to try to get away that night. We confided our plan to McCurry, and he said he would give us any assistance we might need.

That night the Japanese took added precautions against anyone escaping. They stopped the train and pushed up all the windows. These windows were made out of steel and were opened by dropping or sliding them down between two grooves of steel. To close them, someone had to push them up from the outside of the car. When they closed them, we complained so loudly that we couldn't get any air that they finally let the windows down a couple of inches, pounding wedges up underneath them to keep them from falling. This still made it hard to get out, but I knew that if one pulled up on the window hard enough, the wedges would drop and the windows could slide down. Outside the car I knew that there was a little flange of steel that one could stand on while clinging to the bars for support.

At about eleven o'clock that night, I started working on the window with my pliers. There was a bedroll hung from the roof of the car and this partially shielded the upper half of my body as I worked on the window. Every half hour the guard would count us off. One time when he came in, he shined his light twice on me. He must have become suspicious because the second time, he let it linger on me for a while. I knew I was in a pretty tight spot and that he was watching me closely, so I just pretended I wasn't getting enough fresh air and then turned around and sat down. When I sat down, the guard turned his light off. I waited a few minutes in the dark, then leaned over to Jack who was sitting across from me and told him that I thought I was being watched and that we had better wait awhile before I started in on the window again. Jack suggested that I change places with him because the guard was suspicious of me and not of him and he thought he could get the window down without arousing suspicion. So we changed places, and he immediately went to work on the window.

We made arrangements with McCurry to keep his eye on the Japanese guards while one of us worked on the window. His seat was right next to the barbed wire that separated us from the guards.

Fifty men were crammed into each barbed wire prison car, twenty-five on each end. Inside we had a small fold-down seat to sit on. There was only enough room for five men to lie down on the floor at one time. There were four barred windows, and barbed wire was strung across the windows. Wire partitions separated us from the Japanese.

I sat a yard beyond him and Jack, who was working on the window, was only about four feet from me. Only two feet separated Mc-Curry from the Japanese guard. There was not much distance from the guard to Jack at the window—only about nine feet. The rest of the guards were asleep on the floor between the barbed wire that separated us from them and the other prisoners in the other end of the car. During the time we worked, McCurry kept smoking cigarettes. When he inhaled on the cigarette, the glow would light up the guard's face and he could tell by this dim light if the guard was looking at us. If he was looking our way, Mac would reach over and touch me and I would, in turn, touch Jack. When the way was clear, Mac would draw on the cigarette again, this time with the lit end toward us. This was our makeshift signal we had rigged up between us. As I sat there in the dark, waiting for Jack to get the window down, I started to get cold feet. I thought about what would happen to us if we got caught. I thought of the water cure, bayoneting, stabbing, and being shot. Then, as I sat there thinking of these things, my mind suddenly flashed on to something I had read that day in a book that belonged to a friend sitting next to me,

Charley Mayberry. I had picked the book up that morning and while glancing through it had come to a sentence at the end of one of the chapters that went like this, "The best way to overcome fear is by direct action." It seemed to me as I read it that morning and then as I sat there that that sentence had been written especially for me. "The best way to overcome fear is by direct action." Suddenly I felt a slightly cooler breeze stirring through the car and I knew that Jack had the window down. Almost immediately I heard him whisper, "Hey, Bill, pass the pliers over." Reaching in my pants, my fingers came into contact with those precious pliers and I quickly handed them to Jack.

It seemed just a matter of seconds before I heard him whisper, "It's all clear, Bill." As soon as I heard those words, my heart started beating violently because I knew that it was now do or die. If we didn't go now, we would undoubtedly be found out. And you can bet the punishment would be severe. I could just picture the guard spotting the open window and the cut wire and the excitement that would follow. The train would be stopped and a thorough search made. And when no one was missing, the fun would begin. They would find

Mac McCurry watches the four sleeping Japanese soldiers while Bill Taylor and Jack Hernandez escape out of the freight car window in the middle of the night.

us out—they always seemed to be able to get to the bottom of that kind of trouble. These thoughts all went through my mind within a few seconds after I heard Jack's whisper. From out of this tenseness, I pulled myself into action. There were rings all up and down the inside of the roof of the car. To these we had tied our shoes, two or three pairs on each ring. I then discovered that I had gotten hold of the wrong pair. But I couldn't pause at that point, so I took them anyway. Grabbing my supplies, I moved over to where Jack was and sat down to put on my shoes. They were about two sizes too large. I wonder what the guy that got mine the next day thought when he put on a pair of shoes that were two sizes too small. Lacing up my shoes as fast as I could, for time was what we then needed, I imagined how we would feel if the guard suddenly flashed his light on and started to count us. It was just about time for him to do just that. I kept hoping I wouldn't get stuck in the window.

Standing up, I reached over and touched Jack's arm and said, "I'll go first, Jack, and you can pass the supplies out through the window after I get out." Arching my back, I slid my arm, shoulder, and head out the window. Reaching up with my free hand, I grabbed hold of the one bar left in the window. For an awful moment I thought I couldn't make it, and then I was through. I pulled the rest of my body through and then let myself down on a short iron ledge that stuck out about an inch from the car and was about three feet below the window. The night was black, only the stars were shining. I couldn't see the ground below and it seemed as if the whole train was floating in the dark. I knew Jack was hurrying and in a few seconds he passed out our supplies. Grabbing these, I pulled myself as far away from the window as I could, holding on with one hand and in the other, holding our supplies. Soon Jack squirmed out of the hole and then we were both hanging on the side of the train. Suddenly I wanted to be back in that train more than anything else in the world. We couldn't see where we were going to jump or how fast we were going, although I imagine we were going about thirty-five to forty miles an

I jumped first and was followed by Hernandez. Both of us were injured, but Hernandez broke his leg and was recaptured. Little did we know that we had escaped near a large encampment of Japanese.

hour. I told Jack I had better jump first as I was in back of him. If he jumped first there was just a good possibility I would jump on him. Getting a firm hold on our supplies, I swung as far out as I could and let go. There was a second of suspension and I struck the ground. It was eternity in a split second. I supposed this was just about as close to the other side as one could get and then I struck the ground. There was a sharp pain in my left foot and then I was tumbling down the side of the track, coming to a sudden stop. I laid where I was until the train was swallowed up in the blackness. Suddenly everything seemed quiet, and a cold wind was now a breeze, gently blowing across my face. I was exhilarated as the train disappeared and I could no longer see those red lights on the caboose.

Realizing I couldn't stay there, I jumped up only to sit right down again. In jumping, I had injured my left ankle. Getting to my feet slowly, I put my weight down on my left foot and decided it wasn't broken. I suddenly realized that I didn't have my bag of supplies. "Damn, where had I dropped them?" I rapidly looked around for them. But in doing so, I tripped a wire signal that was strung tightly through rings that were welded to short steel rods imbedded in the railroad ties along the tracks. When I disturbed this wire, I could hear dogs barking on each end of the line, not too far away from us. Picking up the food and canteen, I rushed over to where Jack was, tripping the wire again in my haste. Grabbing Jack's arm, I whispered, "Come on, Jack, let's get going." We could already hear voices in the distance on each side of us. Then came the words that I will remember as long as I live, "I can't, Bill. I think my leg is broken."

Oh, what a sickening feeling came over me. Reaching down, I touched him gently on the shoulder and told him to lay back and I would see if I couldn't ease the pain by taking his shoe off. Removing his shoe, I felt his leg and ankle. I knew then that we were stopped. His leg or ankle was definitely broken. I thought, "Why does this have to happen to Jack?"

It was so dark around us that you couldn't see anything beyond a few feet away. Jack said, "You better get going, Bill. You know we're going to get caught." I told him, "We're going to go together." After a minute or so, I got him on my back, and took a few steps west. We had not moved more than twenty feet when we both fell into a huge ditch, which I found out later was an anti-tank trench, about ten feet deep and ten feet wide at the top. I climbed out the other side and then pulled Jack up beside me. In the meantime, we could hear the dogs barking their heads off. Getting Jack on my shoulders again, we stumbled west. After going a short distance, I decided to walk ahead for a few yards and then come back for Jack. After a couple of moves, we came to the base of a tree. We realized the dogs were getting closer. It was so dark.

At the tree Jack said, "Bill, we're both going to get caught. Give it a try. Maybe you can make it. There's no reason to stay." After a few minutes I made the difficult decision to go at it alone. This was one of the hardest decisions I have ever had to make.

Free and Alone

We both knew Jack was going to get caught, so I moved as fast as I could. My left ankle was swelling and my arms were bloody and very painful. But I had no choice except to keep going. There was a steady wind blowing from the north. The only light I had to guide me came from the stars. I started limping west as fast as I could, taking a bearing from the North Star. Soon I was in what I thought was a wheat field. About that time, a dog started barking off to my right. My heart started pounding against my ribs. Slowly, but as fast as I could, I kept going west. In about an hour, I came to a large canal I thought was the Inland Canal. (The Inland Canal runs all the way from North China to Nanking, bordering the railroad in the vicinity. At the outbreak of the Greater East Asia War, dredging on this canal was stopped.) Putting everything that could be ruined by water in my sack, I held the sack above my head and started across without hesitation. To my surprise, the canal was not deep, but rather, very shallow. It didn't reach above my waist. Every movement was an effort, especially for my injured left foot, as with each step I took I almost sank to my knees in ooze. The water was filthy and undoubtedly carried everything in it a cesspool does, including the stench that I was not able to get rid of for days.

Finally, after considerable effort, I reached the opposite shore, a distance of about thirty yards, and crawled up on the other bank, exhausted. I must have blacked out for a few minutes there, because when I came to it was getting pale in the east. Getting up as quickly as I could, I started hobbling off southwest, continuing in that direction for about an hour. While ambling along with my makeshift gait, I happened to look behind me. I saw five men emerging from the darkness in the distance. As I was deep in a grain field, I threw myself on the ground and held my breath. My heart was making such a racket that I thought surely the men would hear it even if they didn't see me. But they passed off to my left and were soon out of sight. Being shaken from the events of the first few hours and because it was getting light in the east, I decided to stay where I was until the next evening. At that time, I ate about half of an emergency ration chocolate bar and one hard tack. After taking a long drink from my canteen, I started removing my shoes. Then I noticed that my left foot had swollen quite a bit and was very painful.

While lying there I summed the whole matter up, deciding that I had butchered the whole escape. My head ached, my foot was throbbing, and I was cold and damp and smelled to high heaven. And not only that, but I knew that I was still in Japanese-controlled territory with little chance of getting out and only about a half of a pint of water left in my canteen. But I had to remember that these are the chances one must take. Oh, how lucky we are in America to be free. There are few countries in the world where one can think, act, and pray so freely. Thinking of these many things, I dozed off into a fitful, troubled sleep clouded with bad dreams.

I awoke with a pain in my foot and a burning thirst in my throat. The sun was shining directly overhead and was very hot. After taking a drink from my canteen, I felt much better. Not daring to sit up, I stayed almost motionless for the next four hours. This is actually a very hard thing to do. First your nose itches, then your back aches, and then you get a small cramp in your leg. Pretty soon you feel that if you don't move, you'll go crazy. But you don't move because in doing so you might lose your life.

Twice during the morning I heard sirens and then a little later, bombings, and once a reconnaissance plane flew directly over me. I finished all my water in the first two hours. For the next two hours, I suffered from a thirst that I hope I never have again. About five o'clock that evening, I figured it was do or die, so I put on my shoes and got to my knees and, after looking carefully around, I started off toward a Chinese village. At that time I figured that I was about seven miles from the railroad.

Chapter Fifteen

FREEDOM AND FRIENDLY
FARMERS

As I approached the village, I noticed a middle-aged man coming to the well on the outskirts of the village. I also saw the dreaded Japanese Military barracks off to the left. Waiting until he filled one of his jars, I approached the man very quietly. He didn't see me until I was about ten feet from where he was hauling water out of the well. I must have startled him, for as he pulled the water bucket out of the well, he turned around and faced me. The expression on his face said, "Who are you?" As I stood motionless in front of him, he looked me over from the top of my black and blue face, to my torn clothes, to my swollen and bloody hands. But what he really stared at was my blue eyes.

We stood there looking at each other for a minute or two. It was very quiet. Neither one of us moved. Finally I raised my canteen and indicated that I needed water. He immediately filled it up for me from a separate container, then took a sip to show me that it was all right. Evidently he had never seen a white man before because he wanted to know what was wrong with my eyes. I almost laughed—the first laugh in a long time—but I held myself in check. With grave concern, I drew a picture of a plane on the ground and

showed stars on the wings and said, "Wo megwa figi de." He knew
what this was, then pointed toward the military barracks and said,
"Bu how," and showed me which direction to go. It being a westerly
direction, I then left this kind man and started on my way, after
quenching my thirst and eating one half of a hard tack.

Running parallel to me, going west, was a low range of hills.
On approximately every third hill was a Japanese blockhouse. I had
been on my way for about a half hour when I started to feel like
someone was following me. Changing my course and backtracking,
I soon discovered that my middle-aged farmer friend was following
me. When he drew near, I stepped out of the path and confronted
him. Looking around, he motioned for me to follow him. But before we started, he took my hand and put it over his heart while
putting his hand over my heart, signifying "friend." I followed him
for about three hours in a westerly direction, skirting the villages.
At the end of this time we emerged on the edge of a huge wheat
field that stretched north and west as far as the eye could see. To the
south was a row of low rolling hills. We stopped on the edge of this
field and I had a chance to size up my Chinese friend. He was about
five feet two, slightly stooped, and of medium build. His complex-
ion was lighter than most Chinese with many fine wrinkles around
his dark brown eyes. He was dressed as a Chinese farmer with thin
cotton wrap-around pants, a shirt, a pair of shiats (sandals), and a
straw hat. As we squatted there on the soft dirt, which covered this
part of China, my heart went out to this man who had been my
Good Samaritan. He could have turned me into the Japanese with
very little trouble and even received a reward, but he didn't. If we
had been apprehended, he would have been tortured and shot. But
he helped me anyway, as much as he could.

Pointing to the sun, which was a flaming red disk just going
down over the horizon, he told me in sign language to keep away
from the blockhouse on my left, travel straight west and not to stop
until I had reached the opposite side, and to go slow on my water.

I attempted to converse with Chinese Coolies by using a "pointy-talky." A series of Japanese barracks are on the horizon.

Rising to his feet and taking his straw hat in both hands, he bowed to me two or three times. I, in turn, saluted him, turned about, and left. After I had gone about two hundred yards, I turned around and he was still standing, watching my departing figure. Over the years I've wondered, "Who was this wonderful Chinese farmer who risked his life for me?"

First Night and Next Day of Freedom

A short time later, I noticed a long line of Japanese troops off in the south. Stirred on by this I quickened my stride in spite of my swollen ankle and made good time. I must have traveled until about one o'clock in the morning when I became so tired that I had to stop. In the meantime, there had been a bombing off in the southeast at about eleven o'clock that night. Moving aside from my original course about four hundred yards, I stopped to rest. Slipping to the earth, I untied my food sack and ate one hard tack, a big handful of raisins, and drank better than half of my water. Then I fell half asleep. I say half asleep because during the night some kind of an animal kept bothering me. I would just get to sleep when there would be a slight rustle at one side of me. I shook the shocks of grain beside me to frighten it away. Finally after two or three attempts to get my food, it stayed away. I believe it must have been some kind of a fox, which, sensing my exhausted condition, was trying to get a free meal. For my bed that night, I gathered two large armfuls of wheat to cover myself. About two hours later, I was aroused by a single shot, close by.

I awoke with just an inkling of light in the east. Getting to my feet, I changed my westerly direction by about a mile. Soon the sky became lighter and lighter. Far in the distance I could just barely make out what looked like low hills on the far horizon. As time went on and I drew closer, I discovered these hills to be clumps of trees. By this time I had drunk all of my water and the sun was climbing higher and higher. By noon I was so thirsty that I had just one continual vision of cold, sweet water. Oh, for a mouthful of water. I had visions of water and all sorts of things cool and sweet. What a terrible experience it would be to die from dehydration.

About three o'clock in the afternoon of May 13th, I reached the extreme western edge of this never-ending wheat field. There were trees about two miles ahead and the outline of a village. Stumbling and half running to the nearest group of trees that enclosed the village, I searched out the closest well. At this point in time I really didn't care if the water was contaminated or not. A farmer was just drawing water from a well. As I approached him, he simply stood still and stared at me. I pointed to my canteen and motioned that I was very thirsty. He stared without emotion at me for a minute, then he nodded his head, bowed, then spoke to a little woman who was near the well. I then noticed that her two small feet were bound with cloth. Without saying a word she turned and shuffled off in the direction of a nearby hut. After she had gone, this Chinese peasant farmer turned back to me and motioned that the water was not good (*bushin*) for drinking but that it would not be very long until I would have water. Standing there watching him draw bucket after bucket of cool water from the well was almost more than I could stand. In about five minutes, the small Chinese peasant woman came hobbling back carrying a clay teakettle in her hand. She filled up my canteen with hot water, then motioned for me to follow her. Upon entering her hut, she went quickly to a small clay pot set and ladled out a small cup of water for me to drink. I drank the water as slowly as I could and never in my whole life had I tasted any water as sweet and good. I slowly drank cup after cup for about ten minutes, gradually feeling better with every cup.

By that time, word had spread throughout the village that a white man had just come from the east. Soon the whole room was full of Chinese people from one to fifty years old, gesturing and clicking their tongues all at once. I became a little nervous because this is the way a lot of pilots were caught by the Japanese. Everybody becomes family, then suddenly the "Japs" walk in and you are caught. I had been told many times previously never to linger very long in the villages, but to keep going so there was less chance of recapture. I was the subject of curiosity to everyone that came to see me and I began to be very nervous. I would be a rich man if I could collect a dollar from all the Chinese who came to see what a white man looked like. After this kind of experience, I now believe that a sideshow is fun for everyone except the person on display. After drinking my water, I thanked the little old lady as best I could, pushed my way through the crowd, and was soon on my way west.

It would be impossible to stay on a straight course west as there are so many villages, so I had to wind my way around them. These picturesque and quaint villages are only about a mile or two apart at the most, dotting the landscape as far as the eye can see. I suppose I was in the southern end of the Shantung province, which is truly a beautiful part of China. In the states, we had farms fenced off from one another, lots of untillable land, telephone lines, and modern equipment. But in China, they had none of this. Throughout the Hopei, Honan, and Shantung provinces, I saw nothing but beautiful farmland. These people had very little material wealth, but what they had seemed to make them very happy.

A Chinese Farmer's Life

The average Chinese farmer—we'll call him "Mr. Wong"—gets up at about five in the morning, carries several buckets of water from the community well, heats enough for drinking and food purposes and then waters and feeds his chickens, a donkey (if he has one), and an oxen or a goat. These animals are kept with his neighbor's livestock in a separate compound. Pigs are also kept in a separate compound. Mr. Wong eats a simple fare of wheat mash and wheat noodles with a piece of hard, dried bread. This food has little or no seasoning. After this simple meal, Mr. Wong goes cheerfully to work, working until the sun rises high in the heavens. Work consists of weeding wheat and vegetables. The Chinese plant their wheat fields differently than we do in the states. They sow their seed row upon row. Their fields have long single rows of wheat instead of one large mass. Due to the type of soil found in this part of China, it is important to keep something growing on it at all times or it will blow away. To keep this dirt from blowing away and turning this area into another Sahara Desert, the Chinese have planted trees in long rows to check soil erosion. They probably had never heard of reforestation, but they certainly knew how to hold onto their land and how to derive from it the maximum amount of benefit.

Before planting the new season, Farmer Wong hitches a plow to his oxen, which pulls a heavy disk, to cultivate the ground before planting the seeds of grain. After planting the grain by hand, he then uses a heavy stoneroller to flatten the grain into the soil. This is a good way to keep the soil down. Many years of experience farming land that is threatened by the Gobi Desert storms has made him successful. Overall, it is a miracle that he can prepare and plant wheat that continues to win the battle year in and year out.

About ten o'clock in the morning he returns to his little clay hut, resting through the hottest part of the day. Then, at about three thirty in the afternoon, he emerges and goes again to the field. In this way he rests not only himself during the hottest part of the day but also his beasts of burden. Just before the sun goes down, Farmer Wong quits for the day. Retiring to his hut he usually eats a bowl or two of unseasoned wheat noodles, a small bowl of bean sprouts, and a good quantity of wheat *meinpao* (bread). After understanding the way the Chinese live in this part of China and after being a prisoner for three and a half years, I am firmly convinced that wheat is truly the staff of life. Man can live and work hard eating almost nothing but prepared wheat.

Returning to "Farmer Wong," let's take a look at his home. The walls are made of bricks formed from a mixture of heavy clay, wheat, and straw. The walls are about one foot thick, rising about eight feet from the ground. The exterior walls are usually about eight feet high and seventeen feet long by twelve feet wide. For a window, Farmer Wong has an opening five feet off the ground about eighteen inches wide by two feet high. In place of glass, he uses a latticework of wood. In the wintertime, paper is put over the window to keep out the cold Gobi Desert air. The floor of his hut is nothing but packed earth. He throws everything he doesn't want into a small container that will eventually be picked up and taken outside. Then the floor of the hut is swept out. Into this space, Farmer Wong puts a small wooden bed with a bamboo mat for a mattress. It is really not uncomfortable and there are even less bed bugs when you sleep on a hard surface. A small cabinet stands about four feet off the ground, four feet wide, and acts as a chest for clothes. The chickens run freely about the place, as do the fleas. In this small room live Farmer Wong's wife and small child. There is no toilet, stove, or sink.

The Chinese in this section of the country were entirely self-sustaining. They had no running water, telephones, transportation (except by foot), paid entertainment, or modern equipment. They had nothing except what they produced themselves. There was no room for slackers. And most importantly—they were genuinely happy. Nowhere did one see signs of unemployment. Everybody had something to do. Food, such as it was, was quite plentiful. If these people could have been more educated about cleanliness and could have been taught about the advanced standards of the world and still have been content with their lot, they would indeed have had a modern utopia. In a primitive way, those Chinese farmers reminded me of James Hilton's *Lost Horizon*. Do you remember the valley of Shangri-la and the wonderful people who lived there? In that part of China, one was in the same atmosphere as that which prevailed around the people in Shangri-la. They had a peace of mind and seemed quite happy—that is hard to find in many places in the world.

Chapter Sixteen

DAY-TO-DAY SURVIVAL
THROUGH CHINA

O n the afternoon of May 13th, I again stopped for water, this time at a very small village of not more than a dozen huts. In this village I was treated with great kindness. I was given food and water, and also water with which to wash my aching feet. To me, this was most welcomed as my left foot at the ankle was still swollen to the point that I couldn't tell where the anklebone started and where my foot began. The food I was given greatly resembled a large flapjack about eighteen inches across and one-quarter inch thick. It was tasteless, but very filling, especially with drinking water. I stayed with them for about an hour.

I noticed the smoking pipes, which the Chinese all over China used. They looked like opium pipes, ranging from about seven inches to eighteen inches in length, with a small bowl at the end that was used for tobacco. The other end usually had a bone mouthpiece. For tobacco, the Chinese farmer had his own mixture, which he grew himself. Everywhere I stopped I was offered tobacco. I wasn't smoking at that time, so I didn't take the opportunity to find out just what this tobacco tasted like. However, I did know that is wasn't opium. Smoking seemed to be encouraged, especially among the young boys.

I saw young boys smoking everywhere—even boys younger than ten years old—puffing away on pipes or smoking cigarettes. The women also smoked—young and old alike. They didn't know how damaging this habit could be to them later in life. What a curse.

Leaving that small village, I again made my way west. At that point I figured that I had traveled about twenty miles. Stopping at another village for water late in the afternoon of May 13th, I got the feeling that I was staying too long, even though I was just on the outside of the village. Airmen that had been shot down that were also imprisoned at the Kiangwan Prison Camp had told us again and again, "Don't go in the villages. Be nice, get water, and move on." Almost every pilot whose plane had been shot down and had been captured by the Japanese was caught because he relaxed and lingered in a supposedly friendly village. You never really knew who was friendly, but if the Chinese didn't cooperate with the Japanese, they would be killed and their families too. Even though the Chinese hated the Japanese, the Chinese were still forced to either cooperate or put their lives in danger.

So while standing on the outskirts of this village, I suddenly got the feeling to move on. When I first arrived to the outskirts of this village, I was alone. Within just a minute, however, there were five or six villagers standing by, then ten, then twenty, and soon the villagers who had all run to see a white man surrounded me. By that time I was becoming uneasy. I felt that I had to get out of there right then. Reaching down to my sack of Red Cross supplies, I must have startled the soldier who had appeared on my left. He probably thought I was reaching for something dangerous like a hand grenade. He jumped up, yelling to the people in Chinese. Of course, I didn't know what he said, but the reaction was immediate. The guy on my right started yelling, then everybody started yelling and running away. Within two minutes, they had all disappeared and I was alone. I noticed that the guys on my right and left had departed; the one on my left walking rapidly away to the left and the one on my right disappearing in the crowd.

I left and walked due west as fast as I could. I figured I had two or three hours of daylight before darkness really settled in. After about two hours I started looking for a place to sleep for the night. Just as twilight started, I found just such a place. Scooping out a hollow place between two rows of wheat, I made myself a place safe from the wind. Then I pulled up the surrounding wheat plants for use as a cover. I had found out that this did very well not only as a cover, but also as a camouflage in case I overslept in the morning. I had just about finished my wheat pad when I noticed two men coming across the field toward me.

The Fight and Flight

As I just had my head sticking out, I figured I had not been seen and, if I had, I would probably be taken for a farmer gathering herbs for supper. I ducked my head and pretended to be very busy. This is where I made my mistake. When I again looked up, they were about twenty feet away, spreading out on each side of me. They both wore the same uniform. (I learned later that they were members of the Wang Ching-wei—puppet troops of the Japanese). Suddenly they both pulled guns from inside their coats and rushed up to me. One was armed with an old bolt-action rifle and the other with a Luger pistol. They motioned me to raise my hands. I complied. They then circled me warily, scrutinizing me closely. I thought my goose was cooked at that time. The troops then told me, in sign language, to take off my sweater, shirt, and undershirt and to take my canteen off my belt and drop my pants to the ground. When this was done, they both seemed satisfied that I was unarmed.

The man with a pistol was going through my Red Cross sack, talking and gesturing. In the meantime, I had pulled up my marine khakis and stood still, shivering in the cold. In about ten seconds, the one with the rifle, a much younger man, was attracted by what his partner was saying and turned sideways. The rifle was no longer pointed at me. Seizing this opportunity, I leaped on the man with the rifle, meaning to trip him, then shove him into his companion. But he was too wary for me and whirled to meet my rush. All I succeeded in doing was knocking his rifle up. But I managed to grab the barrel and stock of the rifle. So now I was fighting with the guy with the rifle. We both had our hands on the gun, with the barrel in one hand and the stock in the other. Now we were facing each other across the rifle. In the meantime his partner with the pistol was circling and trying to get a shot in. Finally he shoved his pistol over the shoulder of his companion and jammed it into my throat. I released my hold on the rifle and immediately my opponent swung around and clubbed me in the head with the butt of the gun. I fell down on the ground and he hit me in the head again.

He thought I was unconscious, but I wasn't. I actually wasn't hurt very much at all. He just hadn't jabbed me in the right spot. I feigned unconsciousness, waiting about one minute and then groaned as I

Captured by the "Wang Ching-wei," puppet troops of the Japanese. After a brief fight, I was able to escape again.

turned over on my side. Through lowered lids, I could see both men were standing about ten yards away, arguing over my bag of supplies they were investigating. The whole episode must have taken no more than three minutes. As I turned over on my side, they hardly gave me a look, for they were so engrossed in the spoils they had acquired. Slowly drawing my legs up under me, I suddenly jumped to my feet, bent low, and started on a zigzag course, running across the field.

The element of surprise was in my favor. Before they knew it, I was fifty feet away and traveling fast. After all, I thought, I would either outrun them or get a bullet. And I preferred a bullet to being recaptured. They yelled and shot, but I just kept right on running. After about a mile, I slowed down to a trot, which I kept up for about ten minutes. Finally, I ran down a narrow path through some bushes and threw myself on the ground behind a small bush and listened. I knew that nothing could be distinguished beyond twenty feet away and as I had on khaki pants and brown shoes and as my skin was tanned brown, I didn't think I would be discovered. I stayed there for about an hour.

During that hour, the night descended. In the dark, with merely starlight, I did a lot of thinking and praying. I knew I was in a tough spot and that it would take much more than mortal power to get me out. I was at the end of my escape through China. At that time, the only means of help for me was to talk to the Lord. My simple prayer went something like, "Father, I know I haven't been an example in many ways, but if you get me out of here and home again, I will try to do better in the future and I'll serve you the rest of my life." I felt as though the Lord was right there listening to me. I also said that I didn't know how anybody could ever get me out of the mess I was in. At that point, I had nothing on but a pair of marine khakis and shoes. I felt better after I had finished my prayer and, with that, I again started on my way, meaning to put as much distance as possible between my would-be captors and myself.

It wasn't long, however, until a chilling wind from the Gobi Desert started blowing from the northwest and soon I was very cold and shivering all over. At that point, my spirit was at its lowest possible level—having no food or water, wearing only shoes and pants in an unfriendly country with no immediate prospect of getting to freedom. I realized that something would have to happen soon or I would get very ill from either exposure or starvation, or I would suffer the very worst—recapture. It was not a very pleasant outlook. The wind was piercing and the colder I got, the more I realized that I was going to get ill very shortly.

I started moving in the dark again and soon I could see the outline of the next village. It was very dark, so instead of skirting the village, I walked very carefully into it. I needed clothes, a blanket, or anything I could find. In this part of China, most of the villages were surrounded by a fifteen-foot mud wall. The huts were connected to the wall and to each other. The door for each hut had no hinges, but was secured by two wooden slabs on the inside that ran across the width of the door frame in two places. And each hut had one small window about eighteen inches by two feet.

I went by each walled hut without arousing the occupants. But all my efforts were frustrated because each of the entrances had a wood door in place for the night. Leaving this village, I tried another village with the same results. In the second walled compound, however, I did disturb a pig that broke loose from its stall and went charging out into the village, overturning pots and buckets all over the place. The pig and I went out of the village at the same time.

A Fortunate Find

At the third village, I felt my way to a doorway that was unbarred. Standing cautiously in front of the entrance to this adobe hut, I listened for signs of occupancy. Soon I distinguished a slight snore from inside the hut. I crossed through the doorway by placing one leg inside the room, then the other. I didn't want to stay in the open doorway because my silhouette could be discerned from inside the room. I stepped back from the door opening and waited. Soon I heard the snore again; it was deep and regular. I could tell it was coming from about six feet away. I moved very cautiously, a few inches at a time, and soon I knew I was next to the bed and the snorer was right under me. I lowered my head sideways until it was about six inches above his. My heart was beating like a drum. The room was dark and quiet except for the man's breathing. Everything seemed suspended.

Again I remembered what I read on the POW train while traveling from Nanking: "The best way to overcome fear is by direct action." If I had stopped to think about what might have happened, I would never have attempted to escape in the first place. At heart, I am no braver than anybody else. In fact, in most instances when it comes to taking the initial step in any dangerous venture, my heart beats so fast and hard that I can feel it up in my head.

Extending my hand out, I brought it gently down above his chest until I could feel what I thought was a blanket beneath my fingers. Gingerly feeling my way along the top of these covers, I finally brought them to rest on the edge of his bed. Gently lifting the edge of his cover, I began to pull it off him. It was a good thing he was a sound sleeper and snored or I never could have managed the job. Every time he hesitated with his snore, I had to stop and wait for it to start again. Finally my arm grew so tired that I just threw caution to the wind and took a firm hold on the bed covers, gave a great big tug, and took off out through the doorway. In a second I was in high gear running away from the village compound.

Within about fifteen minutes I stopped and discovered that it wasn't a blanket after all, but a large Mandarin coat with two shirts inside, one white and one black. I slipped the shirts and coat on and then kept up a steady trot. To this day I'll bet that that Chinese farmer wonders what happened that night years ago, thinking what a fool he was for not barring the door in the frame.

After about an hour and a half of trotting and walking, I slowed down and stopped. By this time I was dead tired and figured it must have been about two in the morning. I went off the narrow trail about fifty yards into a wheat field, pulled up some wheat, and made a soft place to lie down. I was asleep within minutes, but not before thanking the Lord for watching over me. I realized that I never could have made it so far without His help.

I slept until it started to get light. Standing up, I could better see what I had taken from the Chinese farmer the night before: one long padded Mandarin coat, a short jacket, and a shirt. Evidently, at the end of the day the man just took off all his clothes at once and threw them over himself and went to sleep. There were no buttons, but rather the Chinese-style cloth hooks. I had a great surprise when I looked in the pocket of the shirt and found a roll of money that amounted to $1,665 in Central Reserve Bank of China currency, commonly know in China as CRB.

That night after the scuffle with the Wan Ching Wei, I entered a Chinese village and stole a blanket, which later turned out to be a long Mandarin coat with two shirts. Stuffed in one of the shirt pockets was sixteen hundred dollars in Chinese currency.

Continuing on my journey west, I traveled well into the morning of the 14th. I couldn't stop thinking about what had happened in the past forty-eight hours. I went from being practically naked to having a nice wardrobe that was warm and fit me very well, considering the circumstances. I realized that in a way I was better off than before my encounter with the soldiers the day before. I looked like a Chinese peasant, only lacking a hat and Chinese facial features. At the first place I stopped for water I was able to beg a little food and a walking stick. The weather warmed up so I rolled up my coat and tied it after a fashion. Running my stick through the coat, I slung it over my shoulder in the manner of an American tramp.

It was about eleven in the morning when I passed the edge of a village and noticed several men talking together. One of the men yelled for me to stop. Pretending not to hear, I jumped into a ditch in front of the village. After stooping and running along this ditch for a short distance, I stopped, turned around, and peeked over the top to see if I was being followed. Sure enough, I was. And not by just one, but by at least a half a dozen men. They had spread out around me, and I knew escape was impossible in my weakened condition. I later discovered that this ditch was about six feet deep and five feet wide and was actually a moat that ran around the village, so there was no escaping, especially not in broad daylight.

Chapter Seventeen

THE KINDNESS OF THE
COMMUNIST ARMY

Oblivious of the fact that I was headed in a circle around the village, however, I continued running down the moat until suddenly a soldier appeared above me holding a grenade. He motioned me to come out of the ditch then searched me for weapons. Finding none, he returned my clothing and marched me into a small building. There I was surrounded by at least eleven Chinese. I saw that most of them were uniformed soldiers. In about ten minutes, I was led to another small brick building one story high. A Chinese man about my own age greeted me pleasantly and asked me to please sit down. There I stayed for about three hours.

During those three hours I was given more food than I had seen in days. I took advantage of this believing there would undoubtedly be lean days ahead. In time, my charge, whose name I learned was Shia Wong, led me from the village to a little town about three miles northwest where he soon left me. At intervals over the following two hours, I was given paper and pencil to write, "I am an American, my name is William Lorin Taylor." Evidently I was being quizzed about my status. Believing they were going to turn me over to the Japanese, I gave as little information as possible.

There was such a crowd of men in the room during the interrogation that I felt like I could hardly breathe. Finally a man about my age forced his way in the room and sat down beside me. In perfect English he started talking. I told him very little until he said, "Your country and mine are friends." I questioned him regarding that statement, and he told me that I was in the hands of the Eighth Route Communist Army of New China, known as the "Paluchun" (This was my spelling of the term pronounced in Pinyin, a common variant of Standard Mandarin romanization system). When the truth of this struck home, I could control myself no longer. Throwing my arms in the air, I gave vent to a wild yell. The Chinese surrounding me all started to laugh and for a few minutes there were laughs all around. After this I told my questioner about everything I had experienced from 1941 to 1945.

He then left as suddenly as he appeared and in a few minutes I was alone. Soon a large basin of hot water was brought in and I was able to give myself a good sponge wash down. Ah, what luxury! While I was washing, a Chinese soldier brought in a clean change of clothes—specifically Chinese Army clothing. As soon as I had finished dressing, more food was brought in. This time it was fried onions and bread. My interpreter appeared and said I would leave that afternoon for Zwin Cio Meaw, a little town farther northwest. Within half an hour I left my newfound friends for a new destination, not sure what was ahead, but realizing my only choice was to follow.

Tired as I was, I was still glad to be moving again. I figured that I had traveled about seventy-five miles from where I had left the train. But now I was traveling in style. Since we would be passing through enemy territory, they gave me a horse and twenty soldiers as my bodyguards. All afternoon, evening, and night we traveled, disturbed only once by the booming of a cannon in the distance. By this time I was so tired that I almost fell off my horse. When we did stop and I was told to get down, I slid off with great discomfort, as I was plenty sore in the right spots. I was shown to a small hut and given a small blanket. There, I laid down on a wooden platform and immediately went to sleep.

We left at about ten o'clock the next morning and traveled until we reached Zwin Cio Meaw. There I was fed like a king and was given my own room and even warm water for a bath. After bathing, I immediately dressed and went to sleep. I slept soundly for many hours. I could think of nothing I appreciated more at that time than a bed and food.

The Paluchun gave me a notebook, and I decided to keep a daily journal of my activities and to record from memory the events that had transpired during the days beginning just prior to our departure from Kiangwan and finishing with my capture by the Paluchun on May 14, 1945. The following is taken (and sometimes paraphrased) from this journal.

May 16, 1945

Upon awakening, I found myself with a terrific appetite and a Chinese boy name Li. This boy stayed with me until I arrived at Bai Tung on the 26th. He accommodated my every need, washing clothes, bringing my food on a tray, and bargaining with the candy vendor for me. He was about sixteen years old, a soldier of New China.

I became very fond of this lad, and treated him more as a friend than a servant. He appreciated this and did everything he could to make me comfortable. When he first came with me, he had tried to get away with as much as he could, taking my soap, slipping away when I needed water, and doing other little annoying things. On the third day I pretended that I was mad at him and told him in my best Chinese (which was terrible) that I thought he was a thief, a liar, a scamp, and generally, no good. I ended by cussing him out in both Chinese and Japanese. I told him that I had lived too long with the Japanese to not know all the tricks of the trade. At first he tried denying my charges, but when he saw I was serious, he came around to my way of thinking and from that time on, we had no further difficulties.

Upon awakening this morning, Sia Li brought me water to bathe my swollen foot and a tray of food consisting of partly fried meat and fried eggs. He also brought a beverage made from crushed corn meal.

It was tasteless, but good. I was also given cornmeal bread and wheat bread. These people gave me the best in town. It was much better than ordinary Chinese food, and I was given all I could eat.

May 18, 1945—My Birthday

I stayed in this town until the morning of May 18th, when the whole group I was with moved to the town of Hai Li, ten kilometers away. This was my 28th birthday. I awoke with a slight cold. Mr. Yen Po,

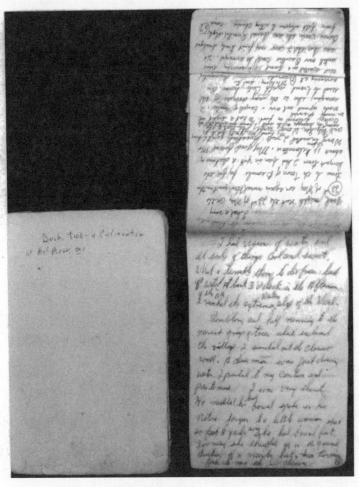

Journals kept by Bill Taylor from May through June, 1945. After his capture by the Chinese Communists, Bill was given writing material with which to record journal entries of his travels with the Communist army through China.

the gentleman in charge of the headquarters of the Eighth Communist Army, came to see me and gave me permission to write to my mother, grandfather, and girlfriend. That night in company of Mr. Shew, I heard the first United States broadcast since 1942. It was a grand thing and hearing the announcer say, "This is the United States of America" gave me a wonderful feeling.

The next day Mr. Yen Po told me that Brigadier General Wong would be back on May 30th, following the which he believed I would be transferred to Megan. At Hai Li, I was given a room next to a farmhouse. Sia Li's bed, which was nothing more than a straw mat on some rough planking, was just outside my door. That night I got no rest thanks to an attack of fleas and bed bugs. Examining myself the next morning, I found that they had eaten me such that I looked like I had the measles. One of my legs had more than 250 bites and my waist looked like one big red welt. Oh, what fun it was! When Sia Li saw what had happened, he laughed so hard tears came to his eyes. But I knew he really felt badly about it because later on the day, he cleaned the room and bed, took all the rugs and mats out, beat them, and then left them to air in the sun. I slept the next night, but only because I was so tired. When I awoke the next morning with additional bites, Sia Li decided to exchange beds with me. His bed having no fleas and my bed being larger, we were both satisfied with our trade. And I had a very good night's rest.

May 23, 1945

On the 23rd of May, we moved headquarters to Bianshi, a town about ten kilometers away. It was by far the largest town I had been in yet. Mr. Wong Shien insisted I ride horseback with Brigadier General Wong and his wife. The rest of the camp followed on foot. My friend, Mr. Yen Po, had to go away on business, so he said. I found out later that he was newly married and had probably just returned to his wife.

What a sight we were—spread out across a couple of miles. I imagine this is the way armies of old used to travel with carts, horses, and women. Upon arriving at Bianshi, General Wong and I dismounted and waited in a local merchandising house until our quarters could be arranged.

It was there that I saw my first truly beautiful Chinese woman. I saw her from across the street. She was dressed in the traditional Asian style from her felt slippers to her tiny Chinese coat. Her hair was in the typical style with a black fringe of bang in front. What impressed me most, however, were her beautiful eyes. They were the largest almond-shaped eyes I had ever seen, almost like a Eurasian's. I stared at her so long that for a few minutes I didn't notice the snickers and laughter going on around me. After that one good look at her, though, I never saw her again.

My quarters in Bianshi were the best yet. Sia Li and I occupied a small brick building. It was about fifteen feet by thirty feet and seventeen feet high with a peaked roof. Late that night, Brigadier General Wong arrived and informed us that the Paluchun were engaging the Japanese in the north. The Chinese Communist soldiers didn't have much, but what they did have they used in the best way they knew how. They had no money except what they printed. They held their own quite well against the Japanese with their outdated machinery and guns. The Japanese often took their supplies and used them against them. The Chinese then waged war against the Japanese to get more guns and ammunition to fight bigger and better battles. It became one continual round of conflict progressing until one side became victorious. Having seen both the Chinese and Japanese in action, I will say that both are brave. The Japanese had the equipment while the Chinese had very little. But I think the Chinese soldier was better at using his head. I believe the Chinese soldier would have given an excellent account of himself every time, especially if it were in China.

Chapter Eighteen

REST, JOURNAL, AND A JOURNEY

O n the 24th of May, I again met Brigadier General Wong at his temporary house in Bianshi. He was thirty-two years old and a big man for a Chinese. He received me kindly and told me that within four or five days I would start home by way of Li Shi. That evening, my friend Mr. Wong Shien, the paymaster, gave me one hundred dollars in the currency of the Bank of West Shantung. I then accompanied Mr. Wong Shien and Mr. Shew into their village where we listened to United States radio over the headphones. On my way home I bought some peanuts and joined Mr. Wong Shien and Mr. Sen Shi Hun in a gluttony feast. I was in bed by about ten o'clock that night.

May 25, 1945

I arose the morning of the 25th, brushed my teeth, washed, and ate breakfast. I worked all day on my journal, taking time out for yasumi three or four hours in the afternoon. That evening, Mr. Wong Shien, the paymaster, came to announce that my presence was requested by General Wong. I had just cleaned up, dressing in clean homespun clothes provided by the Communist Army. The clothes looked rough, but were quite comfortable once I got used to them.

Upon entering General Wong's house I was cordially greeted by the general himself. To my surprise, in the center of the room was a table set in American style with Chinese plates, European cut glasses, and many things I had not seen for almost four years. General Wong introduced me to two colonels and motioned for me to be seated. Besides the knives, forks, and spoons, which were on the table in profusion, there were chopsticks. I had learned to use chopsticks way back in 1942, so I felt right at home here. There were five of us at the table: General Wong, Mr. Wong Shien, the two colonels, and myself.

The dinner began. First they served Japanese Asaki beer, which is supposed to be very good. I had made a resolution, however, not to touch alcohol again, so I didn't taste it. After the beer, servants started bringing in the food. I had heard of Asian feasts, but never expected to sit down to one. There was every kind of meat and fowl in that feast: duck, pigeon, chicken, lamb, goat, pig, beef, and some whose English names I didn't know. We were also served *sho bai tai,* a Chinese spinach; *patoolou,* finely cut meats; *cow row pian,* which tasted something like veal; and *gi dung tung,* a soup with pieces of eggs, greens, and finely cut pieces of meat. There were two plates of bread and many other delicious things, of which I have forgotten the names. For dessert we had sweet cakes and syrup. There were many different kinds of cakes; *gi din gow,* a cake fried up with eggs; *giden beng;* and others, all served with generous portions of syrup and eaten like hot cakes. Along with this feast was served quantities of Chinese tea. All throughout the meal there was a great smacking of lips and sucking in of breath, which was the Chinese way of showing appreciation for good food. They surely enjoyed their food.

They don't have our standard of etiquette, but having experienced both styles, I believe I like the Chinese way of eating as much as I like ours. When you dine out in China, you go to enjoy an excellent meal with little thought about the latest rules of etiquette and without fearing that if you make the slightest mistake, your hostess will lift her eyebrow and for the balance of the meal make you feel like a criminal. A person should be able to enjoy his food.

After dinner I told General Wong that I hadn't enjoyed anything as much as I had this meal in years. He replied that the meal was very poor and that the Chinese were also poor. This man was charming and made you feel right at home. I enjoyed myself thoroughly. Returning to my place of abode, I was met by Mr. Yen Po who stayed up with me until about eleven o'clock that night talking about books, authors, playwrights, and artists of all nationalities.

On the morning of the 26th, I arose feeling wonderful. I did nothing all day but eat and sleep. What I wanted most at that time was a good book to read. In the early evening, the entire camp was moved to Bai Tung Tsi, a small town about five miles west. My new home was in a Chinese farmhouse in very cramped quarters.

The next morning, I was moved to very good quarters in another farmhouse at Mr. Wong Shien's place. I had a new boy now, Ho Gung Qui. Mr. Wong Shien, the paymaster, had decided to change Ho Gung Qui for Sia Li as he thought that Sia Li wasn't giving me the right kind of service. I found out how true this was when young Qui came to handle my affairs. That boy was always doing something for me, from morning until night. He had food and good Chinese tea at my elbow all day long. It was true Chinese hospitality. I consumed at least a gallon of tea every day. He jumped at my slightest wish and spoiled me in every way.

May 28, 1945

On the evening of May 28th, Mr. Wong Shien came to my house to invite me to take a walk with him. Accepting his invitation, I joined him as we strolled from my place of residence to the edge of Bai tung tsi and out through the golden fields which stretched as far as the eye could see, interrupted only by groups of swaying trees that sheltered other villages. It was a most beautiful view.

The Chinese farmers were just finishing their work for the day, bringing in their oxen for the night. They moved slowly down the narrow paths, little puffs of dust rising with each step. In the distance one could hear the lowing of cows and the braying of goats. Taking our time, we walked around the town of Bai tung tsi talking about the future of China and problems confronting her. When we reached the extreme southern edge of town, the sun was just going to bed. We paused to witness this spectacle and it seemed as if all of China were watching and holding its breath. I have never seen a more beautiful sunset; it was a huge blood red ball of fire slipping silently over the distant horizon. As it sank lower and lower, it changed the color of the white clouds in the sky from white to orange and later to a brilliant red and then fading into a deep purple. Finally the sun slipped out of sight and twilight came stealing in. In a few minutes all of China had retired for the evening. The sight we had just witnessed would not soon be forgotten. Having little else to say, Mr. Wong and I retired too.

While I had been away, my boy, Ho Gung Qui, had taken out all my bedding and brought in another bed. He had put a fresh reed mattress on it, made the other bed, and had a hot pot of tea waiting for me. I sat up for about an hour just sipping this excellent tea and watching the moon rise higher and higher in the heavens, thinking about what a wonderful thing it would be to go home again and daydreaming of all the things I most wanted to do.

While I was cogitating on those various things, I couldn't help but think of the marvelous blessings I had experienced up until the present time. In my heart I knew it wasn't just luck. To many people this would sound strange, but I had been in and gotten out of too many tight spots recently to doubt the existence of a Supreme Being. I honestly feel I had been given help from the moment the battle of Wake Island began back in 1941. I cannot deny that I had received an answer to the prayers I offered when I was a prisoner on Wake Island.

It was on Wake Island that I made a commitment to the Lord to serve him the rest of my life, through thick and thin. And now

I couldn't help but realize that what I had survived and what I was going through was just part of my resolution to serve Him forever. There was no vocal voice talking to me during the events that followed my escape from the train, but there was a constant feeling that I was being helped. When I needed to make decisions that were important, the impressions came very strongly. I know that divine guidance influenced me. Without this assistance, I would have never arrived at this point.

That night in the square in front of my quarters, Chinese boys and girls sang the songs of New China. The composition of these new songs has none of the characteristics of the old Chinese classics. The music was very beautiful and helped me to pass the evening.

May 29, 1945

The next morning, Ho Gung Qui told me I was to have breakfast with Colonel Chew. Hurrying through my toilet chores, I was soon at his home, where I had everything to eat I could want. It was here that I was introduced to a Korean by the name of Huang Jhong Yong, a very interesting man about the same age as myself. He had escaped from the Japanese Army at Soochow while en route from Harbin, Manchuria to Shanghai, China. Prior to his escape, he had been an interpreter in the Japanese Army. From 1942 to 1944, Huang Jhong Yong or Nickolai, which was his Russian name, worked in Shanghai. While he was in that area, he acted as the interpreter for the first party to make a break from our camp at Kiangwan. The escapees were later apprehended and brought back to Shanghai for a heavy jail sentence. Colonel Chew, through Nickolai, who understood Korean, Japanese, Russian, Chinese and some English, informed me that I was to leave the next day for a six-day journey by horseback.

Finishing our breakfast, which was delicious, we returned to our separate quarters. Within about an hour, Colonel Chew came to my place, informing us that we were to leave for Lia Shi immediately. This I found to be the Chinese way of giving you plenty of time to get ready. Grabbing my clothes, I hurriedly placed them in a pile. Then a boy came in and gathered everything up, and in about five minutes I was on my way. In front of the main brick building was a brown horse, which was to be mine for the journey north. Soon three soldiers came up the street leading four horses. Shortly afterward, Nickolai appeared. Colonel Chew shook my hand heartily, and told me he was very sorry General Wong and Mr. Wong Shien could not come as they had been called away on business. He apologized in general for the lack of certain refinements that the Chinese in the vicinity did not have due to war conditions. Leading our horses to the edge of town, we mounted and were soon on our way north, traveling until about nine o'clock that night. Boy, was I sore. I was given a place to sleep and informed that there were Japanese nearby, so we were to be very quiet. They also told me that early the next morning we would cross over a Japanese-controlled road. Everyone was a little nervous.

We rose early the next day and began our journey, crossing the road by eight o'clock. Followed by about ten soldiers on foot, I rode my brown horse until late in the evening. It was on this day at about noon that I saw my first "Chinese Indian." I noticed his hairstyle with two braids and was immediately struck by the remarkable resemblance to the American Indian. For the "Chinese Indian," the hair from the ears forward is shaved off and a band about five inches wide from ear to ear is allowed to grow. This hair, as it grows, is braided down each side of the head, similar to the American Indian. Stripped to the waist and with sweat running down his brown face, this Chinese Indian works in the field. Noticing his high cheekbones and hard lean well-developed body, I was struck by the similarity between the Indians from two separate continents. For the rest of the day, we saw Chinese Indians in increasing numbers.

We stopped that night at a Chinese village close to another road we were to cross the next night. This road would also be dangerous and we were told that we would have to move quickly and quietly.

Chapter Nineteen

A GOBI DESERT DUST STORM, ENEMY DOMAIN, AND TRAVEL PARTIES

That next day, May 31ˢᵗ, was hot, dry, and dusty. All that day Chinese boys and men came and went quietly from our room, so there was little opportunity to rest. When we left early that evening, it was a most welcome delivery from our curious onlookers. We traveled west until about seven thirty that evening when we came to another village. Here, in the company of Huang Jhong Yong (the Korean interpreter) and the Communist head of the village, we rested and enjoyed the evening while eating noodles and scrambled eggs and drinking scented tea. At about nine o'clock we were on our way again, continuing west. We had been joined with about thirty-five foot soldiers, so with the three of our own, Huang, and myself, we were a party of nearly forty. I also learned that a small group of soldiers had gone ahead to scout out the section of another road we were to cross. It seemed that the Japanese were very much in need of this road and would stop anyone who crossed it or tampered with it in any way.

As we neared the road crossing I could feel the tension everyone was under, even the horses seemed to feel it. Suddenly the road was in front of us. It was very quiet and there was no wind. We crossed the road quietly and moved on west. We paused several times, crouching low on a path of a ditch to see if we could distinguish anything silhouetted against the sky. The night was dark; our horses and clothes blended in with the ground. We had a hard time seeing beyond thirty feet in front us. We paused often, beginning again on a silent signal.

After we had crossed the Japanese-controlled road, we traveled about a mile when suddenly I noticed a huge cloud coming down from the northwest, blotting out the only light we had, which was starlight. I expected a rainstorm, not being familiar with this part of the country. Suddenly a cool blast of air struck us. The cloud was right above us, threatening to envelop us any minute. A few seconds later I learned that the ominous cloud was not a rainstorm but rather a huge Gobi Desert dust storm.

We stopped and waited a few minutes for the storm to quiet down. The minutes turned into hours. This Gobi dust storm was in control of us and we just had to wait until the storm made up its mind what to do with us. We were then in a gully that was about ten feet wide and eight to ten feet deep. The soldiers accompanying us were all crouched over with their heads between their knees. Those of us riding horses got out of our saddles and waited. The wind was blowing so hard it was impossible to see. I had slid off my horse and moved under its belly. My horse didn't even move an inch while I was under it. The dirt had gotten so blinding and the darkness so dense that it was an effort even to breathe. I can't explain how overwhelmed I was or the feeling of despair that came over me as the wind blew unceasingly. I felt an affinity to the horse I was riding; we both were in a situation we couldn't control. I prayed, knowing the only way we were going to survive was with help from above.

As the hours went by, all we could do was wait. Finally, after more than five hours, the wind died down enough for us to be on our way again. I imagine by this time it was about two or three in the morning. We continued to move west as fast as we could against strong winds, for we were still in Japanese-controlled territory. We stopped several times and I was getting a strange feeling that we were lost.

There was a Kuomintang (Nationalist Party of China) general traveling with us who spoke a little English. After we had stopped for the third time, this general moved up alongside me in his horse and told me, "We are lost, and they have decided if we don't find our way within the next hour they will leave us and maybe even kill us." I replied, "I don't think these people are going to leave us or kill us."

Soon we were on our way again. I couldn't keep my eyes open as they were already smarting and full of dust. I didn't dare rub them for fear of losing my eyesight. Grabbing the horse's tail in front of me and leading my horse by the bridle, I closed my eyes and stumbled blindly on. We stopped to rest about every twenty minutes. How our guides knew where we were going was beyond me. After two hours of this I didn't care. I had no choice; my life was in their hands. All I wanted to do was get away from this suffocating dust. By this time my hair, eyes, ears, and throat were full of dust. My mouth was caked with dust, and my clothes and shoes were full of dust. But we couldn't stop because to stop meant to be apprehended in the morning by the Japanese and that would mean a running fight for us.

June 1, 1945

At about four-thirty in the morning on the first of June, just as it was getting light, one of the Chinese Paluchun officers yelled, "There it is!" He was pointing to a small village that was near a railroad track the Japanese controlled. The dust was still blowing and how on earth the guides found this village was unknown to me.

We hurried to the village military barracks and our officer knocked on the door. Soon someone opened the door for us. They also opened a larger door to accommodate the horses. I soon learned that this was a village that had to support the Japanese. Our arrival had been expected. I was in the enemy domain, only this time the enemy was friendly. Or were they? I could hardly believe what was going on. For some reason, *these* Wang Ching-wei (followers of the Japanese puppet government) were friendly to all of us. How could this have happened? My guess is that it stemmed from a basic Chinese hatred of the Japanese.

We rested here in the barracks until about five o'clock that afternoon. The dust storm had calmed down considerably, but visibility was still not good past two hundred yards. While staying in this village I learned that three days prior to our coming, a different group of Wang Ching-wei troops (not the ones that befriended us) had been to this village and had stolen everything the people had. Each of us were given noodles, three eggs, and tea. We left this little village at about eight o'clock that evening and traveled until one o'clock the following morning, which was then June 2nd.

We wanted to stop overnight at one village, but couldn't as the Japanese had just been there the day before. Coming to another small village, we bedded down for the night. When I say bedded down, I mean horses, men, and almost everything together. I didn't sleep much that night thanks to a headache I had developed from the dust, fleas, bugs, and vermin of every sort, which were infesting the place where we stayed.

That next morning we were up and on our way by seven o'clock. We made good time on this day and crossed the Yellow River about three o'clock in the afternoon. We then arrived at a larger village where we were given accommodations. I rested a few hours and ate a delightful meal. The weather was so calm and even though I was somewhat tired from the previous day's activities, I decided to take a walk out into a huge wheat field that ran right next to our village.

I headed out into the field, marveling at how calm it was as I walked. Entranced by the beauty of the countryside, I must have walked for about half an hour. A few white cumulus clouds were almost stationary in the blue sky above. I was so relaxed that I didn't think about how dangerous it could get.

As I was walking, my thoughts drifted back over the past three and a half years and I was amazed and humbled to realize how fortunate I was to be alive. Musing on these thoughts, I stopped and decided to kneel and give thanks to my Heavenly Father. I really poured out my heart to my older brother, Jesus Christ, recognizing the many, many blessings I had received during the war, prison camp, and the miraculous events since my escape from the Japanese. As I was praying, I felt as if there was somebody, the Spirit probably, nearby. It was a marvelous feeling.

When I finished, I looked up at the sky and realized that I had better get back to the village as quickly as possible while it was still light. I hurried through the grain field to the village and just as I got near, a young Chinese soldier who was the sentry on duty, screamed at me to stop. As I looked at him I could see that he was very young and very nervous. As he continued to yell at me, I noticed that his finger was on the trigger of his rifle. We were about fifteen feet from each other. I raised my hands in the air and said nothing. The soldier was getting more excited, but I didn't know what to do and was afraid to say anything because of my limited Chinese vocabulary.

Suddenly a Paluchun (Communist) officer appeared and yelled at the sentry to put his rifle down. As soon as the sentry saw the officer, he relaxed. The officer apologized to me and it was all over. When this confrontation was over, I realized that in the future I would have to be very careful. There would definitely not be anymore long walks in the wheat fields alone!

When it was time to retire, I decided to avoid my bed because of the vermin. So after shaking the blankets thoroughly, I slept in the open-air courtyard—and very well. But my stomach was still sore and upset because of bad water, changes in diet, and the consistent jogging of the horse.

The next day, June 3rd, we reached Chi Luey in the panhandle of Hupeh Province where the headquarters of the Chinese Communists was located. I was given a clean dry room for myself, my Ko-

rean friend Huang Jhong Yon having departed with other Korean
men who were there under the same circumstances. That day I met
Captain Shen Yiepang, who was summoned from a nearby village,
where he was studying, to come to Chi Luey and be my interpreter.
This gentleman was educated in Singapore and had joined the Paluchun in 1938.

Later in the day I was introduced to Mr. Chung Hah Ryce, a
Korean who had escaped from the Japanese Army in 1944. He was
in charge of Korean propaganda directed at the Japanese. Ryce told
me that conditions in Korea were very bad and had been that way
since the Japanese occupation first started. "Always," he said, "the
'Japs' have kept a large standing army in Korea of over a quarter
million men. When the Japanese went into Korea many years ago,
they stripped the people of everything they possessed that was of
any material value. They then took all the young men away and
put them into service throughout the various parts of the Japanese
Empire and on the islands of Japan. They were forced to work in
the factories of the Japanese. There was no loyalty by the Koreans
to the 'Japs.' The Koreans were beaten, starved, raped, and killed
by them," he said. "My comrades are now fighting the Japanese on
many fronts and are awaiting the day when they will be liberated
and allowed to return to a country under Korean jurisdiction." Mr.
Nikolai Hwong, another Korean acquaintance, told me from his experiences in the Shanghai Gendarme, that the Japanese treated the
Koreans in Japan as they would war prisoners. He told me, "These
men are put with war prisoners in shipyards, factories, or some other military objective. A large barbed wire and electric fence runs
around the area and here they eat, sleep, and live. Japanese troops
guard them in case of unrest during an air raid. In case of trouble
or an uprising of any kind, machine guns soon put a stop to it. Not
a great position to be in, is it?" concluded Mr. Hwong.

On June 4th I had everything washed and took a nice sponge bath.
Oh, how good it was to feel clean again. On June 5th I just slept and

yasumied all day long. That night, in company of Mr. Wong, Captain Shen, and Mr. Ryce, I went to dinner at Brigadier General Chew's home. There I met General Chew's wife, a charming Chinese woman. They extended their hospitality to us and we ate a dinner that was sumptuous and delicious in every aspect. Mrs. Chew presented her little boy, a beautiful lad with large brown eyes. As products of New China, these people are very happy. General Chew graduated from Canton University, and Mrs. Chew graduated from Stephens School for Girls in Hong Kong. After dinner, we congratulated them on the meal and the manner in which it was served. After leaving, we walked for a short time around the town and then back to our various abodes. I moved my bed out under the stars, shook the blankets again, and slept very well through the night.

On the 6th of June I was up at the break of dawn. It was cool but not cold. I worked all that day making another journal for myself. That evening I dined with Mr. Wong Sen and Captain Shen. The next morning Ho Gung Qui brought me some fresh cow's milk, the first I had tasted since 1941. Later he brought scrambled eggs, meat, and various Chinese sauces. For lunch, I had a cold cucumber salad and sliced apricots and pears. That evening a nice Chinese dinner was followed by a walk in the country with Captain Shen and Mr. Ryce. Before I retired for the night, the boy brought water and washed my feet.

On the 8th of June I was told I was going to leave very soon, within two or three days. On this day, Colonel Wong gave me about two pounds of chocolate, which must have cost a fortune. The food we ate on this day was delicious; there was every kind of meat one could want. I was very spoiled, having my every wish carried out. These people were treating me like a visiting potentate.

June 9, 1945

On the 9th of June I received new clothes, a Paluchun officer's uniform. It was quite a treat to wear clean clothes every day. Mr. Ryce came over and we had quite a discussion concerning the future of

China. A graduate of the Imperial Japanese University in Korea, Mr. Ryce majored in economics and spoke Korean, Chinese, Japanese, German, and fairly good English. Ryce told me that after the war was over, American goods and machinery would be imported to China and the Orient. He said the Chinese would learn about the modern methods of farming and all kinds of factory production. He said it would take a space of many years, but in the end, about eight out of ten men and women of the tremendous population of China would be working in the factories and in the large cities of China. He maintained that this could be done and would be done after the war. I contended that the population of China was too great. If modern machinery were brought into the country, China would be in a state of chaos. People everywhere would be out of work. I told him that even if this was introduced into China over a period of years, I believed the population of China too large to be assimilated into the factory and modern life. The production would be too vast for consumption and, in the end, there would be unemployment and starvation. I said, "If the population of China was two hundred and fifty million, then it might be accomplished. But most likely during the short period of time that China was being modernized, the population would expand tremendously. As things stand now in this country, the peasants from the farming areas know nothing about the outside world. They have no knowledge of books and they can't read or write. There is no sanitation and the children run about the villages naked until they are about two or three years of age." At that point I thought about what a humorous sight it was to see a young Chinese boy gathering herbs out in the field with nothing on but a pair of shiats (cloth slippers) and a straw hat to keep the sunrays off. Eventually, our conversation ended with neither of us convincing the other of his views, but it was interesting dialogue.

On Sunday morning, the 10th of June, I had breakfast with General Chew Quong, Mrs. Chew, Colonel Wong, and Captain Shen. We ate Northern China's rice, which is of a smaller grain than the South and Central China rice. The meal also contained several varieties of salads, bread, meats, and sweet sauces, which were served to us in a charming manner by Chinese boys. After the meal, General Chew Quong gave me an autographed one hundred dollar bill made out to the Bank of West Shantung. We, the five us and Mrs. Chew's little boy, then went outside to pose for the local village photographers. I have never seen a prettier little boy than the Chew's child.

General Chew told me that I would leave early the next morning and take a secret route to the mountain Tai Hung Shan. Thanking him and Mrs. Chew for their kind hospitality and waving aside their apologies, I shook hands with General Chew. In the company of Captain Shen, I returned to my little mud house.

June 11, 1945

The next morning we left for Mt. Tai Hung Shan. We did not take the regular route that large parties would travel over a twelve-day period. Instead, we went by horseback on a route used only when fast communication between the two military cities was needed. I learned later the Chinese General accompanying me was a Kuomintang General and was being sent to Yhang Wann as soon as they, the government, could get him there.

We traveled straight west the whole day, stopping that night at a village called Hapto, which was on the borders of the provinces of Hopeh and Honan. Every building there had been destroyed by the Japanese during their raids in 1941, 1942, 1943, and 1944, at which time they had slaughtered over two thousand men, women, and children. The Japanese ravaged the country, destroying crops, men, and beasts. They had nothing left to sell but noodles. Captain Shen had prepared for this, however, by bringing two containers of fried beef and noodles. Not bad at all. That night we all slept out under the stars.

We left at dawn the next day and didn't stop until we reached a village about midday. There we were told we would have to stay for about two days until the underground ahead was notified we were coming. The name of this village was Yong Hai Khew and was right on the edge of Japanese-controlled country. We were welcomed by Mr. Wah, the head of the village, and by a small force of Paluchun. Mr. Wah gave us the best rooms in the village and Captain Shen gave orders for our care. What a thoughtful man Captain Shen was. I don't know how I would have managed at this time if it hadn't been for him. After a delicious meal that evening, General Chang came over and we had a very interesting talk. He spoke broken English and excellent Japanese and I spoke broken Japanese, so between the two languages, we made out fairly well. His story was quite interesting and helped pass the time away. General Chang had been a general in the Kuomintang. I learned later that in March of 1945, he had escaped to the Communist party headquarters in Shantung Province.

That night Captain Shen and I slept on the roof a large brick building. On the 13th of June, we relaxed all day, except for the time I spent washing my clothes. (This was usually done for me by my servant boy, but since I had nothing else to do, I washed them myself.)

My left foot, the one I had injured jumping from the POW train in May, was giving me trouble. The swelling had gone down some but it still was painful, especially after walking a long time. For this reason I was already dreading that stretch of one hundred li (Chinese miles, equal to a third of an American mile), which we had to make between sunset and dawn. Captain Yong said the route had to be kept secret so we could only bring two soldier guards and three horses. We were told it would be difficult to take more horses, as a horse is liable to whinny, snort, blow its nose, or shy away at something. My Chinese companion-to-be was considerably older than me, so it would be my lot to walk. The benefit of this was that now I would have complete freedom of movement. While walking, I would not be leading a horse or carrying anything except my journals and two thousand dollars in the Bank of Shantung currency.

That evening Captain Shen and I went over and had dinner in

a beautiful place in the village. Captain Yong, who was in charge of the Paluchun force here, Mr. Wah, and two other Chinese gentlemen joined us. This dinner was the best food I had eaten yet in China. I was first served wine (which I did not drink), then salads of different types, followed by fourteen courses of meat fixed in various ways, and ten different dishes of eggs. Large steamed rolls were served with many different sauces and other foods I can't even remember. The dinner was served in a little courtyard just before sunset and lasted about two hours. After we had finished, the Chinese boys who had served us brought in damp towels for our hands and faces and a cup of cold water to rinse our mouths. This custom of wiping and rinsing was followed religiously at their meals. As the men then lit their cigarettes, Mr. Wah informed us that we would be leaving the next night. He said that we would stop midway and rest for about four hours. I personally wanted to push on through, but Mr. Wah said that he didn't think we could walk the one hundred li between sunset and dawn. Well, here's hoping we make it. At about ten o'clock that evening the gentlemen left and Captain Shen and I retired to the roof, our beds having been laid down for us by our boys.

June 14, 1945

All the next day we just waited for night to come. At about four o'clock that evening, Mr. Yong brought in twenty young girls and boys and their primary school teacher. We had a pleasant time singing songs. At first the girls were bashful and shy, but after a few songs, a feeling of congeniality permeated the group. The songs they sang were not the old Chinese classical songs, but songs of New China. Some were very good, almost like our own popular music, but with that intangible oriental air. Around six o'clock, Mr. Wah came to our house and said we were to leave immediately for the Tai Hung Shan. He looked at our clothes to see if we had on Coolie dress. Finding we did, the rest of our baggage was taken out, put on the horses, and soon we were on our way.

Here I said farewell to Captain Shen and the others. Captain Shen had only accompanied us this far because no one else could speak English, a Chinese courtesy on the part of General Chew. In our departing party there was General Chang and his servant, two soldiers in Coolie dress, myself, and the horses carrying our baggage.

Traveling west on fairly smooth terrain, we watched the sun go down in a fiery red ball. In about an hour we came to a small gully. It was here we were met by two more Coolie soldiers, three Chinese traveling to Tai Hung Shan, and two donkeys. The men changed from Coolie dress to the Wang Ching-wei Nanking government soldiers' uniforms. The Nanking government, Wang Ching-wei, was the puppet government set up by the Japanese in China. At the time, I became more fearful for the outcome of our venture as we now had ten men in our party, two mules, and two horses. We moved as fast as we could. Soon it was completely dark, the only light coming from the stars and the new moon. We did not hesitate once before we came to the Wei River, which we followed in a westerly direction until we came to a village. Here the guards cautioned us to be quiet. Getting down from our mounts, we waited in the dark for a few minutes while one of our soldiers went ahead.

At this time the moon was just going down over the horizon. One couldn't hear anything except the gentle bubbling of the river, the rustling of the trees, and the breathing of the horses. In about twenty minutes our guide came back and whispered, "tchuba," which means "go." Again we were on our way, this time leading our horses down the bank around trees and across ditches, while the village loomed above us to the left, dark and forbidding. As we came to a fairly level spot next to the river, we stayed and waited while one guard swam the river, about thirty yards wide. In a few minutes we could see the dark outline of a rather large boat. Finally, after much maneuvering, the soldier was able to get the boat about three feet from shore. As far as I could tell, the boat was about seven feet across from beam to beam and thirty feet long.

Taking the reins of my horse, one of the soldiers jumped on the boat and pulled on the reins while another switched the horse across the rump. After a little of this persuasion and not too much noise, the horses were on board. The second horse was a little more stubborn and would not enter the water. Switching him savagely in the rump and pulling on the reins, the soldiers finally made him jump on the boat. When the horse came down on the boat one of his hind legs went through the top deck and in getting his leg out, we made a hell of a racket. The stillness of the night was shattered, dogs in the village began barking and one of the donkeys began to bray. A fine mess! General Chang, his servant, two soldiers, and I jumped on board. Poling the boat across the river, we stopped about four feet from the opposite bank. Taking off our shoes and rolling up our pants, we slipped into the water and waded ashore. The soldiers brought the horses, which jumped off the boat, only too willing to leave it. The strap that went around the horse's stomach and held my clothes broke and everything went into the river. Quickly wading out, I grabbed these garments, which were in a makeshift bag, and made my way back to shore. This time instead of fastening them around the horse's stomach, I simply let them hang on each side of the horse.

In the meantime, the soldier had gone back across the river. Someone in the village had become curious and came down to inquire what was going on. The soldier gave him some answers, then all was quiet again, except for the howling of the dogs which didn't let up right away. Then another problem arose. Getting the donkeys on board the boat was a different matter. The soldiers finally had to tie them to the side of the boat and tow them across. Reaching our side of the river, the soldiers quickly saddled the donkeys, threw the baggage on, and we were on our way. The whole proceeding must have taken better than half an hour. The soldier guards by this time were also a little apprehensive, so we changed our course many times.

After about two hours of this, our guide called the other three soldiers together for a few words. General Chang then told me that we had lost our way again. My heart sank. What would we do when daybreak comes? We would be found out by the Japanese, our identity would be discovered, and things would be bad. I knew which way to go to return to Yong Hai Khew, but I knew that there would be a small chance to escape detection. After their short talk, we changed course, this time traveling due north. We traveled this way for quite awhile, finally veering off to the northwest. Looking over my shoulder I could see that dawn was not far off. By this time we were moving as fast as we could, passing one village after another. Just as the dawn was approaching we came to a village and circled it until we came to a stone compound. A soldier rapped on the door, then ran around the side and rapped again, this time on a large door. This door was immediately opened for him and he motioned us to follow. Leading our horses through the doorway, we found ourselves in a courtyard about one hundred feet by sixty feet, surrounded by a high wall with thorn branches on top. In the dim morning light, I could see that people were sleeping outside. Along one side, for about fifty feet, ran a high one-story stone building. A lamp was lit. I was cautioned not to talk and was led into a small room at one end of the building.

The occupants of the building knew we were going to arrive and everything had been prepared for us. In a moment, they brought in hot water and I washed my face, hands, and feet. How soothing it felt. Taking off my shirt, I laid down on that hard clay bed, which to me felt as good as any mattress I had ever laid on. As one gets accustomed to sleeping this way, it's really quite comfortable. I was exhausted and soon was fast asleep.

At breakfast the next morning, I finally had a chance to look out the window and see what kind of place we were in. To my surprise, I discovered that I was again in a Nanking government (Wang Ching-wei) compound. This time, however, I wasn't frightened. I felt secure. Here I was being taken care of very well by my enemies. These were Chinese who deeply hated the Japanese. At the time there were about fifteen Chinese soldiers in the compound. I had

breakfast that morning with the commanding Wang Ching-wei officer of the garrison, who was very polite to me. Twice during the day
I heard planes bombing the railroad no more than five miles away. I
was also told there were Japanese soldiers in the area. We left after
dinner that night and were again on our way.

We traveled due west, passing many villages, this time with two
Chinese, two donkeys, and eight more horses. The place (which I
will not name for military reasons) was right in the center of a Japanese controlled area. Not a good spot for the Japanese to find us.
In a village, just before we crossed the railroad, my horse balked on
its way down the side of the ditch and I went right over his head. I
didn't get hurt, but I was very sorry that this noise had awakened the
village dogs, of which there seemed to be a hundred. Picking myself
up, I climbed back on my horse (which had been very patient with
me) and rejoined my group, who had been waiting for me. They
were not smiling this time, for we were in dangerous territory. They
wanted us to be quiet and to leave the area right then.

Traveling again, in just a matter of minutes we came to the Japanese-controlled railroad and moving as fast as our escorts could walk,
we soon had many li behind us. Most of the night we traveled, stopping
only for about ten minutes every hour. Everyone was on edge; even the
horses seemed to sense the danger of ambush by the Japanese. After
several hours we found ourselves on a slight grade that got steeper and
steeper as we climbed the rocky slopes of the Tai Hung Shan.

All of us, including myself, were beginning to get more fatigued
as the night wore on. But there was no way we could stop because the
Japanese or Wang Ching-wei could spot us when dawn arrived. There
was starlight and some moonlight, but generally it was quite dark and
whoever was leading us really had to know the trail. The torture for
all of us, including the horses, went on for a long time. It was step by
step, up, and up, and up. I wondered if it would ever stop.

Chapter Twenty

LONG JOURNEYS, SWEET
FRIENDSHIP, AND
A FLIGHT TO YENAN

After what seemed like an eternity, the sky began to lighten behind us. Without any warning and after rounding a bend in the trail, we were on top of Tai Hung Shan. Just as we arrived, the partially clouded cumulus sky behind us turned an orangey red. Then, within just a few minutes, the rays of the sun descended on all of us. For a moment we were all silent. And then smiles and laughter, coupled with an attitude of total relaxation, came over all of us. We were now quite secure from the enemy.

After a forty-minute rest, we climbed back on our horses and started moving down Tai Hung to the village far below. The trail was narrow but from there we could see where we were going. The canyon we were traveling down had pools of clear, still water in which we washed our faces and hands; the water was so cool and refreshing. The air was invigorating. It made me feel like a million dollars. Carefully descending, we came to a village about midmorning. It was quite a picturesque scene with its sturdy stone houses and fields built up the sides of the mountains. On all sides there were walls made of stone stacked one on top of another to keep the ground from caving in. Our guide seemed to know right where to go and soon we found ourselves in a large, clean stone house. After breakfast, the secretary of the Paluchun said that I was to have a room to myself. But General Chang argued that he wanted to stay with me. As I could not speak Chinese, it was rather difficult to say anything to anybody because no one spoke or understood English. When the discussion ended, I found out General Chang was to stay with me.

The room was fine, clean, and fairly large. There was only one problem, my bed was right across from General Chang's. I had a bed on a flat platform with two mats and no window. It didn't look promising. General Chang's bed was right next to the only window in the room and his mosquito net would undoubtedly shut out most of the air from reaching me. I felt a little hurt and annoyed to think that he had taken the only place by the window when, after all, the room was mine. Not only that, but in laying out the toilet articles, his servant placed all of his things on the only table in the room.

Undressing, I climbed into my mosquito net, which General Chew had given me, and tried to sleep. In about ten minutes I dozed, only to awaken a half hour later in a sweat. Not only was I perspiring, but I was being eaten alive by bed bugs. At first I tried to kill them off, but when I moved, they all disappeared. They seemed to know when I was after them. Glancing across the room, I could see General Chang sleeping peacefully. I could feel myself getting really upset. Jerking on my pants, I jumped out from under my net. General Chang's servant, who was resting on a large wooden plank, became startled. He knew I was mad, but just didn't know why. Brushing past him, I was out the door and down the short flight of stairs through the compound and into the party headquarters. This took about thirty seconds. The secretary of the party was playing a war game, similar to chess, with another soldier. Interrupting their game, I motioned for him to follow me. Hurrying back to my room, with the perplexed party head and about ten soldiers tagging along behind, we entered the room. Walking over to my bed, I pointed to the blood spots on the sheets and to the damp places where I had been perspiring. I showed him in the best way I could and told him by using a few Chinese words I knew that I was disgusted with the whole affair.

I asked him, "Why did General Chang get the only spot in the room where one could get any sleep? Look at the welts on my body from the bed bugs and the perspiration on the bed. Can you or will you do something about it?" By this time General Chang had awakened and became aware of what I was driving at and offered to have his quarters moved elsewhere. The secretary asked me if it would be all right. I replied, "Yes! Please ask him to move out of here." He didn't understand what I said, but he knew what I meant.

During the next few minutes, his sheets had been taken away and his net taken down and my sheets taken outside and thoroughly shaken. When General Chang left, my sheets and net were put on his old place. I knew the party secretary felt very bad about the whole situation, but I told him to never mind. Everything was okay. Fifteen minutes later I was asleep, only getting up for lunch and dinner. That evening, with all forgiven, General Chang and I went for a walk up the mountain, which was actually just one terraced field above another. The farmer in this part of the country makes his living from farming terraces that go up the side of the mountain. As time goes on and more people are added to the village, more land becomes necessary. To accomplish this, the farmer has to go higher up the mountain. With stones, he makes a stout wall. This requires hard labor and often takes more than a year to build, as it all has to be done by hand. After this terrace wall is built, dirt is hauled in *yo ho* baskets to the terraced area. This fertile soil is then plowed, fertilized with dry night soil, and planted.

On our way back that evening, we washed ourselves in the stream that ran along the side of the village. The water was cold, but very refreshing. Shortly after that we turned in. As I laid on my bed that night, I felt so good and as I went over my experience since the escape in May, I could hardly believe that this had happened to me and that I was still alive. For the first time since May 11th, I felt secure. The Paluchun was in complete control. There were no Japanese anywhere. I felt, at this time, that I finally was going to see Americans again. That night I slept well. I was so grateful to have made it this far. And so ended the 18th of June.

June 19, 1945—San Leung

The next day we moved to Lin Shi, a larger village about fifteen miles away. My quarters consisted of a large room and a hard clay bed, about two and a half feet from the hard caked mud floor with a reed mat and rolled up covers. Soon two officers of the Paluchun came to my door. I invited them in and they introduced themselves. They were both captains. I was a little surprised when I saw that one was an attractive Chinese woman. I welcomed them in and we talked. Soon I realized that the man could not speak any English and this was somewhat embarrassing to him. But the other captain, the woman, could speak a fair amount of English. In a few minutes, the other officer excused himself, leaving the two of us alone.

When I asked her what her name was she said, "San Leung." It was a wonderful relief to hear my own language and carry on a conversation with someone who could understand me. San Leung and I talked and laughed for over an hour. I could see that besides being attractive, she was very curious about America. I told her how wonderful America was and how wonderful it was to be free. I soon realized that she was different than most of the other Chinese I had met.

San Leung was about five feet five inches tall. Her hair was daintily trimmed, hanging even with her shoulders with some cut just above her eyes. Her skin was as smooth as silk and her brown almond shaped eyes were dark and quite large. Yes, she was attractive. After San Leung and I had talked for about an hour and a half, she said, "Would you walk with me tomorrow?" It didn't take long for me to say yes. Then she got up and said, "I'll see you in the afternoon about three." Early that evening I could hear children singing. It had been so many years since I had heard children laughing, singing, and playing together.

The next afternoon San Leung came to my room to get me. The weather was perfect. We left the village and walked about two miles, finally stopping under a large tree and resting for a while. San was very intelligent and was quite curious about America. After about an hour, we finally got up and went back to the village. Everything was quiet, except for the kids. There were a few white cumulus clouds in the sky. The sun was so comforting. The countryside was very peaceful and quiet. When we reached my room, I started to go in and she said, "Would you go again with me tomorrow?" I replied, "I would be happy to do that."

The next morning San arrived at about eleven o'clock. We then walked about three hours away from our village. The weather was pleasant and peaceful. Everyone we passed politely bowed and smiled at the two of us. After we had walked for some time, San, pointing to a group of trees off to the side of the trail about a hundred yards away, suggested, "Let's go over there, I've brought some food to eat." When we got to the trees, we were a little tired and ready to rest. We just sat down with our backs to the trunk of the tree. Neither one of us said anything for some time. Then San turned toward me, looking me in the eyes and said, "I have had a wonderful time being with you yesterday and today. It has been very special to me. I have learned so much about your America." There was a long moment of silence, then I said, "San, I will always remember your kindness to me." We sat there quietly for a few more minutes. It was so beautiful and quiet. San finally touched my arm and said, "I have something for you." She then handed me a small envelope. I opened it, reached inside, and pulled out a little slip of paper with Chinese writing on it. Glued in the corner of the paper above the Chinese characters was a photograph of San Leung.

As I looked at the photograph of San Leung, I could see that it had been trimmed in the shape of a heart. I didn't say anything for a few moments. Finally I said, "I will keep this picture forever. You have been very kind to me." We didn't talk much after that

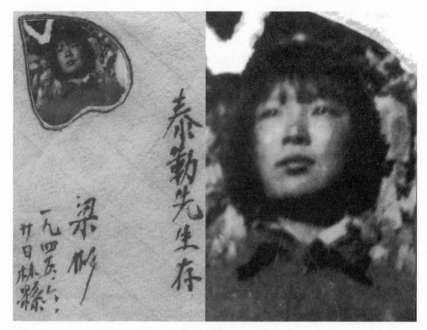

San Leung, June 20, 1945

and on the way back I thought, "What a wonderful three days I've spent with this lovely person," and I felt that we both were going to miss each other. When we finally came back to my room, we just stood looking at each other for a minute. I didn't want to go into my room and she didn't want to leave. Then she said, "Tomorrow you will leave for Lin Shiem. I have enjoyed being with you these past three days, but now I won't see you again." Then she slowly turned around and left. I watched until she walked out of my sight. San Leung was the first woman I had spent any time with for over three and a half years. Yes, I was going to miss her.

June 22, 1945

Early on the morning of the 22nd of June, I was told that we were leaving Lin Shi within an hour. It would be a long walk, about eighty li (nearly twenty-six miles), and there would be no horses. As we were leaving Lin Shi, I turned around hoping to see San Leung. There was

no one that I could see, but I felt she was looking. I will always remember Lin Shi and San Leung as my Chinese *Shangri-la* (paradise).

We walked all day in a westerly direction, even through a little
rain. Just as it was getting dark, we arrived at Lin Shiem. I was given
a room and a meal of wheat and noodles. I wolfed it down; I was so
hungry. By now my clothes had dried off, so I took off my shoes,
pulled a blanket over me, and in two minutes was sound asleep. I
rested the next day, knowing that the next day would bring an even
longer walk west. We woke early on the 24th and ate a large meal of
noodles made from wheat. I don't know what they put in those noodles, but they sure give you a lot of energy. We walked that day until
I thought I would drop. When we finally stopped in the early afternoon where I was told we would be for a few days. Again I filled up
with noodles. Even though I had eaten the same meal in the morning, I could hardly wait for my noodles in the late afternoon.

After I had eaten, I realized I was in a Paluchun Army Compound. Soon an officer walked in and told us in English, "Our national headquarters is in Yenan, which is in Shensi Province, about
350 miles from here. The Americans have an outpost there, would
you like to speak to them?" Man, I could hardly believe what I was
hearing. I immediately responded, "I would be in your debt if I
could talk to an American." He smiled and said, "Come with me."
We walked over to another building, and soon he was on the radio.
In about ten minutes he handed me the radiophone. I could hear a
voice with an American accent asking who I was. I was so excited
I could hardly speak. Finally I said, "I'm Bill Taylor, who is this?"
Then I heard a voice I would never forget, "I'm Captain James Eaton of the Army Intelligence here in Yenan, China." I then said a
dumb thing, "Are you for real?" He laughed and said, "You bet I
am. How in the hell did you get way out here in the sticks?" I just
laughed, then howled, then wept. Finally after regaining some com-
posure, I said, "I am a former prisoner of war of the Japanese. I was
captured by the 'Japs' on Wake Island back in December of 1941. I

spent the last three and a half years as a POW in Shanghai, China. When they moved us from Shanghai in May of this year, I escaped from the prison train, then got recaptured, escaped again, then was captured by the Communist Paluchun who have treated me great. They tell me we're about 350 miles East of Yenan." I paused for a few minutes and then Captain Eaton said, "This is unreal, I've got to talk to my superior, Colonel Brown. I'll call back within a couple of hours." I hung up the radiophone, sat back, and thought, "This is the first free American I have talked to in many years." About three hours later the phone rang again. The Chinese officer picked it up and handed it to me. I said, "This is Bill Taylor." Then the voice on the other end said, "I'm Colonel Brown, Bill. We're so happy you have made it this far. Are you okay?" I said, "I'm okay Colonel, I just can't believe I've made it this far. I've had a lot of help from so many wonderful people, and prayers have really helped too." Colonel Brown then said, "Your walking days are over Bill. There's an Air Strip very close to where you are. A couple of days from now, I'll send a B-25 in to pick you up. Hang in there, Bill. Day after tomorrow, you'll be with us. Congratulations, I can't wait to hear how all this happened." I responded, "I'm so grateful to you, Colonel." I then hung up, leaned back in my chair, and said to myself, "I didn't do this, I never could have done this myself," and silently thanked the Lord for all the help I had received. I hoped that the rest of the journey would go well.

The 25th of June was a day of relaxation. I went swimming, cleaned myself up, and even had a shave before I turned in for the night. On the 26th I was invited to a banquet held in my honor with a group of Chinese officers, including a General K. Yung and many colonels, majors, and other officers from the Paluchun. Where all of the delicious food came from I have no idea. During this banquet, which lasted about an hour, I answered a lot of questions and comments about POW life under the Japanese and about my capture and escape from the Wang Ching-wei.

The conversation later drifted to religion, which went on for about an hour. The general belief of the Chinese that I came across was that man was the end product of evolution and that there is no God. I listened to their discussion and didn't comment at all until I was asked directly about my belief. When I began speaking, a Chinese officer sitting next to me began to interpret. Everything gradually became quiet as I began to voice my personal beliefs. I told them, "I believe there is a God who watches over all of us. And I believe we are here to be tested to see how we will act away from him. We are all given the choice to do what is right or to do what our conscience tells us is wrong. This is called agency. Every man, rich or poor, Chinese, American, Japanese, or African, has this wonderful gift of agency, which we call conscience. We each have within our bodies a spirit that exists within us from birth to death. During this time that we live, we can reject or accept the spirit that is in us. You could be a king or a peasant working in the field, a prisoner who is forced to work, or a landlord over many—it doesn't matter who you are, everyone has a spirit in him. And when we die, our spirits do not die; they live forever. Everyone that is born here on this earth will be judged at the day of judgment, and it will be just. It won't make any difference whether we were rich or poor, but it will make a difference if we were kind or mean. Did we have love and concern for those around us? Did we use our means to sustain those less fortunate?" I spoke for about fifteen minutes and no one moved, there was a good feeling in the room.

I hadn't meant to talk so long but then they had asked and so I gave them a small concept of what I believed. I could tell that they felt the feeling of what I had said. They had asked me for my belief and I know that some wanted to hear more. The dinner finally finished and I went back to my room, in a contemplative mood. I didn't feel that I had stepped over my bounds as a guest. No, I just felt good, and so I went to sleep.

June 27, 1945—Yenan, China

On the morning of the 27th the Chinese officer who could speak English came to my room. "I have good news for you," he said, "Your American friends are coming to fly you to Yenan. They will be here in about an hour." My heart started to beat more rapidly and I was out of my room in about two minutes. There was a small truck outside with the motor running. I jumped in and we were on our way to the runway, about a mile away.

When we reached the landing strip, I jumped out of the truck, waiting to hear the motors. Soon I could hear motors and I looked up to see not one but two B-25 aircrafts. One was flying high, at about eight thousand feet. Soon one swooped out of nowhere a few hundred feet above the runway. I learned later the other B-25 was flying cover. I had never seen a B-25 bomber before and I realized that it was not a small aircraft. It was a twin motor medium bomber. I was almost overcome by the sight of the aircraft. It circled our runway and put its wheels down for a perfect landing. It slowed down at the end of the runway and as it turned to come back, its nose wheel found a hole in the runway, which was made out of clay. That stopped the B-25 dead. It just couldn't move.

I looked up to see what the other B-25 was going to do. We didn't have to wait very long for it, though. Within five minutes it had leveled off and was landing just like the first aircraft. Only this one, after landing, was able to make the turn around and taxi over to where we were. The two pilots talked to each other and soon it was decided to leave the disabled aircraft. When everyone was in the aircraft and buckled down, I noticed that there was a Korean on the plane. He sat just opposite of me.

The plane revved up and taxied to the end of the runway, then turned and revved the motors as high as they could go as we started to make the run to get out of there. I looked out of the window on the side as the plane picked up speed. I thought, "Get this thing in the air." But in moments we were off. Within a minute after we took

This is the first American flag Taylor saw when he landed in Yenan, China, July 1945.

off, the two motors quieted down and we were on our way to Yenan. After we had gained some altitude, I was told the Korean, who was traveling with us, was Kim Il-Sung from North Korea and that he had been with Mao for over three years. (Mao's name didn't mean much to me at the time, but later he became the sole dictator of China.)

After about an hour and a half we landed at Yenan in Shansi Province. Then the aircraft landed, turned, taxied back to a small building, and finally stopped. The hatch opened up and we were told to come down a rope ladder. After I had descended to the ground, I turned around and saw one of the most beautiful sights I had ever seen. For there, about two hundred yards away on a tall pole flying in a gentle breeze, was a large American flag. I started to cry. I could hardly believe that I was in American hands again.

Within seconds an Army jeep stopped in front of me, and two officers approached. They introduced themselves. One was Captain James Eaton, and the other was Colonel Brown. After chatting for a few minutes, Colonel Brown asked, "Would you have dinner with us tonight?" I said, "Yes Sir, it would be an honor for me." We drove to a section of barracks, where I was shown my quarters and given a change of clothing.

The meal that evening was wonderful, not fancy, just all-American, like you would get at home. It was very tasty. There were a number of officers there and I told them about my experience from 1941 to June of 1945. Everyone was quiet as I talked about the battle on Wake, traveling to Japan in the bottom of the *Nitta Maru*, and the years of uncertainty as a POW under the Japanese. I expressed my gratitude to them for flying me to Yenan. They had a hard time believing I had made it all the way from Shanghai to Yenan, which is only about 150 miles from Inner Mongolia. I was very tired and retired to bed shortly after dinner. And so ended the 27th of June.

On the 28th a Chinese officer came and took me to a small warehouse. Inside the warehouse was a room, inside of which were at least a hundred Samurai swords that had been captured from the Japanese. They insisted that I take at least two Samurai swords. I did so gladly. I spent a lot of time during that day being interrogated and resting. That night there was a picture show. On the 30th of June, I met Chu Teh, the general chief of staff of the Paluchun and had dinner with him and other top Communist leaders. July 1st was a Fast Sunday for me. Fasting was just a small way to thank the Lord for being so good to me.

Chapter Twenty-One

THE AMERICAN FLAG,
YENAN, MAO,
AND HOME—AT LAST

On July 2nd a Chinese officer came to my room and asked if I would like to see Yenan. We went down into the main shopping center and many of the people said hello to me. After about an hour, my guide said, "I want to show you something special." We got in his jeep and drove to the outskirts of Yenan towards the hills. When we had arrived at the bottom of the hill, he parked the Jeep and we got out. As I looked up the side of the hill, which gradually turned into a mountain, I noticed a row of what looked like caves. The caves looked big, even from the outside. We hiked up the slope leading to the caves, which were only about 150 feet away. When we got to one of the caves, he said, "This one is quite special." Entering, I was a little surprised. Right before us was a large room with benches, with a few other rooms off to the side.

My guide said, "Come over here." He took me into a room that had a small table and several chairs. It was quite bare. Then he pointed to an alcove where just below a window was a clay bed about three feet wide and six and a half feet long. As I stood looking around the two rooms, my guide told me, "This is where Mao sleeps." When I heard this I was flabbergasted. I said, "So this is where the great Mao sleeps when he's here?" I liked this guide more all the time. He replied, "Yes, this is where he sleeps when he's here. Chairman Mao is a great man. Without him, we would be lost."

I turned to my guide and asked, "Why have you shown me this?" He turned towards me and said, "We know you. You have lived, marched, and traveled many miles on horseback and on foot. You have slept in the same bed with us. We trust you." I turned to him and said, "I will never let you down. I am an American and always will be. But I love the Chinese people, and they know it." We left and he drove me back to my room. We didn't say much as he drove. When we arrived back, I thanked him. As I closed the door of my room, I was filled with gratitude.

I spent the next day waiting for a plane to take me from Yenan. The day after that I spent playing bridge. Surprisingly enough, I heard firecrackers that evening—it was the 4th of July.

July 5, 1945

When I was told on July 5th that a C-47 transport had landed at Yenan and that I would be leaving for home and the United States, I couldn't believe what had happened. That morning a jeep took me to the little airfield where I had landed several days before. Upon my arrival, I noticed a number of Chinese and American officers who were there to wish me bon voyage.

As I was talking to several of the US officers, I heard some commotion as several jeeps drove up with about three or four Chinese soldiers in each one. The soldiers immediately jumped off the jeeps and formed a little circle around us facing out. They all had automatic weapons. Then a sedan drove up and two Chinese Military officers got out and came over to where I was standing. To my surprise, both of these important men approached me, were introduced, and shook my hand. Was I ever surprised! One was Chairman Mao Zedong, the number one leader of all Communist people in China. The other was Chu Teh, the number two man in the Chinese Military.

*Bill Taylor and Mao Zedong: July 1945, Yenan Airport, North China Chairman Mao Zedong led
the Long March of his people from Southern China to the safety of Yenan in Northern China, a
distance of more than six thousand miles. Mao was a tremendous leader who never gave up.*

*Bill Taylor and Chu Teh: July 1945 Yenan Airport, Northern China Chu Teh has never been
recognized for the great man he was. Chairman Mao depended on him, trusting him completely, as he
was invaluable on the Long March to Yenan.*

After Mao shook my hand, he started talking through an interpreter and congratulated me on my escape from the Japanese and Wang Ching-wei and on traveling the great distance between Shanghai and Yenan. He also said that throughout all of the war years, there hadn't been one POW that had escaped from the Japanese and made his way across North China. I was so flattered to have this great leader of the Chinese people visit me, and I told him that I wouldn't be where I was today without the help of the Paluchun. I told him that there were several times I would have been recaptured or killed by the Wang Ching-wei or the Japanese if the Paluchun hadn't protected me at the risk of their own lives. I wouldn't be there talking to him. I said "thank you" in Chinese several times to him and he responded with a smile. I also told Chairman Mao that the Chinese people were a great people and I would never forget the many kindnesses they had shown me over the past months.

Captain Eaton of the US Military, who was standing about eight feet away, stepped up and suggested that we have our picture taken together. Chairman Mao smiled and said "Okay." We then stood shoulder-to-shoulder and had several pictures taken. After my picture with Mao, I had my picture taken with Chu Teh. Chu Teh helped Mao build up the Red Army. I noticed that Chairman Mao and I were the same height, five feet eight inches. He was dressed like any other Chinese soldier, nothing to indicate that he was anything special. I took an immediate liking to the courageous man who had fought for what he thought was right—not only for himself, but for his people. Mao, on the Long March, back in the early thirties, risked his life for his principles. Many others who believed in him and his principles risked their lives as well. Mao and those that accompanied him on the Long March never gave up. Giving up was not in Mao's vocabulary. It was do or die, combined with courage and sacrifice. Before he left, Mao gave me two small handwoven rugs. I thought that was very kind of him. Yes, I felt we did have something in common.

After Chairman Mao and Chu Teh left, the C-47 started its motors and I was told to board. I was wondering by now how I was going to get all of the gifts home. The C-47 taxied down the runway, turned at the far end of the runway, revved up its motors, turned, and then took off. Our next stop was Sian (Xian), a former capital of China, where we stayed in for about two hours. Our next stop was Chungking (now Chongqing). Chungking is located in Szechwan Province, which is probably the most centralized province in China. As we circled the city, I couldn't help but notice how green Chungking was. You could see the mighty Yangtze River that skirted the city.

After we landed, the US Air Force gave me the royal treatment. I was told that we would be staying in Chungking for about a week. I was also told that I would be an honored guest at the embassy the following evening, the 6th of July.

The meal served at the embassy was outstanding. After the service, I was asked to speak, which I did for about half an hour. Everybody sat still and listened intently. After the meal, I answered questions about Wake, Japan, China and the Communists that I had been living with for the past two months. The questions and answers went on for about an hour.

There was a Colonel Dickey, from the Air Force, who wanted me to have lunch with him the following day. We talked about many things, but for some unknown reason, I wasn't comfortable with him. I told him about the Communists and how they had treated me well while I was with them. But I didn't feel comfortable telling him much about the Kuomintang, so after about half an hour after the lunch was over we said goodbye.

When I got back to my quarters, I was given a huge roll of glistening, white embroidered silk. How was I going to cart it all home? There was also a note on my desk indicating that we would be leaving tomorrow for Kunming. On July 8th I boarded a C-47 and we were on our way to Kunming in Yunnan Province. In Kunming I was given nice quarters next to the airport. I was questioned for many hours the next day about Japan, China, et cetera. It was a very friendly interrogation.

July 10, 1945

On the 10th I was sitting in a tent watching the aircraft take off and land. Someone said, "You have to see the way the Chinese pilots fly. They are really nuts." When I asked why, he said, "Just watch the way they take off." The Chinese pilots just get in a cold aircraft, start it up, and take off without warming the motor or motors up. I watched aircraft after aircraft take off like this, and no accidents. (I learned later that they do have quite a few accidents.)

Later on in the day, as I was sitting in the tent out of the burning sun, a pilot came to my tent and wanted to talk. He was a major in the Air Force. When I invited him in, he said, "I understand you escaped from the 'Japs' a few months ago." When I affirmed this, he said, "We have something in common. I was also a POW of the Japanese, and I also escaped from them last year." I immediately became very much interested and asked him, "How did you get away from the 'Japs'?" Then he told me his story, which I will now pass along to you. (Unfortunately, I do not remember his name.)

"I was a second lieutenant in the Army Air Force based in the Philippines when the war started. When the Japanese overran the Philippines, we were forced to surrender. MacArthur was already in Australia. It was a living hell being a POW of the Japanese during those years. On October 11, 1944, eighteen ships with POWs left for Japan. Eleven ships reached Hong Kong, seven were sunk. On October 25th, our ship, the *Arisan Maru*, was torpedoed about two hundred miles north of Formosa. The *Arisan* was hugging the coastline where the ocean was quite shallow. We had 1,800 POWs in the hold, which was divided by partitions, and there were several decks in each partition. We were jammed in and the 'Japs' had battened down all of the hatches. There was no escape. We would be doomed if a bomb or torpedo hit us.

Well, a torpedo did hit us, and the *Arisan Maru* folded into two
pieces. I was swept up by the water rushing in and was miraculously
pushed to the surface. I grabbed a battered, wooden door that had
been blown off from its hinges. The ocean was quiet, and looking
west I could see shore lights burning about two miles away. I started
paddling my wooden float toward the light and in a couple of hours
reached the shore. I staggered into a village. The Chinese saw me
and took me in and treated me as one of them. Freedom, how can
you express freedom? I learned later that out of 1,800 aboard the
Arisan, only five made it back."

We talked for a little longer before he left. His story was another
miracle. And so ended the 10th of July.

Soon we left Kunming and arrived in Myitkyina (pronounced
"Mis-yen-na"), Burma. We stayed there for about four hours, then
took off for Calcutta, India. This meant flying over the Himalayan
mountains, which the pilots and others called the "Hump." Most of
these mountain peaks were twenty thousand feet high and many of
the peaks were even higher. Mount Everest was the highest, twenty-
nine thousand feet-plus—the highest mountain in the world. While
we were traveling over the "Hump," I looked out of the plane window and could see how very dangerous the "Hump" really was.
Our altitude was thirty thousand feet plus and as I looked down
at those treacherous mountain ranges, I could see that if anything
went wrong with our aircraft, and we lost altitude, all would perish.
There would be no landing in these mountains or valleys. But it was
a gorgeous sight, a true wilderness. Once you have seen the Himalayan Mountains, you will never forget them. It is a marvelous sight,
but very dangerous. It was a lovely, spooky day. What a ride!

Calcutta was so different. I had never seen so many people and
so much poverty. On the streets, I was surrounded by a horde of
boys six to ten years of age. They surrounded me and wanted to
shine my shoes, even though my shoes were not the kind to polish.
I noticed that these little lads were starving. Some had blotches of

white hair and others had lost portions of their hair. I couldn't help them; I didn't have any money. It made me very sad.

Next, we flew to New Delhi, India, then on to Karachi. From Karachi, Pakistan, we flew to Abadan, Iran, where we refueled before moving on to Cairo, Egypt. After a few days in Cairo we flew to Tripoli, then on to Casablanca, Morocco, on the Atlantic. From there we flew to Bermuda where we stayed until the morning of the 27th, when we flew to Miami, Florida.

July 27, 1945—America!

Upon landing in Miami, I wanted to hug and kiss the ground. I was alive; and for that matter, The United States of America is the best place in the world to be alive. I called my mother and told her I was home. She screamed and after I had hung up, she started calling other women from Wake telling them that the boys were home. But I was the only one. In Miami, I was met by the Military who wanted to see me in Washington the next day, on the 28th of July.

In Washington I was hustled off to the Pentagon where I met a group of Military officers who asked a lot of questions about the Japanese, but mostly about the Paluchun (Communists). They seemed impressed. I told them that as soon as the war ended, Mao would conquer all of China within a short time. They listened very politely, but didn't believe me. That is, however, exactly what happened. I took the train to New York where I stayed in a fancy hotel. During the night a B-25 flew over the hotel. I jumped out of bed and rushed to the window. I knew the aircraft was very low. A few seconds later, there was a loud boom. The aircraft had smacked into the side of the Empire State Building. The only thing that saved the Empire State Building from burning up was the fact that the aircraft was out of gas.

I arrived in Ogden on the 1st of August. I stayed there with my Uncle Melbourne Douglas for a few days before I left for Boise, Idaho, where I met Esther Packard and other Wake Island women. I was able to tell them about their husbands, children, and friends. It was a precious experience.

On August 6th, while traveling to Los Angeles from Boise, Idaho, I heard that we had dropped atomic bombs on Hiroshima and Nagasaki. That day will long be remembered. It changed the world and saved more than one hundred and forty thousand POWs from a sure death.

I later learned Jack Hernandez was recaptured and the Japanese fixed his injured leg. They told him I had been captured and executed. Jack sent a telegram from Kunming, China, to my mother telling her that I had been executed. I was already home when the telegram arrived—and I opened it. No, I hadn't been killed, so it all worked out well.

In conclusion, I would never, never have made it through those three and a half years without help from the other side. There were so many times I should have been killed, but wasn't. I know the Lord helped me to get through my years as a prisoner of war and return safely to my family and friends in America.

EPILOGUE

J ust before I jumped from the train, I gave Oscar Ray the Book
of Mormon my brother Dick had sent to me and asked him to
send it to my mother in Los Angeles, if he survived the war. He
did just that, believing that I had been killed. I have this book today
and it is a treasured possession.

The Survivors of Wake, Guam, and Cavite group was organized
to enable the civilians of the war to keep in touch. Because Morrison
& Knudsen Construction Company had brought most of the men to
Wake Island from Boise, many of them and their families still resided
in the Boise area. I was therefore able to have contact again with my
POW friends from Woosung and Kiangwan prison camps, "Mac"
McCurry and Chalas Loveland, as well as Oscar Ray and others.

In 1985, the organization was invited by a similar Marine group
to travel with them to Wake Island to dedicate a monument that had
been built to honor the Marine presence on the island during WWII.
Many of the civilians who had been on Wake, including Mac, Chal,
and me, jumped at the chance to return to our place of capture.

Arriving there and witnessing the dedication of the beautiful
memorial to the Marines affected us in an unexpected manner. Real-

ity set in for us—there was nothing there to represent the civilians (a much larger majority of the population on the island in 1941) that also fought, died, and were held prisoners. This feeling was magnified by the presence of a Japanese memorial on the island. We felt that we needed to do something. So, one morning, the Wake Island civilians, with the help of Barney Uhart, the contractor on Wake at the time, dug a foundation. Barney poured a concrete slab into the foundation and we carved words on it about the civilian presence, adding the date and decorating it with seashells some of the wives had gathered off the beach. Then we held our own little private dedication. It wasn't much, but it was something.

Upon return to the United States, Chalas Loveland and others laid out plans for a beautiful granite monument to be designed and built in three sections on Wake Island. These plans were immediately put into motion. This task was not easy, as we needed government approval, government transportation, funding, and someone to return to Wake to install it. Since Morrison & Knudsen Construction

First Civilian Workers' Memorial placed on Wake Island in November 1985

Company had sent most of the civilians on Wake, we decided to approach them for assistance. They were very generous with their assistance in the funding of the memorial.

I was able to obtain a bid from a local company in Provo, Utah, to manufacture the monument for us to pick up, crate, and make ready for placement. Secretary of the Navy John Lehman provided the necessary documents permitting the memorial to be flown by military transportation from San Diego to Wake. He also granted approval for the memorial to be erected on Wake Island.

We would never have received the permission to install the memorial nor the approval for the Military transportation if Congressman Ron Packard from California had not represented our cause to Secretary Lehman of the Navy. Ron Packard had a very personal reason to do this, as his father was Forest Packard, a Wake Island POW, and one of my close friends in China.

On January 1, 1987, I drove a truck with the three granite monuments to San Diego, where I boarded a Military plane that delivered me and our precious cargo to Wake Island. With the assistance of Barney Uhart, who was still the contractor on the Wake, and his work force, an area was developed and the beautiful memorial was erected to finally honor those civilians who lost their lives in battle and in prison camps and those who came home after three and a half years of hell.

In June of 1988, the Survivors of Wake made another trek to the Island to dedicate *their* memorial, a trip that was closure for many of us. Many family members accompanied us on this trip and were able to experience a greater understanding of the stories told of the Battle of Wake Island.

In the summer of 2003, the History Channel flew me and five Marines, who had been on Wake Island during WWII, back to the island. There they filmed a two-hour documentary, *Wake Island: Alamo of the Pacific*, which explains the actual story of the battles that took place at the beginning of World War II.

The company filming the show gave a recap of my escape and final capture by the Chinese Communists. As part of the documentary, they used several of my drawings as well as the photo of me with Mao. This has been replayed quite often over the past years. I have received many phone calls from all over the United States, and from other countries including China and Ireland (the History Channel also has an International station), from former POWs and family members of Wake Island workers.

* * *

There were ninety-eight POWs left on Wake Island who did not board the *Nitta Maru* for China. The Japanese had ordered these civilians to stay on Wake to help fortify the defenses on the island. The US Navy made frequent raids over the next two years and supplies from Japan became limited. Rear Admiral Shigematsu Sakaibara, who

Second Civilian Workers' Memorial placed on Wake Island in June 1988

acted as captain and commander of Japanese forces on Wake Island, was angry with the prisoners—not only could they become a threat if the United States successfully attacked Wake, but they were now reducing the limited food and water supply. Sakaibara thoroughly hated Americans and especially these that were on his island. After a devastating US raid in October of 1943, Sakaibara decided to put in motion the plan he had been formulating in his mind over the past few months. At sundown on the 7th the prisoners were taken to the shore where Japanese soldiers bound their legs, blindfolded them, and forced them to kneel. At the given command, the soldiers opened devastating machine gun and rifle fire into the backs of those innocent men. It was over within two minutes. In September of 1945, Rear Admiral Sakaibara was tried in a War Crimes trial on Kwajalein Island and was executed in June of 1947 on Guam Island.

When the war was over, the civilians from Wake Island who had been taken to China were brought home from their prisoner of war camps. By now nearly all had been relocated to the Japanese mainland. Even though the workers from Wake actively participated in the battles on Wake Island and were held prisoners of war with the military in the various camps for three and a half years, upon arrival home, their efforts were not acknowledged. That situation was not rectified until 1982 when Congress finally passed a bill that authorized the civilians from Wake Island to be inducted into the United States Navy as of December 8, 1941, and honorably discharged in August of 1945. With this bill in place, the Survivors of Wake were finally able to participate in the various military programs afforded other former Navy personnel, including the GI Bill, and were able to receive other benefits, such as health care at Veterans Administration Hospitals.

I was inducted into the United States Navy and given the rank of Gunner Mate 3rd Class as of December 8, 1941 and given an honorable discharge as of July 28, 1945 (marking my arrival back in the United States after my escape).

On December 4, 2001, I was honored at a United States Marine Memorial held in San Francisco where I received the Nation's sixth-highest Military award, which states:

This is to certify that the President of the United States of America has awarded the

LEGION OF MERIT *(with Combat V)*

to

Gunner's Mate Third Class WILLIAM L. TAYLOR, *United States Navy for exceptionally meritorious conduct in the performance of outstanding services*

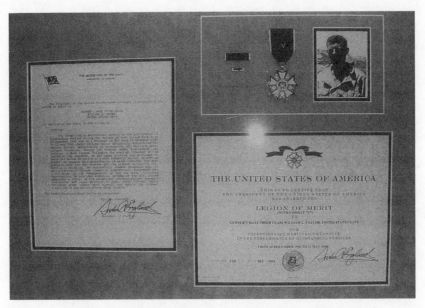

Photograph of framed citation, letter, and medal awarded to Bill Taylor